TIPPING
THE
SCALES
OF
JUSTICE

TIPPING
THE
SCALES
OF
JUSTICE

FIGHTING
WEIGHT-BASED
DISCRIMINATION

SONDRA SOLOVAY, J.D.

 Prometheus Books

59 John Glenn Drive
Amherst, New York 14228-2197

Published 2000 by Prometheus Books

Inquiries should be addressed to
Prometheus Books, 59 John Glenn Drive, Amherst, New York 14228–2197.
VOICE: 716–691–0133, ext. 207.
FAX: 716–564–2711.
WWW.PROMETHEUSBOOKS.COM

04 03 02 01 00   5 4 3 2 1

Library of Congress Cataloging-in-Publication Data

Solovay, Sondra, 1970–
    Tipping the scales of justice : fighting weight-based discrimination /
Sondra Solovay.
          p.   cm.
    Includes bibliographical references and index.
    ISBN 1–57392–764–3 (paper)
    1. Body image. 2. Overweight children—Psychology. 3. Obesity—
Psychological aspects. 4. Obesity—Social aspects. 5. Self-esteem in children.
6. Body image—Social aspects. 7. Physical-appearance-based bias.
8. Discrimination against overweight persons. I. Title.
BF697.5.B63 S65 1999
306.4—dc21   99–048231
                                                                    CIP

Printed in the United States of America on acid-free paper

This book is dedicated to
Christina Corrigan.
I wish I had known you.

CONTENTS

FOREWORD
BY MARILYN WANN

I GET THE CALLS ALL the time: "My son tries really hard in PE class and suits up every day, but the coach calls him 'lard butt' and says he's going to fail him. My son needs that class to graduate!" "I went on a job interview, and they said I was perfectly qualified, but they couldn't hire me because I don't have 'front office appearance.' Can they do that?" "I don't have any history of health problems, but every company that I apply to for insurance turns me down because I'm 'morbidly obese.' Is that legal?"

My answer is invariably: You need to talk with Sondra Solovay. She's the only person in the legal arena who knows anything about weight-related law.

Isn't that stunning? I can't think of any other legal topic—especially one that involves so many areas of individuals' rights and so many areas of the law—that has gotten such consistent lack of attention from legal scholars. (The government's latest figures classify 97 million Americans as "overweight" or "obese." That's 55 percent of the population! But why quibble? When flight attendants can be fired for gaining 5 or 10 pounds, we're *all* at risk from weight-related discrimination.) The only explanation I can imagine for this gigantic blind spot is that discrimination itself; as Sondra demonstrates so thoroughly and brilliantly, lawyers and legislators and legal scholars and the courts themselves are not immune from the arbitrarily antifat attitudes that pervade our society in general.

I'm eager for the fat revolution. I'm eager for the day when fat people (and thin people) will stop trying ever more ridiculous diets in hopes of being one of the so-called lucky 5 percent who may actually maintain weight loss. I'm eager for the day when fat people of all sizes refuse both the self-hatred and the societal prejudice that has kept us all down for so long. I'm eager for the day when people of all sizes start throwing their weight around, demanding equal respect and opportunity in society, regardless of the number on the scale. I'm eager for the day when the public bullies run a very real risk of getting righteously sat on if they say something rude about a person's weight. But until that glorious day, some 97 million-plus Americans desperately need this book . . . to stand up for them. Because no one else is. In most cases, not even the victims of weight-based discrimination themselves.

Hey Sondra, I've got another call for you . . .

Flabulously!
Marilyn Wann
Author of the book *Fat!So?* and editor of the magazine *Fat!So?*

ACKNOWLEDGMENTS

T HIS BOOK WOULD NOT EXIST without the committed activists who, years ago, had the vision to recognize that fat discrimination was wrong and the courage to speak out against it. The work you did made the world a better place.

A special thank you to Marilyn "Rolodex-Goddess" Wann for being so wonderful (and for going through it all six months ahead of me) and to Alice, Christie, Maria, Sabrina, Leah, and especially Joe, for your help with the drudgery.

The book makes Boalt worth it, so thanks to Ellen, Robin, April, Nevada, Mark (it was your idea!), Matt, Sabrina, Michael Adams, and Jake for making it bearable.

And much appreciation to: Bill Fabrey and Judy Freespirit (you both rock!), Alice for everything, Bob at the law library, my boy (and all the bits), Christie Johnson, DVM (Villa Wilda vet extraordinaire!), Carole, Corky, the disability rights community, Nancy Dunbar, Diana, Elena, every FaTGiRL collective member and contributor, Frances, GaGa, Grandma Bea and Gramps, Giorgio (Cult leader of the millennium!), Hanne, Jo, Joanne Ikeda, Jody, Leah the Research Queen, Marlene and the Corrigan defense team, Mark for the late-night conversations, Max (cute and gives good keystroke), all of the amazing people at NAAFA (who deserve much more thanks than just this little acknowledgment), Nomy, Peggy, Sandra, Toni, *every* size acceptance author (especially Charlotte Cooper, Paul Ernsberger, Laura Fraser, Susan Stinson, and Marilyn Wann), those who bravely and generously volunteered time to be interviewed, and all the activists and educators, fat and thin, out there making art and turning the world into a better place.

Please note: *Tipping the Scales of Justice* documents much of the legal history of prejudice against fat people. This book cannot substitute for legal advice or information. Laws and rights change in time and vary by jurisdiction. Some of the decisions in this book may have been overturned before publication, but are included to give an understanding of the field. Anyone who has a legal question should seek the advice of a qualified, licensed attorney immediately.

CHAPTER 1

PREJUDICE IN PRACTICE

The Felony Trial of Marlene Corrigan

A Case Study of Fat Bias in the Pursuit of Justice

Nobody will ever know why Christina Corrigan died.

She was a bright, friendly child. Like many teens and preteens, she had a stubborn streak. She loved to swim and to read. She collected music boxes and talked about boys. And she had dreams. She wanted to be a marine biologist. She wanted to visit Australia.

Christina never got to see Australia, but Australia, like the rest of the world, got to see her. A private teenager, she suffered in death what she tried so desperately to avoid in life: the public eye. Her death made headlines worldwide. Nobody was interested in who Christina was. They were interested in what she weighed. Over and over, thirteen years of life was summed up in three digits: 680. She weighed 680 pounds.

*   *   *

Nearly eight months after the death of her daughter, Marlene Corrigan was charged with violation of California Penal Code 273a(a)—felony child abuse/endangerment. The prosecutor alleged, "Under circumstances likely to produce great bodily harm and death, [Marlene Corrigan] did willfully, unlawfully, and feloniously cause and permit a child . . . to suffer unjustifiable physical pain and mental suffering and permit the health of that child to be injured."[1] The charge carries a maximum prison term of six years.

Was Marlene Corrigan guilty of a crime? Normally, a trial determines the answer to this question. Marlene had two trials: one in the courthouse, the other in the media. In both, the thread of prejudice is woven tightly into the fabric of the case.

Images of a 680-pound girl lying nude on the floor, fast-food wrappers strewn around her, covered in feces and bedsores was the world's introduction to Christina. The majority of the print media pronounced Marlene guilty from the start. At the very least, she was guilty of having a fat child. Despite hundreds of stories and hours of coverage, very little investigation was done. Once the story hit the Associated Press, the same inaccurate sensationalism was repeated in progressively larger papers with almost no news added and little fact checking done, or even possible. These later stories relied heavily on the original newspaper report, often repeating it word for word while ignoring courtroom testimony. Attorney Robin Adler, at that time with the Public Defender's office in the area, had heard of the reporter who wrote the first story—he had a reputation among defense attorneys for writing "prosecution-favorable" pieces. His story, which first painted a picture of Marlene for the public, was based on the police reports. According to Marlene, he did not talk to her and he could not see her apartment to confirm it was as police described. While some facts were accurate, the story became such a twisted combination of fact and fiction that the truth was difficult to distinguish.

The full story began years earlier, in the doctor's office. Christina had a history of seizures as a baby and was placed on Phenobarbital, a barbiturate that depresses the central nervous system. Though her weight was just barely above average at around three months and then dipped below average, Marlene recalls being told not to use whole milk in her bottle. Noted University of California San Francisco endocrinologist Dr. Diane Budd, who testified in Marlene's defense during her trial, believes that putting Christina on her first diet was irresponsible. It may have altered her metabolic rate early on, leading to her tremendous weight gain. Diets, she says, make people fat. In this case particularly, the weight gain was too fast to be explained by simple overeating. A second childhood obesity expert believed the amount of weight was too high for her to have been able to "eat" her way up to it. By three years of age, Christina was the weight of an average eight-and-a-half-year-old. At age five, after two more years of dieting, her weight was equivalent to the average thirteen-year-old. At seven, she was over 180 pounds. Before she turned eight, her weight was completely off the charts.

The doctors with her health plan did some very basic tests and found nothing unusual. They could have done better thyroid tests and taken a picture of her brain. She could have been sent to a geneticist. Instead, they assumed it was her eating habits in combination with a family tendency to be heavy. Marlene repeatedly asked about her daughter's weight during those early years of exponential gain. Christina was referred to a dietitian, put on a diet, and was given ceramic food to practice with to be sure she understood portions. She was an active girl and stuck to the diet but still gained weight. She went in to be weighed every two weeks. Often her grandfather took her to be weighed because Marlene worked during the day. Christina's last weigh-in was at the age of eight. She weighed almost 240 pounds. The hospital still claimed her weight was due to her eating.

For Christina and her mother it was a period of endless frustration. They shared in a cruel hope that all the effort would pay off and Christina would lose weight. Christina made plans for the future while her mother banned potato chips from the house. Christina's only sibling, Chad, had to sneak them into his room to avoid tempting Christina. Marlene shared a "cookie" joke with her sister. The joke was, if you wanted cookies at Marlene's house, you had better bring them yourself because you would not find any there. For all the denial Christina endured, the numbers on the scale kept climbing and climbing.

As a mother, Marlene was concerned about the weight, but she was also worried about Christina's emotional health. The hospital visits were taking a toll. Professionals told Christina if she would only control her diet she would lose weight, but it was not happening that way. Perhaps they did not believe her. Maybe Christina herself felt she was not trying hard enough. The weigh-ins were reminders of what she could not become, conveniently scheduled every other week. To make matters worse, the scale was not private. Nurses, staff, patients, all could be milling around, overhearing Christina's personal business. Like the medical staff, the judge presiding over Marlene's trial had little concern for the damage such humiliation caused. He prevented Marlene's attorney from asking the pediatrician about the effects of the weigh-ins saying, "Whether she was embarrassed won't change the facts of the case." Understanding what Christina went through and why she was resistant does not change facts, but it explains them. Perhaps doctors, lawyers, judges, and reporters will not consider Christina's daily pain important, but a good mother will. Each week Christina knew that the scale would not hold good news. The year of her death, a study came out which showed that even thin people, when weighed and compared with bogus "norms," show an immediate increase in their depression and decrease in their self-esteem. Still, without that official confirmation, the effects are predictable. As Christina's weight went up, her spirit went down. It was a lot of shame, failure, and blame for a little girl to handle and for a mother to enforce.

Hostility by the medical establishment toward fat people is well documented.[2] Fat adults have refused to go to the doctor, preferring even to die rather than face the medical profession's excruciating bias. By the age of eight, Christina probably experienced more humiliation and stress in the doctor's office than most people do in a lifetime. Perhaps someone said something specific to her, or maybe it was just too much. Finally, Christina refused to go back. Marlene saw no point in continuing the futile visits. They had not worked at all. Marlene had been told that she was doing the right thing by putting her daughter on diets and to keep it up. She continued to help Christina diet, but in the privacy of their own home. They did programs like Richard Simmons's Deal-a-Meal® and exercise tapes, and other popular diets. They had the same success rate as working with the doctor—none. Neither the hospital nor the pediatrician ever wondered what happened to her or followed up. The newspapers reported that it was five years since Christina had been to the doctor's office. They did not mention that during the first eight years of her life, she went about one hundred times.[3]

Newspapers also reported with disgust that Christina had not been to school in over a year. At the age of thirteen Christina, who had been a good, capable student at the Fairmont School, was a junior high drop-out. How could something so outrageous happen?

Marlene had been an active parent, known and liked by the faculty at the elementary school. Christina had friends there. One even wrote to the local paper after her death. That is not to say that she was not ridiculed. She was. Writing for the *San Francisco Chronicle*, Catherine Bowman quoted Christina's schoolmate Hector Rodriguez, "Everybody used to pick on her. . . . When the other kids didn't finish their food, they would give it to her. She just pushed it away."[4] Besides harassment, Christina had another impending problem. All of her friends separated, going to different junior high schools. Christina was scheduled to go to Portola Junior High, a school she knew because her brother had also gone there. Her mother arranged to have her stay for sixth grade at Fairmont, but as Portola got closer, her options quickly closed in around her.

Portola is at the top of a long hill. The campus is built into the hillside, rising several stories from the lowest point to the main entrance, which is wheelchair accessible via the driveway.[5] For a student who needs to avoid stairs, getting to the main level entrance requires walking up the entire hill, rather than cutting across the lawn, turning left, and continuing up the hill until the driveway is reached, and then following the driveway down to the school door. For someone of Christina's size and limited mobility, neither option was practical. Even if she could make the walk by getting there very early and going at her own pace, she would have been on display while making the circuitous route.

Marlene Corrigan says she contacted the school about Christina's problems navigating the campus. She says representatives of the underfunded school told her that there was nothing they could do because they did not cover "obesity"—it was not a disability.

Even if the school had agreed to help Christina get onto the campus, she would still have had problems. The school is covered with stairs, many with no handrails. The only part of the school that does not require use of stairs is the main three-story building, which has a somewhat dilapidated elevator on the side. Had she attended, she would have been essentially limited to the central building. The socialization problems she would experience because of her weight would be magnified by her inability to participate in the mainstream of student life.

Not only was the school physically inaccessible for Christina, it was psychologically unsafe. Children from that school had already been harassing her on the bus with her mother and on her travels to her elementary school.

When it became clear that her daughter could not attend the school, Marlene says she contacted the school system about home schooling. After a bit of a runaround, she says she was told that she could hire a private teacher for Christina, but that she could not teach Christina herself unless she became certified. A single working mother, Marlene says she could not afford to hire the tutor for Christina, and she was not able to get the needed certification while working full time. She bought some grade-appropriate workbooks for Christina, had her read books, and write book reports. According to a school spokesperson, once they believed Christina would be home-schooled, they did not follow up.

Christina faced relentless harassment outside the home. When she went out in public she was the subject of comments from children and adults. Marlene chose to move into the apartment complex because it had a pool which she thought would be a good way for Christina to be active. Often after work they would swim together. Christina enjoyed swimming and was seen in the pool a few months before her death. As she grew older and gained more weight, she withdrew from the outside world.

Media reports focused on the fact that Child Protective Services (CPS) was called by Marlene's sister when Christina was six years old. It was reported that Marlene was overfeeding Christina and that her house was filthy. The slender sister said she noticed overfeeding when the family went camping together. The group had gone on a hike and at the end Marlene rewarded Christina with a piece of a Hershey bar. Marlene's sister was concerned because they were cooking around 5 P.M. when they had eaten a large meal at 1 or 2 P.M. that she thought should be sufficient for the day. At the trial she testified that CPS said they would not go over to investigate weight. They then asked her if the child was living in filth. She responded by asking them if they would go over if she was. She then said that Christina was living in filth. When CPS went to the home they found no problem. Marlene asked the social worker for help with weight loss. He told her he would send her some pamphlets, but never got back to her.

Doctors anticipated Christina's difficulties, but did not reach out to help Marlene. School staff were told about her difficulties, but nobody offered any help to Marlene. Even the social worker, called by Marlene's sister, did not respond to Marlene's request for help.

While Marlene was unable to elicit help from services around her, she was herself helping out a lot. Not only was she working full time and raising two children by herself, she was also caring for her elderly parents. She shopped for them and ran the household. She would make midnight runs to their house when there were problems. In the months before Christina's death, Marlene's father died of congestive heart failure and her mother responded with full-blown dementia. A few months later, because Christina was feeling sick, Marlene stayed home from work to be with her. She went out to the market to buy iced tea, and returned to find her daughter unresponsive. She gave her CPR, but to no avail. A few months later, Marlene's mother also died.

The prosecution's charge was always somewhat confusing. Whether Deputy District Attorney Brian Haynes was misquoted by the press or hesitant about his position, the exact basis for the criminal charge was unclear. It was widely reported that overfeeding and "allowing" Christina's weight gain were factors. The police proceeded with those as focal points of their investigation, but Brian Haynes would occasionally deny that weight had anything to do with the charges, basing them instead on the living conditions and on the condition of the girl's body. Nevertheless, they certainly were the indictments in the court of public opinion, and they seemed to factor centrally in the court of law both in the actual trial and the preliminary hearing. The police investigation included crime scene photographs of a pizza box just the way they would snap a shot of a used bullet casing in a shooting. Pictures were taken of the contents of the refrigerator and freezer and trash was removed from bags and spread out on the living room floor for photographic purposes. The judge in the hearing concluded that there was evidence of guilt of a felony saying, "The mother was the food source, [she] had ultimate control over what was being provided to the child."[6]

If the charges were about the condition of the body—the presence of multiple pressure ulcers and potential hygiene issues—then weight should only have been an issue as it related to the bedsores and cleanliness. Factors that were the natural result of being that fat should not be "evidence" of a crime. Since few people reach Christina's weight, very little is known about caring for bodies that size. The judge or jury would have heard evidence about whether, given the high weight, such sores could be prevented, how they should have been treated, and whether they were life-threatening.

More investigation could have been done to determine whether fecal matter and urine near the body were the result of the body voiding at death or Marlene's apathy. Then it would be possible to decide if Marlene had caused or permitted her daughter to suffer unjustifiable pain or damage to her health which was "likely to result in great bodily injury or death."

If the charges were based on the child's weight, then the district attorney was unleashing a huge civil rights issue. The precedent would suggest that having a fat child was a crime. As has happened in other jurisdictions, judges and social workers, with the support of biased medical personnel, could try to enforce weight-loss schemes and remove children who did not lose weight from their homes.

The lack of clarity for the basis of the charges infected the entire quest for justice. All children, fat or thin, have a right to humane treatment. Because of the approach by the district attorney's office, the crucial question of whether the atypical actions of Christina's mother were protective or abusive was obscured.

The cause of Christina's death was critical to the debate over what should happen to her mother. Perhaps the greatest fault of the prosecution was its satisfaction with an appallingly poor autopsy—a problem the press failed to report entirely.

Nobody will ever know for certain why Christina Corrigan died. Nobody will ever know what caused Christina's weight gain. Dr. Brian Peterson conducted a visual autopsy only. He never performed an internal examination on Christina Corrigan.

Marlene wanted answers about Christina's mysterious life and death. She says she called and requested an actual autopsy. Dr. Peterson, the forensic pathologist, said normally he would honor a parent's wishes, but in this case he never received the request. Doing an actual internal autopsy on such a large body would be physically demanding and could take a good deal of time. The autopsies he and his three partners perform for the county are on a fee basis. During an internal autopsy, they pay a diener (an assistant). The fee for an internal autopsy is $400 and does not change even if the examination takes a particularly long time. If he performed an external, or visual, autopsy, the doctor's time would be significantly reduced yet the fee is a full $200. Christina was given an external autopsy. It took Dr. Peterson ten minutes.

During the ten minutes he spent examining Christina's naked body, he measured the circumference of her thighs at the request of a police officer. Under oath he admitted he took photos, without the mother's permission or knowledge, for his own purposes. He did not take time to accurately note the position of the body, first saying the body came in positioned on the right side, and later saying the body was on the left side. This contradiction was not a mistake. He did not know what side she was lying on. He defends this inaccuracy saying, "Side was very difficult to determine in this case. There were protrusions. There were angles from this body that one does not normally see. So it's just hard to say, and I believe my report accurately reflects that uncertainty."[7] There were no "protrusions" and "angles"—the body was fat. Dr. Peterson, like most people, was so unaccustomed to looking at a supersize body, all he saw was fat, eclipsing even the most basic observation possible—the position of the body. Despite the fact that he could not identify which side Christina was on, he said he could ascertain whether the girl had been mobile. Relying on the fact that the soles of her feet were clean and smooth, he ascertained that she could not get around.

Of the many disturbing parts of the autopsy, most troubling is the cause of death determination. The doctor's autopsy report listed pink "edema-*type*" fluid in the mouth and on the face (emphasis added). Though many things Dr. Peterson testified to were taken directly from his report and not from an independent recollection of the eight-month-old autopsy, when he testified in court he added that the fluid was "frothy." Edema and edemalike fluids can result from things other than heart problems.

Even if there was frothy edema fluid present, it would indicate pulmonary edema, which means fluid in the lungs. The leading cause of pulmonary edema is heart failure, but it is by no means the only cause. Pulmonary edema can be caused by asthma, aspiration, some infections, shock, or other causes. There is a limit to what can be determined just by looking at the body. To confirm left-side heart failure, the heart and lungs should be examined. Additionally, the determination of congestive heart failure must be accompanied by a reason for the failure. Even if this case was an example of pulmonary edema from heart failure, the cause of the heart failure must be provided. Fat people are not immune to all types of heart failure and death except those brought on by weight. While "being fat" is frequently assumed to be related to heart failure, it is not a sufficient explanation. Marlene's attorney asked, "And you just looked at the size of this young girl and said well, it must be due to her morbid obesity, correct?" The doctor answered, "That's correct."[8]

Despite the fact that Dr. Peterson began the autopsy by reviewing the short, written coroner's report, he did not know about Christina's seizure history when he performed the autopsy. The police officers who were present at the time did not tell him about the seizure history, either. When he was told in court, he said he would have been more inclined to do an internal exam if he had known about it. Asked earlier in the hearing about the possibility of a brain tumor, he dismissed as absent, among other things, seizure activity.[9] He based his assumption that Christina died from "heart failure due to obesity" partially on the fact that he thought she was found lying on her back, which would put pressure on the chest. In fact, she was found on her side and back, propped up slightly by a couch.

While newspapers were eager to run headlines like "Girl Fed to Death" and all printed that she died of heart failure due to her weight, none were interested in the story that a determination of heart failure was made without opening the body and without even knowing the child's seizure history. "Fat Girl's Death Unrelated to Weight" is not likely to make any headlines. Not only was the media silent on this key point of the case, they did not flinch when the doctor said he made his pronouncement based on "medical certainty," which he defined numerically, and without citing any authority, as 51 percent. To believe something is "more likely than not" to have caused a death seems a far cry from a determination made "with medical certainty." With this definition, it is far more reasonable to say that dieting is medically certain to fail, since 10 percent or fewer are successful, than to say Christina died from her weight.

Marlene chose a trial by judge rather than jury. She hoped to avoid some of the prejudice she might otherwise face about Christina's size. Without a reliable cause of death, it is hard to know what constitutes a fair judgment. Had Christina died from a seizure, Marlene may have been innocent. Had Christina died from a sore which caused a massive infection to her body, Marlene may have been guilty of a felony. Either way, Marlene lost the daughter she referred to repeatedly as her "best friend" in the same year she lost both her parents. And either way, no consequences were going to befall the doctors, the school system, the bullies, or the culture that isolated Christina and forced her to make a small apartment her whole world.

The judge found Marlene Corrigan guilty of a misdemeanor, not the felony she was charged with. She was sentenced to community service, counseling, and probation. Under California law she is a candidate for having her record cleared in the future. Long after the trial has concluded, a question asked by a founder of the fat feminist movement, Judy Freespirit, remains unanswered: "Who is really on [trial] here? Who among us is not responsible for the incredible injustice, the miserable life, and the terrible death of Christina Corrigan?"[10]

NOTES

1. *People* v. *Corrigan*, No. 161417-1, DA No. X 97 000238-6. Municipal Court of CA, County of Contra Costa Bay Judicial District (July 15, 1997) and CALJIC 9.37 (Pen. Code, s 273a[1]a.) (The word "willfully" means "with knowledge of the consequences" or "purposefully.")

2. See chapter 14.

3. Though there are no records to prove it, Ms. Corrigan claims that she took her daughter to see doctors at the clinic about an ear problem less than two years before her death.

4. Catherine Bowman, "680-Pound Girl's Shocking Death," *San Francisco Chronicle*, 19 July 1997, A13.

5. When I visited the school, the accessible entrance was closed and dark, apparently being used for storage.

6. *People* v. *Corrigan*, preliminary hearing transcript, Action No. 161417-1, 22 September 1997, Judge Laurel Lindenbaum at 209.

7. *People* v. *Corrigan*, preliminary hearing transcript, Action No. 161417-1, 22 September 1997, 67.

8. *People* v. *Corrigan*, preliminary hearing transcript, Action No. 161417-1, 22 September 1997, 59.

9. *People* v. *Corrigan*, preliminary hearing transcript, Action No. 161417-1, 22 September 1997, 57.

10. The full text of a press release from Judy Freespirit, Coordinator NAAFA Feminist Caucus:

Being the mother of a severely disabled child is a difficult, full-time job.

Being the single mother of a severely disabled child, having to work full time as the sole support of one's family, is an impossible job at best.

Add to this the lack of support from the school system which refused to accommodate this child's disabilities

Add to this a medical system which doesn't even have a category of treatment which seeks the wellness of fat children but offers blame and demands, deprivation and starvation as its only solutions

Add an overburdened social service system which has no time or energy to assist the family

Add to that a general attitude of blame and hatred for people who weigh more than is currently determined to be "normal"

Add the cruelty of children who torment any child who is in any way different and particularly feel entitled to persecute fat people since they see adults doing it with impunity everywhere they look

Take a coroner who doesn't bother to do an autopsy but automatically declares this child died of heart failure due to obesity

Take a prosecutor who denies the reality of this child's life and death when he denies that this case has anything to do with her weight

Take the atmosphere of a carnival freak show with which this case is being portrayed by much of the media

And you tell me:

Who is really on [trial] here? Who among us is not responsible for the incredible injustice, the miserable life, and the terrible death of Christina Corrigan?

CHAPTER 2

THE FOOD POLICE

An Introduction to Fat Prejudice

Being fat is about knowing it. It is about a round-the-clock awareness that the fat person's body overflows the strict boundaries imposed on it by Western social and cultural norms. To be a fat woman means to carry a double burden, for women are expected to conform to a more rigorous and stereotyped aesthetic ideal than are men.

—Shelley Bovey, *The Forbidden Body*[1]

FIVE-YEAR-OLDS PREFER TO LOSE AN arm than be fat.[2] Formerly fat weight-loss surgery patients almost all agree they would rather lose a leg than be fat.[3] The stigma against fat is consistent and severe. Fat people are the daily recipients of significant hostility. Frequently they are victims of discrimination and abuse in employment, social settings, places of public accommodation, and peer groups as well as in their own homes from their own families.[4] This treatment drains self-esteem and severely affects quality of life.

Attitudes and architecture form barriers to a normal life for fat children and adults. For larger fat people, the daily physical discomfort of a world not built to accommodate their bodies can be tremendous. For example, the everyday task of commuting by bus or train imposes a substantial burden on a person who does not fit in the seat. Fellow passengers often react to this predicament with disgust or anger. Smaller fat people may not have difficulty with the fixtures in the bus or train, but may have problems nonetheless due to the attitudes around them. They may be singled out for verbal abuse from other travelers, or they may be heading to a job that will be given to a less-qualified thin person.

The financial consequences of being fat are not restricted to loss of employment opportunities and lower salaries. Being fat costs more. Fat people often must travel farther to find stores that carry their clothing size. They pay more for their clothes, with some retailers increasing the price of the garment by size.[5] Fat people pay more for health insurance, when they can get it at all. A study of discrimination against fat people in rental housing shows that fat people have a harder time finding available units and are quoted higher prices than their thin counterparts.[6]

Discrimination against fat people disproportionally affects groups that are already oppressed. Fat is more prevalent among Mexican Americans, African Americans, white women, and poor people, and has been associated with Jews and Italians.[7] Almost 30 percent of women with a yearly income below $10,000 are fat while only 12.7 percent of women earning over $50,000 per year are.[8] The Harvard School of Public Health conducted a study involving 10,000 women over the course of several years. It found that fat women are more likely to lose socioeconomic status than thin women regardless of their achievement test scores or family wealth. The average fat woman can expect her household income to be a full $6,710 lower than the average thin woman's.[9] Thin subjects with chronic conditions including birth defects, asthma, and diabetes were also tracked to provide a comparison. Unlike the fat subjects, they did not suffer economic and social consequences compared to the thin subjects, despite their disabilities.

People discriminate all the time. The ability to discriminate well is prized. To do so simply means to distinguish, to differentiate some things from other things. It involves noting a difference, deeming it unfavorable, and usually taking some action consistent with that negative opinion. Certain types of discrimination are odious and unjust. They contravene the fundamental ideology of the United States and offend basic principles of humanity. Many of these have been outlawed. Should the law allow or even compel a person to lose weight before receiving protection from discrimination? What is the difference between reasonable discrimination and unfair discrimination? Where is the line between equal rights and unfair advantage?

There are three fundamental ideologies behind antidiscrimination law and theory.

1. It is wrong, generally, to discriminate against a person for a characteristic they cannot control.

2. Capable people should not be prevented from contributing to the economy and society.

3. It may be wrong to discriminate when the result is an impingement on fundamental rights, freedoms, or human dignity.

The acceptability of fat prejudice and much of the hostility directed toward fat people is supported by the widespread belief that fat people can become thin if they choose to. Scientists have called for massive public education about the complex nature of "obesity" for decades, realizing it is necessary in order to dismantle the prejudice and stigma surrounding fat. They have not been successful. Contrary to popular opinion, scientific evidence over the past twenty years continues to point to the fact that, for the most part, weight is not within the control of the individual. A recent study with subjects living as inpatients at a Rockefeller University lab for up to two years showed, "There are biological mechanisms that regulate weight loss. This is contrary to the notion people have that obesity is a disorder of willpower."[10] Even through the use of powerful, potentially dangerous, new diet drugs, the amount of weight lost is low and temporary, with weight returning upon the cessation of medicine. According to a study published in the *International Journal of Obesity*, up to a full 95 percent of dieters regained all the weight they lost (and sometimes more) within three years.[11] Evidence indicates this process of losing weight and trying to become thin may be damaging in and of itself due to dangers associated with repeated weight loss and gain as well as psychological trauma from repeated "failures."

Others do not want help losing weight, rejecting the medical model altogether. They see the medical establishment as profiteers exploiting a vulnerable population. Some argue that fat is intimately connected to identity, just as race is. A member of the early fat liberation group known as the Los Angeles Fat Underground wrote a letter to the medical community in the 1970s, "You see fat as suicide, I see weight-loss as murder—

genocide, to be precise—the systematic murder of a biological minority by organized medicine."[12]

Of course, it is not just the medical establishment that has an interest in keeping fat unacceptable. At $33 to $50 billion per year, the weight-loss industry is a powerful market force completely dependent on convincing people that losing weight is so crucial it is worth braving the high failure rates.[13]

Prejudice against fat people, perpetuated by a powerful wave of money and industry, has resulted in second-class citizen status for many. Fat people have the same range of social and economic contributions to make in society as any group of people, but often they are prevented from realizing that potential because of bias. This bias can breach basic notions of human dignity and unjustly deny them rights enjoyed by their thin counterparts.

Decades ago, author Peter Wyden exposed the military's policy of denying promotions and reenlistments based on being "overweight." Now the military is even more stringent about weight. After serving in the National Guard for years, Nyleen Mullally started being denied promotions because of her weight. Finally she decided to resign rather than lose her "sanity" or her "life." Less than a year later she was told that the weight standards were suspended for the duration of Operation Desert Storm. She was called to involuntary active duty during that time. Not only promotions, but dismissals from the military can result from weight violations. The air force discharged a man, after over seventeen years of service, for his weight even though he had been allowed to enlist and was recruited while exceeding the standard weight. Had he made it to twenty years, he would have received retirement pay.[14]

Back in 1965, Wyden warned prophetically of the potential for culturewide discrimination, "Some authorities have predicted that similar policies will eventually be adopted by industry. . . . And it seems likely that insurance companies . . . will increasingly discriminate against the obese. . . . The psychiatrists are concerned about this relatively new discrimination against overweight adolescents. . . . 'They become minority groups; they're shunned!' "[15]

The courts have not been silent regarding the civil rights of fat people. Sometimes because of the law's apathy and sometimes because of the law's action, all of these predictions have come true. Courts have tended to treat fat as a mutable condition. They have not only demonstrated a willingness to tolerate requirements by employers and others that fat people reduce, judges themselves have issued the order to diet. Given the overwhelming failure of weight-loss efforts, the dangers of weight loss drugs and dieting, and the lack of "any scientific justification for the continued use of dietary treatments of obesity," is it appropriate for the legal system to continue on this course?[16] As the growing trend to resist weight-based discrimination, the renewed vigor to eradicate fat, and the backlash against civil rights combine, a tension is developing that will have to be addressed in the courtroom. Discrimination against fat people is the civil rights hurdle of the new millennium.

NOTES

1. Shelley Bovey, *The Forbidden Body: Why Being Fat Is Not a Sin* (Great Britain: HarperCollinsManufacturing, 1994), 1.

2. Nicole Campbell, "Weighed Down," *Daily Californian*, 16 May 1995, 9. Reviewing a *20/20* television interview of several five-year-old children, their choice to lose an arm rather than be fat was unanimous.

3. Gina Kolata, "The Burdens of Being Overweight: Mistreatment and Misconceptions," *New York Times*, 22 November 1992, A1.

4. The word "fat" is used throughout this book whenever possible instead of the terms "overweight," which assumes an ideal weight, and "obese," which is a loaded, medical determination. The fat-activist community largely embraces the term. They explain that "fat" is an adjective like "tall" or "thin" and should not be offensive.

5. Note: The custom of the fashion industry is not to differentiate in price between "regular-sized" garments, despite the fact that technically there is an increase in cost between a size 3 skirt and the identical skirt in a size 12. This practice, like the practice of charging women more for the identical haircut or dry cleaning than men, is not motivated by industry need, but instead by industry greed. Just as women are sometimes charged more because they are women, fat people are sometimes charged more because they are fat.

6. Lambros Karris, "Prejudice Against Obese Renters," *Journal of Social Psychology* 101 (1977): 159–60.

7. Hillel Schwartz, *Never Satisfied: A Cultural History of Diets, Fantasies, and Fat* (New York: Doubleday, 1986), 143; and "The World in Medicine," *JAMA* 278, no. 2 (1997): 106.

8. Examiner Staff, "Weight Bias Ruling Starts Fight For Law," *SF Examiner*, 5 September 1993, A16 (quoting National Center for Health Statistics).

9. News Service, "Obesity's Burden," *Star Tribune*, 30 September 1993, A7–A8.

10. Quoted from the *Boston Globe*, "Body of Evidence Proves Dieters Can't Win," *Oakland Tribune*, 9 March 1995, A1.

11. F. Kramer et al., "Long-Term Followup of Behavioral Treatment for Obesity: Patterns of Weight Regain Among Men and Women," *International Journal of Obesity* 13, no. 2 (1989): 123–26.

12. Schwartz, *Never Satisfied*, 324.

13. Naomi Wolf, *The Beauty Myth* (New York: William Morris and Co., Inc., 1991), 17.

14. "Service Members Reach Out to NAAFA," *NAAFA Newsletter* 23, no. 6 (May 1993): 5.

15. Peter Wyden, *The Overweight Society* (New York: Pocket Books, Inc, 1966), 259. This passage quotes Dr. Trulson from Harvard.

16. David Garner and Susan Wooley, "Confronting the Failure of Behavioral and Dietary Treatments for Obesity," *Clinical Psychology Review* 11, no. 6 (1991): 767.

CHAPTER 3

BUT NAMES
WILL NEVER HURT ME

Growing Up Fat

Birthdays were not usually a big deal in my family, but this one was different. I knew it would be good. I was about to turn sixteen. I had been looking forward to it for months, hoping my parents would give me a bike or a puppy. When I saw my present, I was crushed. They gave me a Weight Watchers cookbook and a scale. It was devastating to me.

Years later, when I was in college, my mother acknowledged how terrible it had made me feel. She explained to me that, at the time, she was very depressed about my weight. I was getting fatter and she did not know what to do. The irony is I was in the best shape of my life then. I could run two miles. At sixteen I was 5'4", weighed 145 pounds, and had a 32-inch waist.

Near the end of her short life, the walls of Christina Corrigan's two-bedroom apartment marked the borders of her world. It had not always been that way. Christina never knew what it was like to interact with the world as a thin person. Her experience was of an overwhelmingly hostile landscape where she managed to carve out a few small oases of safety. One oasis was grade school in the company of her friends who knew and cared about her. They would look out for her, defend her, and make sure nobody sat in her special seat. Another safe haven was her home, where she and her mother shared a room and talked like best friends. In the cool water of the apartment swimming pool she would swim with her brother. While moving between those places she faced constant torment.

At first, Christina's quick thinking and bold tongue held back the anger around her. When adults would approach her and demand, "Why are you so fat?" she confidently and proudly responded, "Why are you so rude?" But eventually it was too much for her. When she reached puberty the characteristic pluck gave way under the pressure of the world and she started hiding. Riding the city bus to school with her mother she encountered verbal abuse from strangers sitting behind her. When her mother moved to respond, it was a very different Christina who pleaded desperately, "Shhhh. Please be quiet. Just ignore them. Please."

The United States has declared a War on Fat. With no study to demonstrate even the possibility of long-term successful weight loss, but backed by diet industry money, this war is both under-researched and overfunded. And fat children are the most innocent casualties. Those who survive the abuse of strangers may still be brought down by friendly fire from their own well-meaning parents, teachers, peers, and care providers.

Threatened with ill-heath and a limited future if they resist, children are battered by unrelenting pressure to be thin at a time in their lives when they are most concerned about fitting in. People are counseled that it is acceptable, even imperative, to intervene in the lives of fat people, offering advice and judgment freely. Fat kids and teens endure repeated physical, verbal, and emotional abuse because of their weight.

When does childhood abuse on the basis of weight become an issue worth pursuing through the law and the legal system? When the abuse curtails certain rights, opportunities, and liberties like the right not to be assaulted, to receive an equal education, to be safe, to have reasonable self-esteem, to use places of public accommodation, to have bias-free healthcare, and to lead a full life, the abuse then necessarily involves justice, and thus, deserves the attention of the law.

The law fails fat children most often not because of what it does, but because of what it does not do. It is not enough that fat children are allowed to go to school. The same approach was taken with women's rights but it failed as well. For example, civil rights law has not completed its task simply because it has forced the all-male military school known as the Citadel to accept women. That is a meaningless victory if the actual women who attend the facility are not getting the same treatment and opportunities as the men. When the women leave in droves because of harassment they experience because of their sex, they are not getting the same opportunities as the men who do not have to deal with that specific kind of treatment. When the harassment is not so great that the women leave, but sufficient to cause them to be unable to perform to the best of their abilities, justice has yet to be achieved. Similarly, the fact that fat children are not barred from the classroom does not support the conclusion that they are getting equal educational opportunities.

Fat children and teens suffer serious discrimination. Past prejudice, like the denial of letters of recommendation and lower college admission rates, has been documented by the National Education Association (NEA) and various studies, and future discrimination is absolutely foreseeable. Abuse of fat kids both during and outside of school hours is an everyday occurrence. It is generally neither seen nor treated as a problem by the courts, nor taken seriously by the school's staff. But it is a serious problem.

The prejudice fat kids face can be predicted by studying the framework espoused by author and researcher Ann Hill Beuf. She outlines the level and effect of stigmatization on, as she describes them, "appearance-impaired" children in the United States. Beuf recognizes several factors that predict the likelihood that children will suffer stigmatizing and objectifying experiences.[1] They include:

- *Sociocultural system*: What is the cultural backdrop or environment like? How concerned is the society with the type of appearance in question?
- *Developmental age*: She asserts the five-year-old will be less disturbed by disfigurement than the adolescent.
- *Visibility*: How serious is the impairment? Children with visible impairments fare far worse than others.
- *Severity*: How serious is the impairment? The more severe the problem, the more stigmatization.
- *Psychological resources*: Humor, self-esteem, intelligence, creativity, etc.
- *Social resources*: Economic status, parental status in the community, ethnic-group support, parental education, social isolation, family solidarity, etc.

- *Level/location of social interaction*: What is the availability of support at the place and time of the interaction?

These elements are at their worst extremes for many fat children.

SOCIOCULTURAL SYSTEM

The sociocultural backdrop for fat children in the United States is grim. Thinness is the religion of American culture. This is easily apparent by viewing a few hours of television. A plethora of scholarly books and studies document the incredibly negative attitude toward even the slightest amount of "overweight." Terry Poulton, author of *No Fat Chicks*, is one of the many authors to gather proof of this trend. Among her findings: the ideal for women, as measured through beauty pageant contestant, actress, and model weights, has dropped to at least 25 percent under the weight of the average American woman; in one study, almost 30,000 women identified weight loss as so important they would choose losing weight above the achievement of any other goal; eating disorders are rampant among children, teens, and young adults; and millions of women choose to abuse their bodies and health in an effort to avoid weight gain by smoking, taking laxatives, and refusing birth control pills.[2] Another study shows girls avoid critical asthma treatments for fear of gaining weight.

Even while certain studies have documented less body dissatisfaction among black girls than white girls, likely due to a healthier cultural attitude toward body image, anecdotal evidence confirms that black children are far from immune to fatphobia, and that fatphobia exists within the black community. A study published in *Pediatrics* in 1996 found no differences between black and white nine- to ten-year-old girls in their efforts to lose weight and to engage in chronic dieting.[3]

Societal pressure to be slender is so strong that formerly fat patients say they would rather be blind, deaf, or lose a limb than be fat again. With fat comes stereotypes of laziness and stupidity. Beuf's own research shows that people link chubby kids with attributes like, "sulky, spoiled, impatient, and a show-off."[4] On the whole, mainstream American society is as hostile toward fat as it could possibly be short of criminalizing it. (And

some would say that the case against Marlene Corrigan was a criminal-
ization of fat.)

DEVELOPMENTAL AGE

Although Beuf suggests that five-year-olds may fare significantly better than
teenagers, there is much evidence that, where weight is concerned, body
image problems start very young. By the age of six to nine years, children
acquire an "active dislike" of fat bodies.[5] A San Francisco–based study of
500 girls showed that almost half of the nine-year-olds were dieting.[6] By
age twelve, this number had jumped to 80 percent. Teens were dieting at
an even higher rate. While studies of younger children were not available,
Joanne Ikeda, renowned nutritionist at the University of California,
Berkeley, is concerned about the effects on younger children. She describes
an incident where her very thin three-year-old daughter stuck out her
stomach and exclaimed that she was too fat.[7] In a New York study involving
over three hundred high-school girls, the teens were divided into groups
based on their weight. Thirty-six percent were "underweight," 17 percent
were "overweight," and almost half were "normal" weight. In all three classifications a majority of the girls reported being terrified of being overweight.[8] When weight-consciousness and body-image problems start so
young, there are years left for them to fester, growing more severe and
increasingly paralyzing.

VISIBILITY AND SEVERITY

The visibility component is extreme for fat children. Obviously, fat is a
completely visible condition. Even the most moderate fat is difficult to
disguise (though fashion magazines are full of tips about style and color to
conceal "problem areas" while perpetuating body dissatisfaction). People
will go to extremes to hide fat. One report, published in Largesse's
newsletter, *Food for Thought*, found 88 percent of American women avoid
wearing a bathing suit. Adolescents and teenagers may be particularly
attuned to noticing and exaggerating even the slightest weight variation.

Studies of adults and children demonstrate that the severity of the discrimination increases with the amount of weight. A 1994 study of pre-adolescents found the heaviest children reported the most discontent with their bodies. And while the severity of the weight condition varies in each individual case, even thin children are made to feel fat through comparisons with the modern shrinking American ideal.

PSYCHOLOGICAL RESOURCES

Studies indicate the psychological resources of fat children are compromised as a result of society's negative views about fat. Children who fall victim to these stereotypes may experience intense self-hatred and begin a psychologically dangerous pattern of disordered eating. At Leeds University in the United Kingdom, an investigation into the attributes that young children link with fat measured weight-based perceptions about health and social functioning. Drawings showing the silhouettes of a thin boy, a fat boy, a thin girl, and a fat girl were given to 188 nine-year-olds. The children completed a series of ratings, and their own height, weight, and dietary restraints were measured. Researchers found that, "The overweight body shape was associated with poor social functioning, impaired academic success, and low perceived health, healthy eating and fitness."[9] The weight and gender of the rater had little impact on their perceptions, but the girls' judgments about themselves showed that they had a greater relevance of weight to their own perception of their personal attributes. The study concluded that the prejudices and stereotypes against fat people voiced by society are perceived and internalized by children. So while all fat children are at risk for internalizing these messages, girls are particularly vulnerable.

Much concern is expressed about the self-esteem of fat children, though many of the studies are drawn with an eye toward improving weight loss. A 1995 review of the literature on fat and self-esteem in children and adolescents examined evidence from thirty-five studies to determine whether and in what ways self-esteem is tied to weight. Though many of the studies were methodologically weak due to small sample groups and few comparison groups, of twenty-five cross-sectional studies,

thirteen demonstrated a clear relationship between fat children and adolescents and lower self-esteem.[10] Since then several new studies have been
conducted. A 1996 study of 1,278 seventh and ninth graders showed an
inverse relationship between body-mass index (an indicator of fatness
which involves height and weight) and physical-appearance self-esteem in
both boys and girls. For fat girls in particular, global self-esteem is lower
than their thin counterparts, and even three years later physical-appearance
and social-acceptance self-esteem were inversely related to body-mass
index.[11] As weight increases, esteem decreases. A 1997 study looking at
eating problems and self-esteem of fifteen- to sixteen-year-old girls looked
at questionnaires from 609 girls, studying a subgroup of 31 of the
teenagers. It found 32 percent scored above the Hospital Anxiety and
Depression Scale threshold for anxiety and that 43 percent had low self-
esteem according to the Rosenberg Self-Esteem Scale.[12]

SOCIAL RESOURCES AND THE AVAILABILITY OF SOCIAL SUPPORT

Les and Gabi Voss are an average young Arizona couple thrust into a very
unusual situation.[13] Their baby, born a normal weight at 7 pounds 3 ounces
and fed a normal diet, has gained almost a pound per week, reaching more
than twice the average weight for a baby her age. At fourteen months,
Lyndon is a beautiful, cheery, curly-haired, playful child who weighs
nearly 50 pounds. Her parents continue the frustrating and so far unsuccessful search for medical answers while her mother keeps working with a
nutritionist.

Until the Vosses find the answer to the mystery of their daughter's
weight, the couple has decided not to have any more children. This decision is perhaps one of the most telling sentiments about the underlying
social climate for fat children. It is not that fat children are not loved by
their parents once they arrive. Fat children absolutely can be and are loved
by their families. But like many disabled children, the love covers a complicated truth—that they were not exactly what their parents had hoped
for, envisioned, and dreamed about. In her book *Losing It*, investigative
writer Laura Fraser reports that a full 11 percent of people would abort if

they found out in advance their child would have a genetic *tendency* to become fat.[14] While most parents will treat their fat children as well as they can once they have arrived, they may still think it would be better if fat people were never born at all.

Once the fat child has arrived, it is unlikely that she will have a wealth of social resources to help and support her. Because fat often runs in the family, large children are likely to be exposed to the severe negative financial and emotional consequences their fat parents suffered as "overweight" people in a biased society. (A child from thin parents has a 3 to 7 percent chance of becoming fat. A child with one fat biological parent has a 40 percent chance of becoming fat. A child from two fat biological parents has an 80 percent chance of being fat.[15]) Fat people are more likely to be from a low socioeconomic status than thin people.[16] Fat women are ten times more likely to be poor than their thin counterparts. Their household income is nearly $7,000 less than the household income of thin women.

On the whole, families headed by fat people will have less economic standing in the community and fewer economic resources available to assist their fat children than will thin families. Many fat people suffer a double blow because fat is more prevalent in certain minority groups and these groups are already financially disadvantaged. (Fat minority women may be triply disadvantaged by their weight, ethnicity, and gender.) Not only do women earn less than men in general, and not only do fat women earn less than thin women in general, but spending on costly weight-loss services and medications is largely the arena of women. While, according to U.S. Census data, only 13 percent of the 3.8 million people earning over $75,000 are women, Marketdata Enterprises reports that 95 percent of the two billion dollars spent annually on commercial weight loss programs are spent by women. Similarly, 90 percent of the diet pill prescriptions are made out to women.

The medical establishment focuses aggressively on the eradication of fat. Fat children are often victimized by this medical system, which refuses to acknowledge that weight-loss efforts during childhood are largely unsuccessful and can be harmful physically and psychologically, replacing normal childhood goals with the improbable aim of lasting weight loss. A prominent physician at Stanford University's childhood obesity treatment project is aware of the minuscule "success" rate for medically supervised programs, but admits he continues to recommend low- or very-low-calorie diets hoping that one of his patients will be in the "lucky" 2 to 5 percent.

Because of these attitudes, parents are consistently encouraged by medical professionals to start their children on reduced-calorie diets, which are the gateway to disordered eating later in life. This despite the fact that a longitudinal study published in *Obesity and Health* reported, "Caloric intake was not positively associated with childhood obesity at any age [and] children who became obese were not more likely to have consumed more calories."[17] Dieting alters the metabolism and may affect normal satiety signals. Warning that childhood dieting only makes children fatter or brings about eating disorders, Bill Fabrey, founder of the National Association to Advance Fat Acceptance, writes: "Surveys reveal children as young as the fourth grade are dieting, and are developing eating disorders. Yet public health statistics tell us there is an ever-increasing proportion of fat kids in the population, despite well-intentioned efforts by millions of parents to encourage weight loss in their offspring. Obviously diets, medications, and weight loss camps . . . have not resulted in slimmer teenagers. . . . The solution advocated by many educators: work harder at the same methods that failed in the past!" Eerily, his words hold as true today as they did when written in the 1980s.[18]

More and more, doctors and nutritionists are questioning why children should diet at all. In her 1998 concept paper, *Children and Weight*, Patricia Crawford, codirector of the University of California, Berkeley's Center for Weight and Health, clarifies, "Overweight children do not experience the extent of medical complications of obesity which are experienced by obese adults. . . . Weight loss is inappropriate for children before they have completed puberty. More appropriate goals are increased physical activity/fitness level, improved dietary habits, improved self esteem and body image (or decreased body dissatisfaction), and improved physiological measures such as decreased lipids, blood glucose or asthma complications. . . . The need to equip the child with skills to cope with stressful situations and develop self-esteem is often overlooked."[19] The *New England Journal of Medicine*'s New Year's editorial recognizes, "As common as efforts to lose weight are in the general population, they are virtually ubiquitous among adolescent girls and young women. . . . Although many girls caught up in these practices [bizarre, severe diets and anorexic and bulimic behaviors] are well aware of the hazards, they would rather risk death than fall short in their attempts to attain the contemporary esthetic ideal of extreme thinness."[20] Eating disorder expert and therapist Ellyn Satter explains that by the time parents come to her for counseling to help their children lose weight, "They have already developed a highly charged, negative response to their kid's eating habits. They have tried withholding certain foods, under-feeding, and offering bribes without success. The child is usually preoccupied with food and afraid of having to go hungry. Food has become the source of conflict and mealtime is a nightmare for everyone."[21]

Whether the parents are fat or thin, fat children often do not receive the support at home that they need. The internalized self-hatred that many fat adults have developed after years of unsuccessful dieting can be passed on to their children. Whereas children who are members of other oppressed minority groups often enjoy a sense of pride or at least acceptance from their parents and community, fat children tend not to share those benefits, many times being blamed for their condition by their loved ones. Author Charlotte Cooper describes a family member's reaction to her nephew, "At a recent birthday gathering one of the older relatives commented disparagingly, 'No wonder he's so big, shoveling that food away.' Sam is one year old, he has only just learnt to walk, and already the obsession is starting."[22] Fat parents can be extremely oppressive about fat and food issues. They may be desperate to make their children slim to help their kids avoid the harassment and lost opportunities they learned about firsthand.

Fat or thin, parents who have not reeducated themselves stand to permanently harm their kids. Parents today have grown up in the era of the fad diet. This may lead them to engage in abnormal eating patterns. Those who have not been able to come to terms with their own disordered eating can put incredible pressure on their children while setting an unhealthy example. Jason Advani★ grew up with parents plagued by eating and body-image problems. He says, "I am not blaming them for my lifetime problems with food, but I first learned the pattern of using food as a stress reliever from my mother and then feeling horrible about it from my father." Jason never had body-image problems until he was forced to engage in crash dieting—his parents' favorite pastime—in the third grade.

★Name changed to protect privacy. Private interview, 1998.

The fact one of his parents was a doctor did not save him from the long list of weight-reduction strategies: the Rotation Diet with its alternating daily caloric allowances, the diet shakes, the constant salads, the cabbage soup, and the exercise binges. "My father was getting pressure from his colleagues who said I was too fat. He would say 'We are such fat slobs. We are disgusting.' He tormented me with exercise. If I resisted he would try to bully me. He would start yelling insults at me, saying, 'God damn it! I am your father and you need to do this. You are fat, lazy, and stupid!' When I did try, he would say, 'You're fat. Move it! You've got to go faster!' " Jason certainly was not going to learn confidence or self-esteem from his family at home. His only hope for normalizing his eating and salvaging his body image was an enlightened school environment.

Fat family members can become weapons in a household facing a weight crisis. One fat woman of thin parents remembers being repeatedly warned not to eat because "You'll end up looking like Aunt Kaye." This common behavior has a negative impact not only on the child, but also on the devalued fat family member.

Anecdotal evidence shows that incredible family pressures are often heaped on the back of the fat child. Profiling lifelong dieter Janet Zuckerman, writer Deanne Stone reports that during her childhood, Zuckerman's weight had a profound impact on the family's dynamic. "Family life revolved around Zuckerman's eating. Each morning began with her weigh-in. On days when she was down half a pound, the mood of the family was optimistic. But on other days when her weight was up, gloom prevailed."[23]

Another woman recalls how her well-meaning parents decimated her self-esteem in their quest to help her lose weight. Prue was unusual. While people like Jason learned to hate their bodies early, as a teenager Prue would still look at herself in the mirror and feel good about the way she looked. When she expressed satisfaction with her body to her parents their response was that if she liked the way she looked, she "must not be seeing right." Her parents, both members of the medical profession, were very concerned about her weight. The eating pattern of the whole family was changed to help her lose weight. There was no more sweetened cereal kept in the house. They switched to low-fat milk and stopped having "real" desserts. Her siblings resented the dietary changes in the household and she resented being denied food that her siblings were allowed. With sci-

entific accuracy, her mother would weigh her once a week. When the 5'4"
teenager's weight exceeded 150 pounds, her mother would cry in front of
her. She remembers, "When my mother got too depressed about my
failure to lose weight she'd take it out on me for a week and make me eat
cabbage soup. And it was so ironic because I was very active in the sports
program at my school, running sprints each day."[24] Since she was not losing
weight even when she tried, she explains, "I knew I wasn't succeeding and
that I couldn't so it became easier to lie. Once my parents accidentally
bought regular soda. I was so relieved. I finally could yell back at them and
say 'No wonder I'm not losing weight. You bought the wrong soda and
I've been drinking it for a week!'"

Zuckerman's parents also restricted her food intake, forbidding her
from eating the same food as her siblings. Both young women had the
same reaction. They began sneaking food. Joanne Ikeda predicts this
response, "Therapists working with children whose food intake is being
restricted often find that these children are begging, scavenging, and even
stealing food because of their fear of hunger."[25]

Having spent many years conducting weight-management programs
for adolescents, Ikeda stopped when she realized she was making their distress worse by reinforcing the idea that there was something wrong with
their bodies. In the California guidelines she authored, she encourages
parents of fat children to give the kids love and attention. She warns that
they must not be pressured to lose weight. She says it is important not to
limit the child's food and not to segregate their food from the rest of the
family's, while being sure to encourage the child to get physical activity
like walking the dog or playing outside.[26]

Fat children are frequently left without a safety zone where they are
accepted unconditionally. Prue recalls her father's treatment of her inside
the family home: "My father, a world-renowned doctor, quipped that he
wished I would 'catch anorexia' and then took it to the next level when I
was older by stating flat out, 'I'm ashamed to be seen with you.' He thought
this would help me. He thought the pain would be so intense that I would
stop eating. It just made me seek comfort and of course, I ate more."[27]
Another teenager writes about her experience with her father. "[He told
me] 'No boy is ever going to like you if you don't lose some weight.' I still
can't believe he said that, but I was naive enough to believe him, and even

to stay and finish a conversation that deserved to be walked out on."[28] The failure of even medically trained and educated parents to provide a comfortable home where their fat children can be safe from the fatphobia and harassment of the world emphasizes the vulnerability of fat children in the current social climate. Unlike other appearance-impaired children, and unlike most racial minority children, home is rarely a safe haven for the overweight child. Ikeda describes the hurt some fat children in her group experienced because they had no place where they would receive full and unconditional support: "We needed . . . levity to ease the pain—the pain of knowing that your parents would love you more, your teachers would like you more, and your life would be more wonderful if you could just look like the kids featured in *Sassy, Seventeen,* or *Young and Modern.*"[29]

Though researcher Ann Hill Beuf's framework foretells this reality, it remains intuitively obvious that fat children growing up in this culture will be singled out as the subject of many stigmatizing experiences based on their size and shape. Teasing is one of the most common and arguably the most acceptable of these behaviors. Joanne Ikeda and Priscilla Naworski find, "Larger children are often teased or called names. Put-downs that refer to a child's size may be heard in the classroom, on the playground, in the gym, in the neighborhood—anywhere children have time and an environment that permits hassling or ridiculing others who are different from the norm. Children are very sensitive to such teasing and name calling." Adults can be very callous about verbal abuse. This indifference has consequences. Ikeda and Naworski continue, "Teachers, parents and other caregivers who allow children to tease each other about physical traits or abilities should realize that such teasing contributes to low self-esteem and poor body image."[30]

The severity of the pain caused by these verbal assaults is consistently underappreciated, but the effects of even very limited harassment can be extremely long-lasting. Sometimes it is literally a matter of life and death. *Fat!So?* author and Fat Speaker's Bureau cofounder Marilyn Wann is motivated to reach out to children in part by memories of her own childhood. She recalls, "I had a different background than most fat kids because I did not grow up dieting. My self-esteem was good. Still, when I got teased, it was heavy. Twenty-five years later I still remember very clearly certain kids and what they said. And I remember those certain moments when I just did not want to be who I was. And how much I wanted to be anywhere but there."[31]

Fat children do not only suffer the unkind words of their peers. At home, siblings are notoriously cruel about weight when one child is fat compared to the others. Even when parents are effective at curbing sibling name-calling in their presence, fat kids commonly report being harassed by their brothers and sisters for the hours before the parents return. Fat children also receive verbal abuse from adults, even when the kids are behaving exactly as the experts say they should. The only advice for fat children that all the professionals agree on is that fat children should lead active, not sedentary, lives. Problematically, being active in traditional ways makes fat kids visible and vulnerable to repeated verbal assaults. A fat child jogging down the street can expect to be called names from passing cars. Fat children walking on the boardwalk can expect to hear nasty comments from the people they pass. These interactions alienate fat kids from their bodies and from activity, denying them the benefits of exercise that their thin peers enjoy. The experiences are humiliating, especially when they occur in public. Making fun of the fat kid is such an acceptable practice, that it is not limited to the sphere of personal interaction. Reporting on a fat high-school football player, a San Diego newscaster concluded the story by drawing out his words with barely veiled contempt, "He may not be the best player, but he's the biggest!" As the camera pulled back from the shot of the reporter and the fat boy, to a wide shot of the news team, the reporters shared a laugh at his observation and bid the city a good night.

Fat kids will suffer objectifying and stigmatizing events because of their weight. The discrimination is entirely predictable and the resulting devastation is foreseeable as well. These experiences result in lower self-esteem, alienation, and denial of the benefits of activity while unnecessarily curtailing the kids' future opportunities. Protecting every fat child from all harassment is impossible, but some basic improvements need to be made. Specifically, parents and the public need to be educated and to educate themselves about fat prejudice in order to alleviate some of the intense cultural pressure put on children to lose weight no matter what the cost. It is unfair that children be treated differently by their families, peers, care-givers, and teachers just because they come in "a larger package." Improving the quality of life for fat children must become a priority for all people interested in a just society.

NOTES

1. Ann Hill Beuf, *Beauty Is the Beast: Appearance-Impaired Children in America* (Philadelphia: University of Pennsylvania Press, 1990). See "A Model for Understanding Children and Stigma" at 22–25 and "Vulnerability to Stigmatization" at 59–62.

2. Terry Poulton, *No Fat Chicks: How Big Business Profits by Making Women Hate Their Bodies—And How to Fight Back* (N.J.: Birch Lane Press, 1997), 13–14.

3. Patricia Crawford, Nutrition Research Coordinator, School of Public Health, University of California, Berkeley. (Workgroup members: Laura Brainin-Rodriguez, Lucy Adams, Joanne Ikeda, Rita Allhoff Mitchell, and Karen Pertschuk) *Children and Weight: What Health Professionals Can Do About It*, Concept Paper, 1998, 21. Referring to G. B. Schreiber, M. Robins, R. Striegel-Moore, and E. Obazanek. "Weight Modification Efforts Reported by Black and White Preadolescent Girls: National Heart, Lung and Blood Institute Growth and Health study," *Pediatrics* 98 (1996): 63–70.

4. Beuf, *Beauty Is the Beast*, 59.

5. Crawford, *Children and Weight*, 22. Referring to M. Feldman, E. Feldman, and J. T. Goodman, "Culture versus Biology: Children's Attitudes Towards Thinness and Fatness," *Pediatrics* 81 (1988): 190–94.

6. Ben Davis, "Fatphobia and Children/ Myth and Reality," *Size and Self-Acceptance* (Sacramento, Calif.: NAAFA, 1995).

7. Ibid.

8. Frances Berg, *Children and Teens in Weight Crisis* (N. Dak.: Healthy Weight Journal, 1995), 5.

9. A. Hill and E. Silver, "Fat, Friendless and Unhealthy: Nine-Year-Old Children's Perception of Body-Shape Stereotypes," *International Journal of Obesity and Related Metabolic Disorders* 19, no. 6 (June 1995): 423–30.

10. S. French, M. Story, and C. Perry, "Self-Esteem and Obesity in Children and Adolescents: A Literature Review," *Obesity Research* 3, no. 5 (September 1995): 479–90.

11. S. French, C. Perry, G Leon, and J. Fulkerson, "Self-Esteem and Change in Body Mass Index Over Three Years in a Cohort of Adolescents," *Obesity Research* 4, no. 1 (January 1996): 27–33.

12. E. Button, P. Loan, J. Davies, and E. Sonuga-Barke, "Self-Esteem, Eating Problems, and Psychological Well-being in a Cohort of Schoolgirls Aged

15–16: A Questionnaire and Interview Study," *International Journal of Eating Disorders* 21, no. 1 (January 1997): 39–47.

13. Karina Bland, "At 47 Pounds, Infant Is Both Concern, Puzzle," *San Diego Union-Tribune*, 6 February 1999. Information about the Voss family is also from an interview conducted with them on the *Maury Povich Show*.

14. Laura Fraser, *Losing It: False Hopes and Fat Profits in the Diet Industry* (New York: Plume, 1998), 47, referring to a survey by the New England Genetics Group.

15. Joanne Ikeda and Priscilla Naworski, *Am I Fat? Helping Young Children Accept Differences in Body Size* (Santa Cruz: ETR Associates, 1992), 17.

16. Jerome Kassirer and Marcia Angell, "Losing Weight—An Ill-Fated New Year's Resolution," *New England Journal of Medicine* 338, no. 1 (1998): editorial.

17. Patricia Crawford and Leona Shapiro, "How Obesity Develops: A New Look at Nature and Nurture," *Obesity and Health* (May/June 1991): 41.

18. William Fabrey, "Size Acceptance—Where We Are Today," *Radiance* (Fall 1987): 7.

19. Patricia Crawford, *Children and Weight*, 17, 19.

20. Kassirer and Angell, "Losing Weight—An Ill-Fated New Year's Resolution," editorial.

21. Deanne Stone, "Enlightening Trends: Weight Programs for Kids," *Radiance* (Fall 1987): 27.

22. Charlotte Cooper, *Fat and Proud: The Politics of Size* (London: The Woman's Press, 1998), 39.

23. Deanne Stone, "Desperate to Be Thin: A Woman's Lifelong Struggle to Please Others—And Finally Herself," *Radiance* (Fall 1987): 23.

24. Private interview, 1999.

25. Joanne Ikeda, "Promoting Size Acceptance for Children," in *Children and Teens in Weight Crisis*, ed. Frances Berg (N. Dak.: Healthy Weight Journal, 1995), 24.

26. Joanne Ikeda, *If My Child Is Too Fat, What Should I Do About It?* Publication 21455, University of California, Department of Agriculture and Natural Resources.

27. Private interview, name withheld by request.

28. Lorca James, "Fat or Not: A Teenager Reports," *Radiance* (Fall 1987): 40.

29. Ikeda, "Promoting Size Acceptance for Children," 25.

30. Ikeda and Naworski, *Am I Fat?* 37.

31. Marilyn Wann, interview, March 1999, San Francisco, Calif.

CHAPTER 4

EDUCATION AND THE FAT CHILD

For fat students, the school experience is one of ongoing prejudice, unnoticed discrimination, and almost constant harassment. From nursery school through college, fat students experience ostracism, discouragement, and some-times violence. Often ridiculed by their peers and discouraged by even well-meaning education employees, fat students develop low self-esteem and have limited horizons. They are deprived of places on honor rolls, sports teams, and cheerleading squads and are denied letters of recommendation.

—National Education Association[1]

IF ONE MOMENT MARKED THE beginning of the end of Christina Corrigan's short life, it was when she could no longer go to school. Christina was comfortable attending her middle school where she had friends and teachers who knew her and supported her. Her mother was always concerned that Christina be as active as possible, so she encouraged her to walk to and from the middle school. During those walks, Christina got more than just exercise. She got a preview of what lay in store for her at her new school.

Christina confided to her mother that, as she made the walk home, she was sometimes accompanied by a very unwelcome escort—a boy from the school she was scheduled to attend. This boy rode his bicycle to and from junior high. On his way, he made it a point to travel with Christina. As she walked, he circled her repeatedly on his bicycle. As he rode around her, he mercilessly made fun of her, calling out terrible names and hurling dreadful insults. And he was not the only older child to make fun of her.

The verbal harassment Christina endured from the junior high kids affected her profoundly. It did more than damage her self-esteem and her dignity. It strangled her spirit and robbed her of her future. To imagine a school experience where these teenagers would have even more access to her, where she would be even more vulnerable, was unthinkable.

Anyone who understood what Christina faced would understand her desperation and fear. Marlene directly witnessed only some of her daughter's pain, but what she saw was enough. Schools are legally required under disability laws to be physically accessible, yet when Marlene made inquiries about access assistance for Christina, she was met with total disregard. If the school was apathetic about that most basic need, they were not going to understand or be concerned with this more subtle problem. Average caring parents would be stymied by the problems Christina faced. Marlene Corrigan was not like most parents. Taking care of her aging parents and working as the sole provider for her son and daughter, Marlene was overworked and had few economic and social resources. While it is convenient to say she should have done more, it is unfair. Therapist and dietitian Ellyn Satter observes, "Fat children grow up to think less of themselves when their parents think less of them. Fat children and their parents need help in learning to deal with the prejudice and social and emotional challenges associated with obesity."[2] While people around her were telling Marlene to make every aspect of Christina's entire life about weight loss, Marlene was dead set against tying Christina's self-esteem to the success of her attempts at weight loss. She witnessed Christina's inability to lose weight on many diets and came to understand that Christina was a worthwhile person who "came in a larger package." Having come to this conclusion with no support, information, or sense of community is impressive itself. To expect Marlene to have the wherewithal and experience to shoulder the huge prejudice Christina faced *and* turn it around, is unrealistic. Schools, especially underfunded ones, are not eager to take on the challenge of making their halls safe places for fat children. Why should Marlene be able to institute change that scores of activists, lots of other parents of fat kids, and the National Education Association itself were unable to accomplish? And so Christina's new school failed her in two ways. Not only was the campus physically inaccessible, but the school itself was psychologically inaccessible and unsafe. Physically, Christina could not navigate the campus. Emotionally, she could not survive its hatred and hostility.

The start of school is an important event in the lives of children, but it can be a particularly difficult transition for fat children. Now a successful grantwriter, Christine Ianeri explains, "I can remember a time when I didn't feel shame about being fat. I was four or five. Once I hit school, I became aware of the strange power of the word FAT. It could come at me anytime; for no reason I could see, and it immediately drained me of my sense of worth. There was so clearly a consensus around me that being fat negated me as a valid human being."[3] Her perception is backed up by extensive sociobiological and sociocultural research.

Parents must be prepared and must insist on compassion and training in schoolteachers. Numerous studies show that kids reject obese children. In these studies, young subjects are presented with average-looking children and with children who have appearance-related physical stigmas like facial scars, deformed hands, fat, and wheelchair usage. The subjects are then asked to rank the kids in the order they would most prefer to have as friends. The fat-child option is consistently chosen last or next to last.[4] Educators must address this reality because, while these studies have implications far beyond the schoolyard, the immediate effect of this fat-hatred on peer socialization and engagement in the education setting is monumental.

This prejudice manifests itself in the school environment in several ways. Fat children consistently undergo prolonged name-calling, teasing, and verbal harassment while at school or traveling to and from school. Like thousands of fat children, Christine Ianeri and Lorca James each distinctly remember being called names like "Orca" at school. For Lorca the problem was so bad she persuaded her parents to allow her to officially change her name on school records to the name "Laurie," though she still worried her schoolmates would find out her real name. From "watermelon" to "fatso" to "Fat Albert," the names change with each generation but the attitudes persist with little if any parent or teacher intervention.

Having spent significant time with fat children, renowned University of California at Berkeley nutritionist Joanne Ikeda agrees that teasing is a serious problem but explains, "A lot of teachers do not have any idea how to handle it." After leading a workshop for teachers, an instructor came up to her and shared a problem they were having at the school where she worked. Between classes a group of boys congregated at the bottom of the school stairs. From there they would loudly pass judgment on each girl as she walked down, calling out "fat ass" or "big boobs." Not only did Ikeda find the behavior shocking, but she was amazed that the teacher who related the story felt no embarrassment about her own lack of action to prevent the daily harassment.[5] In their book, Ikeda and Naworski talk about the problems children face about their weight in school and encourage school administrators, teachers, and staff members to take an active role in promoting a safe and accepting school environment.[6]

When teachers do decide to act on their own to help fat children, without first taking the time to educate themselves, they may do more harm than good. Lorca James describes what happened to her in fourth grade. Promising that none of the other students would find out her weight, the teacher brought Lorca to the front of the class and had her step on a scale. Lorca's teacher then informed her that she weighed "at least thirty pounds more than anyone else in the class."[7] She told Lorca that she needed to diet and that she would help her. Similarly a California mother has been fighting with her son's chemistry teacher who forced her students to weigh themselves and exercise in a manner that caused humilitation. She believes the teachers retaliated by giving him a "D" in the chemistry class. The National Education Association, in its report on Discrimination Due to Physical Size, recounted other teacher interventions including telling parents of fat children to put the kids on diets, prizes offered to fat children for weight loss, keeping fat children off the honor roll, and refusing letters of recommendation to fat students.[8]

The 1998 Concept Paper on Children and Weight emphasizes that weight loss is an inappropriate goal for intervention in fat children, stating, "Efforts should be made to take the stigma of weight problems off the child and the family." Experts advise educators and parents to work on improving children's self-esteem. Rather than dieting, kids of all sizes should instead be carefully encouraged to increase activity and fitness levels. Care is needed, explains Ikeda, because it is critical to impart the love of movement and the enjoyment of activity. This philosophy, which is the California physical education mandate, primes children to continue using their bodies actively for the rest of their lives.[9] Condoning weight harassment through active participation or inaction, along with efforts to "help" fat kids through dieting, can contribute to self-esteem problems and leave children vulnerable to many other difficulties. About her teacher's actions Lorca writes, "I realize now that my teacher was probably trying to help, but she only made me feel worse. I was even more frightened to play a sport or speak up in class because I thought the other kids would make fun of my body. For a long time after that I felt isolated."[10]

Transferring to a new high school, senior Cordelia Moon describes her first day in gym class. She relates that, over her objections, "They measured me with calipers. Then the gym teacher told me, loud enough for everyone to hear, that I had the highest body fat of the class! The teacher went on to say it was surprising because I didn't 'look that fat,' but suggested I start a restricted-calorie diet immediately."[11] Cordelia was not the only student to receive this treatment. After class a girl confided to her, voice wavering, that she was relieved that she was "no longer the fattest in the class." Cordelia's reaction was predicable. She says, "I never went back to the gym class after that day. I felt guilty disappointing the poor 'second-fattest' girl by never showing up again and making her number one again, but it was just too yucky to ever go back."

Like Cordelia's reaction, Lorca's fear of public ridicule and lasting feelings of isolation are a predictable result of her teacher's misguided action. Weighing, charting, and comparing people by weight is not a benign procedure. A study, published in 1996 by Ogden and Evans, was designed to investigate the effects of weighing and comparison with social norms on self-esteem, mood, and body dissatisfaction. The researchers took seventy-four "normal" weight subjects and weighed them. Referring to a fictional height-weight chart, the researchers then divided the subjects into three groups irrespective of those measures: an "underweight" group, an "average weight" group, and an "overweight" group. Researchers found the subjects allocated to the fictional "overweight" group showed an immediate decrease in self-esteem and an increase in depression compared with the subjects allocated to the fictional "average weight" group. Those subjects fictionally labeled "average weight" demonstrated improvement in their self-esteem and depression.[12]

Lorca's experience being labeled "overweight" by her teacher caused her to fear playing sports. The most vivid memories of school alienation that many adults have stem from problems they had as fat kids in gym class. Ikeda and Naworski warn, "High-quality school physical education classes have the potential to help all children feel good about themselves, regardless of body size or physical ability. On the other hand, poor programs can cause children to hate gym class and, consequently, hate physical activity for the rest of their lives."[13] In practice, lasting weight loss will not be attainable for most people. Nevertheless, people of all sizes and ability levels can benefit from physical activity. Because of this, a small group studying children at a school conference sponsored by the National Heart, Lung, and Blood Institute instructs the emphasis should not be on making children lose weight, but on making all children healthier whatever their weight. People attending the conference were told, "Goals for public education programs targeted at adolescents must recognize that the physiological and psychological hazards of dieting outweigh the possible benefits."[14] Most important is to help children have fun with their bodies to promote continued fitness throughout life.

Fat students may have some additional, basic concerns in physical education classes. Failing to anticipate or ignoring these worries is unjust and can have serious ramifications for the student. Sharon Hendrickson describes her experience:

> On the morning of graduation from high school, I stood in line holding my breath . . . because I was afraid I had "failed" gym class again. I frequently blew off gym because I refused to wear the gym suit . . . I was mortified to think of my classmates laughing at me as I jumped around in a too-tight sky-blue, polyester gymsuit. . . . It is a sincere and sad irony that a bright girl who was given the opportunity to skip two grades in elementary school was ten years later quaking in fear that I would not graduate from high school because I was so ashamed of how I looked in my gymsuit.[15]

Inadequate or humiliating gym uniforms can contribute to body-image problems for fat and thin children. Feeling uncomfortable about mandatory clothes can make kids avoid and loathe physical activity. Some fat children describe fear that the ill-fitting outfits will tear, so they do not exert themselves to avoid strain on the clothing.

Problems can arise before and after activity time in the locker rooms and showers, which can be humiliating and dangerous places for fat children because teachers may be absent and the protection of clothing unavailable, emphasizing body differences. In these situations Ikeda advises, "Be an advocate for your child. There is nothing wrong with being larger than usual. You and your child do not have to put up with discrimination."[16] When one parent found out his son was being teased mercilessly in the locker room at gym class, he talked to the physical education teacher. The teacher generally was in his office during those times, but recognized the situation was unfair and took decisive steps. He confronted the students, told them that that sort of behavior would not go on, made it a practice to supervise the kids during those times, and moved the child's locker to be close to his office. The teacher continued to address the unfairness issue by overhauling the class. The grading system was changed so it was based not on pure skill, but on effort, attendance, and participation. Consequently, some of the "jocks" got lower grades than the less coordinated and athletic kids.

Many parents of fat kids are fat themselves and may have a hard time speaking up for their child because they themselves suffer from low self-esteem or blame themselves for their child's weight. Some parents succeed in turning these feelings around. Watching their children repeat the suffering they survived can give some parents the confidence to take a stand. One woman was distressed to find out her daughter was being subjected to the same embarrassment she herself had experienced as a child. As a result, she fought the school's mandatory weigh-in policy on behalf of her daughter. When she confronted the school, the administrators explained to her that they were required by state law to gather the weight information on all students. The mother suggested a compromise. She promised to keep the information on record with the child's physician and release it if necessary. She was lucky. The school relented despite the fact that they had little to gain by agreeing to the compromise. Apparently even without the benefit of the Ogden and Evans study results, the school officials recognized the damage the weigh-ins were doing to this girl and cared enough to go out on a limb and violate state law to protect her.

Poorly designed and misguided government rules about weight measurements and activity requirements can cause a lot of problems for generations of even mildly fat teens. For example, passing the Presidential Physical Fitness Test was required in the public schools of many states, and used in many private schools as well. Some of the exercises that the students were judged on were biased against fat children. A thirty-year-old woman recalls:

> They were all exercises that lighter kids excelled at, with the exception of sit-ups. . . . Running backwards was much harder for the heavier kids—we seemed to have a center of gravity problem that the thin girls without breasts didn't have. The fatter children would often fall during this exercise. I remember one time where I fell more than once, and I was a very skilled athlete. The fact that I had problems with the test was a direct result of my size, not my fitness. After all, I was recruited out of the eighth grade by the field hockey coach to play for the varsity high-school team.[17]

Interestingly, her school required an especially high score on the Presidential Physical Fitness Test before a junior high-student received permission to play on the high-school varsity teams. The student's coach had her retake the test in private and conducted it in such a way (she left the room and allowed the girl's teammate to score the test) that she could "pass" the heightened requirement and would be allowed to play. Clearly the coach believed in her student's skill and fitness despite the results she achieved on the fitness test. Just as one school had to violate state law for the good of one of its students, so, too, this coach had to risk breaking the rules so that her fat, fit, and talented student was allowed to take advantage of the opportunity she deserved.

While fat children with excellent physical skills had it rough, fat children who were uncoordinated, in poor shape, or awkward were devastated. They were the victims of public abuse not only by their peers, but, disturbingly, by their teachers.

Thinking back to her school days, one woman remembers the treatment two fat girls in her gym class received. The two frequently avoided gym, sometimes forgetting their shorts or for other reasons. "You were required to wear a uniform to gym class. Thinking back on it, I don't know if they could have gotten uniforms that fit. They did not come in very big sizes. Sometimes these girls would come wearing shorts, not the required uniform. Then they'd get in trouble, and be lectured in front of everyone. This encouraged them not to come in those shorts, of course, so they would just 'forget' their gym clothes entirely. Their punishment for not being prepared to participate was being forced to walk backwards around the perimeter of the gymnasium while the other students played volleyball. It was clearly designed to make them stand out. If they fell or tripped, people would laugh and point."[18] Other fat children report being punished for problems in gym class by being made to "duck walk" (an awkward "squat and waddle" step) or literally twiddle their thumbs while the rest of the students played, looked on, or did other activities.

The ostracism and humiliation experienced by fat children performing these acts is far greater than for thin children. Being called offensive nicknames by teachers and being screamed at in front of the class for being fat, uncoordinated, or slow is a common experience of many fat people during school gym classes.[19] Ikeda admits, "In the past, physical education teachers were not enlightened. As a result, kids [of varying sizes] were not treated with respect." Now experts recommend physical education teachers set new goals. They should make exercises fun and find multiple activities that each individual student excels at so they enjoy the time they spend being physically active. Of course, informed, caring physical education teachers do exist, especially at higher levels. As one fat woman reports, they can provide phenomenal benefits to fat students: "I loved my college African Dance class. The dynamic could have been really weird because there were plenty of itsy-bitsy ultra-thin dancer types in the class. In fact, I did not even think I would get chosen to be in the class because it was always overenrolled and very competitive. But luckily my teacher, Michelle Bach, never made me feel bad about my size. In fact, it was obvious she was genuinely enthusiastic about my participation, as were many of the other students. I actually felt respected and valued in that class, like people appreciated the diversity of having a fat person there dancing, too. Her attitude made a world of difference to me, and it was so different than the theater department faculty who would never cast a fat person in a play."[20] Learning active skills that are both enjoyable and practical outside of a classroom setting will be of help in keeping active later in life for people of all sizes.

As with other minorities, abuse and disrespect against fat children in the lower grades can lead to abuse and disrespect in high school which can spiral into lost opportunities for more education later. The National Education Association (NEA) in the 1994 Report on Discrimination Due to Physical Size calls the school experience for fat kids one of "ongoing prejudice, unnoticed discrimination, and almost constant harassment." Children who suffer this torment may be less likely to want to continue their education. The NEA recognizes that, because of the rampant prejudice and bias they face, fat children's chances for continued education are limited. Bias may result in fat kids receiving lower grades. The NEA recognizes that, because of fat hatred, fat students are denied letters of recommendation, ranked last for receiving scholarships, and are regarded as having lower leadership abilities and energy levels. The extent to which fat prejudice hurts students is hard to calculate, though it clearly also affects employees. A former NEA member from Maryland speculates, "I have had a guidance counselor in this system tell me that he would rather be dead than look like me. I have wondered how he related to fat teenagers."[21]

When bias against fat kids leads them to underachieve, and as a result they get fewer opportunities, it is unfair. But, as in the case with college admissions, discrimination against fat kids is often more straightforward and blatant than that. Even adjusting for high-school records, evaluations, and motivation to enter college, a smaller percentage of fat high-school students are admitted to college than average-weight students.[22] Christian Crandall, a psychologist with the University of Kansas, notes that fat women, as compared to other men and women, more often pay their own way through college. He believes this is because parents refuse to pay college costs for them, not because they cannot afford it, but rather to insist on "self-reliance and self-control."[23] For those who go on to college but have had traumatic or abusive physical education experiences in high school, their choices may be even more limited when all colleges with physical education requirements automatically get crossed off their college lists.

Once in college they may still have socialization problems. For example, a college freshman at a prestigious university reported being excluded from membership in all of the school sororities because of her weight.

Another woman remembers being excluded even from a fraternity party. Walking with two of her friends, several frat boys were hanging out of the house windows to greet the guests. They yelled out their invitation—the other two women were welcome to come in, "But not the fat one!" Several University of California at Berkeley students reported being excluded from the cheerleading program because of their race and appearance. They offer as proof one of the judge's scoring sheets which complained that the cheerleading contestant was "large" and had "big hips."[24]

Most college-age young adults are desperate not to get fat. A survey of one thousand women between eighteen and twenty-four revealed that 54 percent would rather be run over by a truck than be very fat. Two-thirds of the surveyed group would prefer to be mean or stupid than fat.[25]

When students of all ages diet, they may be putting themselves at an educational disadvantage. Many studies show reduced calorie consumption has a negative impact on performance and psychological state. Dieters are more likely than those who are not dieting to perform poorly on mental tests.[26] Their drop in performance is roughly equivalent to the drop in performance resulting from the ingestion of two alcoholic beverages. Of those studied, the largest deficiency in performance was seen in those who failed to lose weight. While a 1997 study failed to confirm previous studies that showed sustained attention and immediate memory problems as the result of dieting, it did show the slowing of reaction time to be a short-term and long-term consequence of calorie restriction.[27]

Another study theorized that objectifiying oneself produces body shame, leads to restrained eating, and monopolizes attentional resources, actually diminishing women's math performance, though not men's.[28] In their article "Time Spent Thinking About Food," Dan and Kathleen Reiff explain that thoughts about food, hunger, weight, and body image preoccupy people who choose to restrict their caloric intake or have eating disorders: "This obsession is one of the most noticeable and potentially disruptive effects of achieving a weight or attempting to maintain a weight below one's biologic set-point range."[29] One student recovering from an eating disorder shares how all-consuming thoughts of food become: "I thought about food, weight, and hunger 99 percent of the time. I'd sit in my classes and figure out how many calories I'd had so far and how many I was going to have at lunch."[30]

This type of negative effect from calorie limitation is not news and it is not restricted to women. In the 1944 Keys experiment, discussed at length in chapter 13, the effects of "semistarvation" on young men showed similar but more dramatic results. They were restricted to 1,570 calories per day, which actually is more calories than most modern diet programs allow. The men became completely preoccupied with thoughts of food to the exclusion of being able to concentrate on other things including sex, and exhibited serious personality changes. Though the tests did not confirm their feelings, the men perceived themselves as being less able to concentrate and understand and felt impaired in their ability to judge and stay alert.[31] This type of self-perception, whether it is accurate or not, can be deeply distressing to students. Women are overrepresented among dieters and underrepresented in math and the sciences. If calorie restriction leads to a loss of confidence in intellectual pursuits, it could be having a serious impact on the academic choices women and girls make.

Fatphobia and fat hatred impact the education experiences of fat children so that their future opportunities are curtailed. But for some unlucky fat children, it is not only their future opportunities that are affected. They may lose their opportunity to have a future at all.

Apathy toward the school environment experienced by fat children has repeatedly resulted in tragedy. A devastating, preventable incident, the result of unchecked teasing, occurred in a Georgia high-school classroom in 1994. Fifteen year old Brian Head knew what he faced each day at school. He had been tormented about his weight since the seventh grade. The smart, shy, drama club member was regularly made fun of and sometimes beaten up. Teachers and staff did nothing. On March 26, right before his economics class, while being slapped and having his hair pulled by another student as a teacher lingered right outside the door, Brian pulled out a gun and shot himself in the temple. The last thing he said was, "I'm tired of it."[32]

At the age of twelve, Samuel Graham was almost Christina Corrigan's age. Like Christina, he was desperate to avoid the incredible strain of being teased and harassed as the fat kid in a new school. Brian made it to school before he snapped. Samuel did not. The night before the start of school, Samuel killed himself. His two younger brothers were the first to find him. He was hanging from the tree in the backyard of their Florida home.

Schooltime harassment and violence often continue outside of school hours and off school grounds. Thirteen-year-old Kelly Yeomans had been tormented about her weight for years by schoolmates. Her victimizers not only poured salt in her lunch, made her uncomfortable at gym time, and threw out her clothes during school hours, but they continued their aggression at her home. They hit her house with stones, butter, and eggs. Despite the fact that Kelly was involved in her community, she could not survive the abuse. Playing in the local Salvation Army band and volunteering with the elderly proved no match for the hatred she faced daily. She killed herself in her home, as her parents slept, on a Sunday evening before the start of the school week.[33]

Not only are fat kids ridiculed in school, they are singled out for physical attacks. Apathy toward the plight of fat kids results in a lack of statistics on their dropout rate, but anecdotal evidence abounds. Often, fat children quit school to avoid the violence and abuse. Brandi, a fat thirteen-year-old girl, describes being forced to leave school because of the treatment she received due to her weight. She said, "They throw stones at me and hurt me bad. . . . I quit school 'cause I could not take the pain."[34] At twenty-two, James Airre talks about his horrific school experiences in a quiet, controlled tone. The worst of the continuous weight related abuse he suffered was physical violence. Despite the fact that he was not only fat, but also large stature, for two years during seventh and eighth grades James was targeted because of his weight by a pack of between four and six fellow students. Whenever they saw him they would punch him in the stomach and arms. Like scores of other fat children in his situation, he kept the abuse a secret for a long time because he was so ashamed.

Many fat kids exist on a steady diet of shame and self-hatred fed to them by their teachers. Even while James was being attacked by his classmates, several of his teachers were busy trying to help him stop "overeating," as if overeating, rather than regular beatings, was his problem. He believes that they were trying to empathize with him but could not because none of them were fat. They just assumed he ate too much and so they would watch him and comment on what he ate until he ended up not eating at school at all. At least once a day the football coach, who was eager to entice him to play because he was a big kid, would bully him, "We could turn some of that blubber into muscle if you played football."

James tried to tell his sister about what he was going through, but she did not grasp the severity of the problem. Finally he confided to his mother that he was being repeatedly hit by these particular boys. She contacted the administrators of the small, prestigious private school. Their solution was to have a teacher talk to the boys. Just as James had warned the staff, the action by the school made the attacks worse. They continued the behavior, but with more force because he had "ratted" on them. Luckily for James, one of the ringleaders of the group left school. The other became distracted when his mother, who appeared to have suffered abuse herself, murdered his father and new wife. Careful intervention could not only have saved James a lifetime of suffering, but might have also identified the other boy as a child in need of assistance because of his family situation. When James snapped and threatened another boy in the group, they finally left him alone.

The damage to his self-esteem was profound. "I started to expect those comments. I felt shitty about myself all the time. I always expected men to yell at me. It was not until I was fifteen that I started to realize it was not acceptable for people to yell at me." Like other survivors of weight-based prejudice, he would find the lasting effects inescapably influencing his opinions of people. James comments, "Basically, I assumed people would be unkind to me. That was the general assumption I had about people."

James continued at the school for a few more years during which time his bulimia gave way to anorexia fueled by compulsive exercising. A smart child, he never had the peace he needed to reach his academic potential in that environment. He left high school before graduation, choosing to pursue a high-school equivalency outside of the school system.

Distressed about the education landscape in store for fat children, Marilyn Wann, author and editor of *Fat!So?* started working on the Fat Speaker's Bureau, a project that educates teachers and students about the effects of fat prejudice and trains volunteers to give talks in schools. The program is designed to promote healthy eating and exercise, combat weight-related teasing, and boost the self-esteem for children of all sizes. She gave her first talk when she heard about Brian Head's suicide. Like Ikeda, Wann recommends taking active steps when children are victimized in school. She suggests telling the child clearly, "You are lovely as you are. These people are wrong and what they are doing is wrong." Revisiting the classroom not only offers some relief to fat children, it gives the volunteers the chance to speak up. Wann explains, "Every time I give a talk in a school I revisit the painful moments, but now I am putting right something that was wrong. It's kind of a rush to know I can now defend myself, that I now have good answers. And I have so much important information to pass on. For the kids in the classes, it is a huge benefit because most have not met a happy, unapolagetic fat person. They may not even have met anyone who is happy with their body, fat or thin."[35]

The alienation and exodus of fat children from public places of education is a problem not just for concerned parents and activists, but for the law. When the school environment is so hostile to fat children that the decision to leave school is reasonable, courts, the legislature, the public, and school staff *must* intervene. Schools that continue to allow this level of abuse, violence, and victimization should pay for it through financial (civil) judgments against them. In repeat cases of repeated violence and victimization, criminal prosecution of apathetic staff may even be justified. Lawyers may be unwilling to take these cases, however. Commenting on Christina Corrigan's case, an attorney offers this explanation: "These cases are losers. The school district is bankrupt. And even if it wasn't, no jury will make a decision they see as taking money out of the classroom and putting it into someone's pocket."

NOTES

1. Statement included in the National Education Association's 1994 report.
2. Ellyn Satter, "The New Paradigm of Trust," in *Children and Teens in Weight Crisis*, ed. Frances Berg (N. Dak.: Healthy Weight Journal, 1995), 21.
3. Interview with Christine Ianeri, 15 March 1996, Oakland, Calif.
4. Linda Jackson, *Physical Appearance and Gender* (New York: State University of New York Press, 1992), 168 (citing the following studies: Alessi and Anthony 1969; Giancoli and Neimeyer 1983; Goodman et al. 1963; Maddox, Back, and Liederman 1968; Richardson 1970; Richardson et al. 1961; Richardson and Royce 1968).
5. Faced with this consistent behavior by these boys, the school's lack of action is telling. While it may not be illegal to harass people about weight, it is illegal to subject women to sexual harassment. Yet even in the face of potentially

serious legal consequences, the school and staff are so apathetic about "teasing" that they ignore the problem.

6. Joanne Ikeda and Priscilla Naworski, *Am I Fat? Helping Young Children Accept Differences in Body Size* (Santa Cruz: ETR Associates, 1992), 35.

7. Lorca James, "Fat or Not: A Teenager Reports," *Radiance* (Fall 1987): 9.

8. National Education Association (NEA), *Report on Discrimination Due to Physical Size* (1994): 10 (citing Esther Rothblum et al., "Results of the NAAFA Survey on Employment Discrimination Part II." *NAAFA Newsletter* 17, no. 3 [April 1989]).

9. Joanne Ikeda, nutrition education specialist, interview, 25 March 1999, University of California, Berkeley.

10. Lorca James, "Fat or Not," 9.

11. Private interview, April 1999. Name changed upon request.

12. J. Ogden and C. Evans, "The Problem with Weighing: Effects on Mood, Self-Esteem and Body Image," *International Journal of Obesity and Related Metabolic Disorders* 20, no. 3 (March 1996): 272–77. Interestingly, the group fictionally labeled "underweight" showed decreased depression but also exhibited some "deterioration of their self-esteem."

13. Ikeda and Naworski, *Am I Fat?* 43.

14. Frances Berg, *Children and Teens in Weight Crisis*, summary edition (N. Dak.: Healthy Weight Journal, 1995), 20.

15. Sharon Hendrickson, interview, 12 March 1996.

16. Ikeda, interview.

17. Interview, 26 February 1996. Name withheld upon request.

18. Private interview. Name withheld.

19. Fat and formerly fat people also report refusing to attend various classes after the abuse they experienced.

20. Private interview. Name withheld.

21. National Education Association (NEA), "Report on Discrimination Due to Physical Size" (1994): 11.

22. Jackson, *Physical Appearance and Gender*, 170.

23. National Education Association, "Report on Discrimination Due to Physical Size," 8.

24. Devra Polack, "You Mean I Can't Be a Cheerleader," *FaTGiRL* 3: 60.

25. Glenn Gaesser, *Big Fat Lies: The Truth About Your Weight and Your Health* (New York: Fawcett Columbine, 1996), 19. Citing a study published in the 1994 issue of *Esquire*.

26. Lillian Langseth, "Dieting Impairs Mental Performance," *Nutrition Research Newsletter* 14, no. 11/12 (November/December 1995): 130. Their source: Andy Coghlan, "Dieting Makes You Forget," *New Scientist* 148 (1999): 5.

27. M. Kretsch et al., "Cognitive Effects of a Long-Term Weight Reducing Diet," *International Journal of Obesity and Related Metabolic Disorders* 21, no. 1 (January 1997): 14–21, U.S. Department of Agriculture.

28. B. Fredrickson et al., "That Swimsuit Becomes You: Sex Differences in Self-Objectification, Restrained Eating, and Math Performance," *Journal of Personality and Social Psychology* 75, no. 1 (July 1998): 269–84.

29. Dan Reiff and Kathleen Kim Lampson Reiff, "Time Spent Thinking About Food," *Healthy Weight Journal* 12, no. 6 (November/December 1998): 84.

30. Ibid.

31. For an interesting recap of the Keys experiment see David Garner, "The Effects of Starvation on Behavior: Implications for Dieting and Eating Disorders," *Healthy Weight Journal* (September/October 1998).

32. Sondra Solovay, "Fat Doesn't Kill, Fat Hatred Does," *Fat!So?* Issue 2 (1994): 19.

33. "Bullied Thirteen-Year-Old Kills Herself," Associated Press, London, 2 October 1997.

34. "Media Watch," *FaTGiRL* 4 (October 1995): 61.

35. Marilyn Wann, interview, March 1999, San Francisco, Calif.

IF THE CHILD IS FAT,
IS THE PARENT UNFIT?

Do you feel, if I took you back tomorrow, you would lose weight? If you would, I will.

—A mother to her daughter on national television

ARE THESE WORDS UNCARING? SUPPORTIVE? Abusive? Loving? Reasonable? Whatever else they may be, they are the words that could save a mother from prosecution and jail time for child endangerment.

Like Christina Corrigan, Amber Meck* was a teen who could not lose weight.[1] At 350 pounds, she, too, was more than twice the size of her classmates. Unlike Marlene Corrigan, often criticized for her acceptance of Christina, Amber's mother refused to accept Amber at her weight. When that attitude meant relinquishing custody of her daughter to relatives, that is exactly Amber's mother did. Amber was separated from her siblings and sent to adapt to a different family in a new town.

Each mother prioritized her daughter's well-being in different ways. In the face of Christina's pain, Marlene Corrigan made a private place for her child in the home, as far from the world's hostility as she could. Ms. Meck was aware of Amber's misery and attempted to use that as leverage for an

---

*Name changed to protect privacy.

64

ultimatum that she hoped would enable her daughter to be one of the few to defy the odds and lose weight. The importance of getting her child to lose weight seems to have eclipsed the emotional devastation her daughter would suffer. With a thin child, the courts would consider the parent's actions and the emotional and psychological consequences to be a priority. With a fat child it can be tricky to get a judge to see past the number on the scale. This was Dorothy Smuller's concern when it came to her son.

Ms. Smuller was living with her son Zack who had been overweight for several years.* Her husband worked in a different city and was usually only able to spend weekends with the family. During the time Mr. Smuller interacted with Zack, he often harassed him about his weight. Although the father intended to aid his son in losing weight with this behavior, the result was ongoing stress for the child and did not result in weight loss.

These facts did not seem significant until the Smullers decided to divorce. Ms. Smuller felt it imperative that she retain sole custody of their son in order to protect him from the verbal and emotional abuse he received from his father. As with many parents, custody became her primary concern during the divorce settlement. She reevaluated her need for divorce when her husband's lawyer phoned: "He called me on the telephone and said because my son has certain health problems, being overweight was particularly bad for him. He said they would use the fact that he was fat in court as evidence to prove I was an unfit mother."

Ms. Smuller took the threat very seriously. "It scared me a lot. . . . It's not hard to prove that an overweight kid is overweight. Whether or not it would work would depend on the standards [of parental fitness]." According to Ms. Smuller, the motivation behind the threat was not a genuine concern for the health of the child. His weight was simply being exploited to secure a more advantageous bargaining position for her husband.

Although the Smullers settled their divorce out of court, Ms. Smuller had legitimate reason to be concerned about a judge's reaction to her parental fitness had they gone to court. Courts tend to look toward the child's best interests in determining custody on divorce, though the trial judge is virtually unlimited in the ability to determine the custody arrangements.

---

*Name changed by request.

There is no uniform, consistent family code, but the proposed Uniform Marriage and Divorce Act identifies generally some of the issues that can be considered in determining what is in the child's best interest. It is recommended that the judge rely on the desires of the parents; the wishes of the child; the relationship between the child and each parent, siblings, or other people; adjustment to home, school, and community; and the mental and physical health of "all individuals involved."[2]

Because Ms. Smuller's child had a physical condition that made his weight a particular risk according to experts in the medical field, the judge might have determined that his health was compromised by his weight. The judge could easily decide that while the child spent the week with his mother he had not lost weight so, in the interest of losing weight, he should be given to the father.

Here both parents were thin, but had Mr. Smuller been thin and Ms. Smuller fat, this could have impacted the court's decision. Defining a stigmatizing disability as a "condition or lifestyle perceived by society as making a person less than totally capable of caring for a child," Michael Gassner warns, "The probability of a poor [custody] decision is exacerbated when the stigmatizing 'disability' of a parent is inserted into the facts. . . . The 'disabled' are especially in need of protection when their fitness as parents is evaluated, for they are particularly vulnerable to conscious and unconscious stereotyped conceptions which may prejudice them in court."[3] The judge might have determined that Zack needed to lose weight and Ms. Smuller was a bad role model because of her own weight, basing his custody determination on that opinion.

Even in cases where the child is without the added risk of a specific condition worsened by weight, the courts have shown a willingness to consider the weight of the child when making custody and guardianship decisions. Whether the court will make a negative custody determination based on the child's weight depends on the particular state's laws or case law, and on the individual judge's opinions and prejudices. It can and has happened.

In Alabama the appeals court stated this simply, "The child's obesity [is] a proper concern for the court."[4] They conclusively determined that Jimmy Fillingim's obesity was within the domain regulated by the judge. There was very little Jimmy's mother could do to change the judge's mind, though she tried.

Fillingim v. *Fillingim* came before the court because Diane Fillingim was unwilling to allow her ex-husband full visitation rights for their son, as ordered in the prior custody decision. She returned to court to argue this determination based on the fact that both parents had moved.

The Fillingims' son Jimmy, then between five and six years of age, had a medical history of infrequent but severe grand mal seizures. After the divorce, the Fillingims moved. Ms. Fillingim, thinking about Jimmy's condition, became very concerned about the location of her ex-husband's new home should Jimmy need medical help. A specialist testified that he had advised Ms. Fillingim to have an accessible medical facility available to her son, even though the condition had not recurred in over a year. Jimmy's pediatrician testified that he had never met the father during multiple years treating the boy and could not comment positively or negatively about the father having visitation rights.

The court determined that the change of location for each parent's residence was sufficient grounds to change the original custody order. Despite the specialist's opinion and the fact that Jimmy's father had never even met his son's pediatrician, the judge chose to substantially increase the father's visitation rights, adding overnight stays to the original decision. He then adjudged Ms. Fillingim to be in contempt of court for the previous refusal to allow visitation.[5]

The purpose of the trial was to discuss visitation changes. The court elected to alter visitation. Even when a court would like to spend extra time on a case, it resists. Courts are already overburdened so, in the interest of judicial economy, normally the Fillingim story would end there. But Jimmy weighed more than normal.

Without prompting of any kind, the judge opted to impose restrictions on Jimmy and Ms. Fillingim in an effort to reduce the boy's weight. The court ordered Ms. Fillingim to start Jimmy on a weight-reduction regimen. Additionally, the court required Ms. Fillingim to report Jimmy's weight to the court each month. She decided to appeal.

In general, appellate courts are hesitant to overturn the custody determinations of trial courts. The written records they have access to do not impart the physical impressions on which trial judges often base their decisions, so the higher courts grant significant deference to the lower-court custody decisions. Although Ms. Fillingim felt the lower court had overstepped its bounds and abused its discretion, the Alabama Court of Civil Appeals disagreed. Ms. Fillingim and her lawyers argued the court had acted erroneously, or, at the very least, exceeded its authority when it instituted the weight-loss and reporting requirements. The higher court said she failed because the evidence did not show that the trial judge was "plainly and palpably wrong and unjust" and thus her appeal was denied. In words that suggest a punitive facet to the judge's order of a weight-loss regimen, the appellate court concludes, "The same circuit judge has been saddled with hearings and decisions in this case since its inception in June, 1978. He could have ascertained from the evidence that the plaintiff [Ms. Fillingim] was, on the whole, *underconcerned* about Jimmy's weight problem" (emphasis added).[6]

Jimmy was four feet tall and weighed seventy-five pounds in February of 1980. During the next seven months, he experienced a weight gain of twenty five pounds. The judge, apparently relying on his own medical opinion, deemed this weight gain unusual. Ms. Fillingim was consistently taking Jimmy to his own doctors. Although one doctor did discuss the fact that Jimmy was overweight with Ms. Fillingim, no diet was prescribed. Jimmy's pediatrician had been regularly making note of the boy's weight, but had never felt the need to discuss the issue with the boy's mother.

Ms. Fillingim responded to Jimmy's increased weight as she thought best. According to both courts, the mother "diminished the size of her son's meals" and also "eliminated some objectionable foods therefrom."[7] Inexplicably, the court goes on to state that the mother "has not placed him on a diet." The court offers no insight into its definition of "diet." If not the reduction of food intake and the elimination of "objectionable" foods, then what does a diet entail? More importantly, what authority does the court have to determine that Ms. Fillingim's program is not a sufficient diet? And why is the court prescribing a diet for a five-year-old boy when the two physicians in charge of the boy's care chose not to?

Perhaps when the court says "diet" it means the popular definition during the time that the ruling was handed down. Two years before the case, Dr. Edwin Bayr wrote in his book *The Thin Game* that the "vast preponderance of modern health problems" were caused by overeating. He called for a "concentrated, coordinated assault on the nation's leading health hazard."[8] As early as 1970, the White House Conference on Food,

Nutrition, and Health recommended screening for obese preschoolers.[9] The rising fear of fat led directly into the diet-centric 1980s, where a poll asking people what they feared most in the world resulted in 40 percent reporting that they were most afraid of getting fat.[10]

This poll, conducted close to the time the Fillingim decisions were handed down, demonstrates the social atmosphere surrounding the case. Maybe Circuit Court Judge Don Bennett pictured himself a soldier in Dr. Bayr's army of diet gurus. It may be that for the judge, like many of his contemporaries, the word diet meant "Pritikin," the Protein Diet, the related Liquid Protein Diet, the Grapefruit (or Rice or Potato) Diet, the Rotation Plan, Weight Watchers®, or any one of the many other commercial weight-loss programs springing up around the nation. The resulting deaths and health problems from the severe, often starvation-ration diets were unknown, ignored, or determined to be worth the risk.

Although the appeals court largely stood behind the lower court's decision, it made two important rulings. First, it curtailed the judge's power, indicating it might be unlawful for him to prescribe "any medication, diet, exercise, or the type of weight program to be undertaken."[11] The court was not distressed that the lower court judge had dismissed as inadequate the diet Ms. Fillingim put her child on, despite the fact that this would most likely have been precisely the diet a sensible doctor of the time would have prescribed (reduced portions and elimination of certain foods). Nor was the court troubled by the judge's requirement that the child lose weight without making any attempt to ascertain the cause of the weight gain—was it normal? Was it due to his seizure medication? Was it a symptom of a hidden metabolic disorder? Was it a psychological reaction to the stress of the divorce and his father's new family? Similarly, the court did not require the judge to check with a medical professional to be certain weight loss was even appropriate and safe for a five-year-old. Today, responsible endocrinologists and nutritionists would not put the child on any diet as they have come to realize the particular dangers of dieting for young children. Even then a doctor would likely have vetoed the judge's order, opting to let the child "grow into" his weight. Instead, the appeals court states definitively, "The judge had a discretion to exercise in Jimmy's best interest, and he did so."[12]

Second, the appeals court curtailed Ms. Fillingim's parental right to determine what her child could eat by saying the specifics of the weight-loss program were "Matters within the province of [Jimmy's] physician."[13] Normally, what a child ingests and what activities a child participates in are firmly within the province of the custodial parent or guardian. This only changes if there is neglect or abuse. Ms. Fillingim neither abused nor ignored her son. She was in constant contact with the doctors regarding her son's health and, taking her at her word, even disobeyed the court's visitation orders out of concern for it. She was not the kind of mother who needed a judge or a doctor telling her how to feed her child. Since the court was not proposing the weight of the child was, in and of itself, abuse, the court had no grounds for interfering with her parental rights.

In Kansas City, Missouri, a judge did insist that a child's being 'overweight' was a violation of parental responsibility severe enough to disrupt the parent's custody right. Fueled by this assertion, the court not only set out to regulate the child's weight and eating, but even supported surprise refrigerator inspections to enforce the order.[14]

Jane Scott★ was considered by most a happy, healthy teenager even though she had lost her mother to cancer two years before. Her thin aunt, however, disagreed, arguing with Jane's father that at 350 pounds, Jane needed to be placed on a diet. When Jane's father refused, the aunt called child welfare, insisting the child was in danger and reporting her brother-in-law for neglect.

Although Jane was allowed to stay in her father's home, she was removed from his legal guardianship, lessening his legal rights over his daughter. In an effort to comply with the court, Jane spent a year on the Deal-a-Meal® program. She was required to go to the hospital weekly to have her weight measured and recorded by a nurse. Jane was then required to present these slips to the court on a monthly basis. Caseworkers made surprise visits to the household to inspect the refrigerator contents and to investigate her failure to lose weight.

Eventually, with her father's consent, Jane refused to continue the emotionally devastating weekly weigh-ins. The judge over-seeing the case felt Jane had not lost enough weight and planned to commit her to an inpatient treatment facility. There she would be placed on an 800-calories-a-

★The name of the family has been changed to protect their privacy.

day-diet. The judge further stated that she was to lose five pounds a week and would not effectively be eligible for release until she lost 150 pounds. Even if Jane was able to lose weight at that impossible pace, she would still be a prisoner within the hospital for a minimum of almost a year.

Luckily for Jane and her father, the judge was forced to hold a hearing before the court could enforce the order. Many anti-diet activists and health professionals appeared before the court in opposition to the plan. It was only when the director of the hospital program admitted that his in-patient treatment facility was not meant for someone of Jane's size that the judge stayed his order, temporarily saving Jane from commitment.

Much like Ms. Fillingim, Mr. Scott found his parental powers usurped by the court ostensibly acting in the best interest of the child. In both cases, an otherwise happy child without any weight-related health problems was forced into a medically unsound plan of action through the intrusive ignorance of the court. In both cases the children suffered. Jane's grades plummeted during her ordeal with the court. Respected University of California at San Francisco endocrinologist Dr. Diane Budd reports that calorie restriction for a child Jimmy's age can result in lifelong metabolic malfunction and weight problems.

In each case the court reacted viscerally to the child's size, using it as justification for changes in legal guardianship and creating the potential of removing the child from the home. For Ms. Fillingim, the court left an unspoken threat hanging over her head. For Mr. Scott, the only thing that prevented such an order was direct intervention of activists with medical professionals backing them up. Jane was saved from commitment by a phone call to the National Association to Advance Fat Acceptance (NAAFA)* from her late mother's friend. The case received no publicity and thus no public scrutiny. Both the ACLU and Legal Aid refused to take Mr. Scott's case, and he was unable to argue the case himself. A blue-collar worker who financed his daughter's private school, he could not afford an attorney and would have been powerless to save his daughter from commitment on his own. The arrival of fat activists and supportive health pro-

---

*NAAFA is a national organization based in Sacramento, California, whose mission is to fight size discrimination and improve the quality of life for fat people through advocacy, education, and support.

fessionals may very well have seemed like the cavalry arriving from beyond the hills. But those saving forces never arrived for Natalie Thomas and her daughter Liza.*

In 1991, an Iowa juvenile court judged ten-year-old Liza to be a "child in need of assistance." In conjunction with this decision, the court ordered Liza to be removed from her mother's care and placed in a residential treatment center where she would be treated not only for depression and personality disorder, but also for obesity. Her mother, Natalie, objected strenuously and appealed the decision.[15]

Ms. Thomas had been married to Liza's father, Loren, for twelve years. During that time, Natalie was frequently abused by Loren. The violence was witnessed by Liza. When Natalie left the home in 1990, she took both Liza and Liza's half-brother with her. The terms of the 1991 dissolution left Liza in her mother's care, but allowed for weekend visitation with Loren.

After Ms. Thomas had escaped the marriage, Liza's doctor expressed concern that Liza was psychologically disturbed. He recommended counseling and an inpatient weight-loss regimen. At the time, Liza was five-feet-three-inches and weighed 270 pounds, eighty of those pounds having been gained during the last two years of the violent marriage. As the court-mandated weekend visitation at her father's persisted, Liza continued to gain weight and suffer from depression. Her mother contacted the department of human services and requested assistance.

The family was provided with a caseworker who referred Liza to a hospital-based weight-loss program and arranged for weekly counseling. A child psychiatrist recommended hospitalization for Liza and in accordance with this advice, Natalie allowed her daughter to be hospitalized for one month. During that time Liza was suffering from a yeast infection on her skin, which presumably was treated at the hospital. Over the period of thirty days, Liza lost twenty-four pounds. Doctors generally recommend weight loss not exceed two pounds per week. They are particularly concerned about the effect of rapid weight loss on growing children. Liza lost almost a pound a day. Ms. Thomas reasonably might have felt that continued hospitalization was not good for Liza. At the conclusion of her month in the hospital, Liza's psychiatrist recommended continued, long-

---

*As in the court documents, these names are fictional.

term, inpatient treatment for her weight as well as emotional problems. Natalie declined to place Liza in the program and stopped scheduling diet appointments at the hospital. Meanwhile, she kept other appointments, regularly driving Liza to multiple doctors. Nevertheless, the court initiated a "Child in Need of Assistance" proceeding.

In light of a medical exam which revealed no "physical cause" for her obesity, Liza's psychiatrist determined that her depression was causing her to overeat and said she needed a long-term residential treatment program to address her "potentially life-threatening obesity."[16] Many health professionals in the obesity field believe rapid weight loss is dangerous and that, "Until more is known about safe, effective obesity treatments, appropriate advice for many large persons may be to maintain a stable weight and simply avoid further weight gain."[17] Liza's mother was strongly opposed to her daughter being removed from home. The court, moved by its belief that Liza's weight "already interferes with her participation in the socialization a child requires to develop physically, mentally, and emotionally," ignored Natalie's opinion and instead listened to the psychiatrist.[18]

Ironically, it was on the same day the state of Iowa was initiating the procedure to force Liza into an extreme residential weight-loss program that New York Attorney Burt Bauman brought suit against Nutri/System® on behalf of eighteen clients. The people were arguing that they had been inadequately warned that it was "innately dangerous to rapidly lose weight because of gallbladder damage."[19]

Nevertheless, the court ordered Liza to be placed in residential treatment foster care. After reviewing the decision, the appellate court validated its decision by noting that Loren, Liza's abusive father, who appeared to be causing much of Liza's depression and anger during their weekend visits, agreed with the decision.[20]

Unlike the Fillingim and Scott cases, where the trial judge simply made a ruling, the appeals court of Iowa had to uphold the Child in Need of Assistance order with "clear and convincing evidence."[21] Only then could the court remove Liza from Natalie's care.

Under Iowa code, a child in need of assistance is: "An unmarried child who needs medical treatment to cure or alleviate serious mental illness or disorder, or emotional damage as evidenced by severe anxiety, depression, withdrawal or untoward aggressive behavior towards self . . . *and* whose parent, guardian or custodian is unwilling or unable to provide such treatment" (emphasis added).[22] This is where the appeals court's reasoning becomes confused. Liza falls under the code because she suffered from depression—a "mental illness or disorder." But there was no evidence presented that Natalie was unable or unwilling to get Liza treatment for her depression and anger. On the contrary, the court noted that Natalie got Liza treatment and took her to multiple appointments regularly.

The court insisted that Ms. Thomas refused to treat Liza's obesity. But, under the statute, obesity does not qualify Liza as a Child in Need of Assistance. The court got around this by using a statement from her psychiatrist essentially theorizing that Liza ate to relieve her of that depression and thus was fat.[23] This is an overly simplistic understanding of the relationship between fat and emotional stability. In actuality, the causes of obesity are complex, involving interactions of metabolism; fat storage mechanisms; hormones; fat cell proliferation; and possible social, economic, and environmental factors.[24]

The court however, relied on the psychiatrist's statement to insist that the obesity was a psychologically created condition. Despite discussing her psychological problems, the court focused on Liza's weight. The court mentioned her weight seventeen times in the two-page decision. By contrast, the court pointed to her "other" psychological problems (the alleged cause of her extreme weight) only eleven times. Writing about her weight at length, the court said: "Liza's mother, Natalie, has been unable to effectively assist Liza with her problem of obesity. Under her mother's care, Liza has failed to lose weight and has failed to attend dietary classes. Further evidence indicates Natalie has actively provoked Liza's adverse feelings for her father and has encouraged Liza's eating habits as a method of coping with the resulting stress. On one occasion, following a session with a treatment professional, Natalie suggested giving Liza food to reward her and to relieve Liza's stress."[25]

Although the appeals court does not actually assert that being fat is an aggressive behavior toward oneself, it is clearly headed in that direction when it states that Liza's obesity is "potentially life threatening . . . likely [to] result in a significantly increased risk of hypertension and decreased life expectancy."[26] Here the concern is not about Liza's actual health or her immediate mortality, but about the risk of future problems even though these heightened risks do not kick in for years—until Liza passes the age of eighteen. Luckily for the citizens of Iowa, the court stopped short of declaring obesity an aggressive behavior toward oneself in light of potential future problems. Otherwise, all fat children not successful at losing weight could be forcibly removed from their parents' care and placed under the state's authority based on their appearance alone.

That the court does not make this assertion has consequences, though. Without this step of reasoning, the court has no right to remove Liza from Natalie's care on the basis of her weight. The court cannot simply reclassify obesity as a mental disorder. Natalie has demonstrated her willingness to treat Liza's mental disorders, therefore there is nothing in the statute granting power to remove Liza from Natalie's custody and care.

For example, if a child blinks furiously as a means to deal with depression, she can only be removed from her guardian's care if the guardian is unable or unwilling to seek treatment for the depression, not if the guardian is unable to control the blinking. The blinking is merely a symptom of the depression.

The injustice in the Thomas case is profound. After surviving and successfully leaving a domestic violence situation, Ms. Thomas herself enlisted the help of state agencies for her daughter. She did what they asked until they asked for her child. When she refused, they took Liza from her. The court did not even make a provision for Ms. Thomas to get her daughter back, nor did it impose a time limit or success requirement on the people "treating" Liza.

Even when children and their parents are united in agreement that forced diets and commitment to an inpatient diet program are inappropriate, the family is still nearly powerless in the face of a judge who disagrees. But parents and children do not always agree on what is in the child's best interest. Children who are alone in their desire not to be forced into a diet program have even less power. At the age of thirteen, Max Airborne was forced into a psychiatric hospital for a year and a half. She was placed on a 500-calories-a-day diet to lose weight. Even after her release her life was governed by the institutionalization. She was required to travel 200 miles round-trip two to three times a week for weigh-ins under the constant threat of again being locked up.

Many children are physically and emotionally abused because they are fat. Yet, being fat is not the same thing as being abused. For a court to equate fat with abuse is unconscionable. It does a disservice to actual cases of child abuse and makes a mockery of the few rights children have. It is important not to let the extreme cases of weight based court intervention eclipse the myriad subtle injustices that happen on a daily basis. Small changes in behavior proliferate in such a hostile legal environment—a mother accepts a less favorable divorce settlement, a father is afraid to ask the government for help with his child, a parent fears letting a child attend school—all worried that, if the courts become aware of their fat children, they will take them away.

NOTES

1. Interview on the *Montel Williams Show*, as reported in "Media Watch," *FaTGiRL* 4 (1995): 61.

2. See the Uniform Marriage and Divorce Act §402.

3. Michael Gassner, "In Search of a Friend: Custody Hearings and the Disabled Parent," *Journal of Juvenile Law* 5 (1981).

4. *Fillingim v. Fillingim* 388 So. 2d 1010, 1011 (September 24, 1980).

5. *Fillingim v. Fillingim* at 1010.

6. *Fillingim v. Fillingim* at 1012.

7. *Fillingim v. Fillingim* at 1012.

8. Hillel Schwartz, *Never Satisfied: A Cultural History of Diets, Fantasies, and Fat* (New York: Free Press, 1986), 254.

9. Ibid., 295.

10. Ibid., 246.

11. *Fillingim v. Fillingim* at 1012.

12. *Fillingim v. Fillingim* at 1012.

13. *Fillingim v. Fillingim* at 1012.

14. The case that follows is from an interview with Russell Williams, Cochair of the National Association to Advance Fat Acceptance Activism Task Force, January 31, 1994. The name of the family has been changed to protect privacy interests.

15. *In the interest of LT, NT*, 494 N.W. 2d 450, 1992, at 451.

16. *In the interest of LT, NT* at 451.

17. Frances Berg, "Health Risks of Weight Loss," *Healthy Weight Journal* (formerly *Obesity and Health*) (1994): 61.

18. *In the interest of LT, NT* at 452.

19. Bis. Trip, September 11, 1991.

20. *In the Interest of LT, NT* at 451. (Liza is still [2 years later] reported to be angry about her father's behavior, including his drinking and frequent assaults on her mother.)

21. Iowa Code, section 232.2(6)(f)(1991).

22. Iowa Code, section 232.96 (2)(1991).

23. *In the Interest of LT, NT* at 452.

24. Berg, "Health Risks of Weight Loss," 58.

25. *In the interest of LT, NT* at 453.

26. *In the interest of LT, NT* at 452.

CHAPTER 6

VERBAL ABUSE AND BEYOND

I am sorry they divorced. I really am. Because she did a lot of things to help Newty. She tutored him, she took care of the children . . . and she didn't have nice furniture. . . . But we often wonder, if she would have lost some weight, if it would have helped. She was quite heavy.

—Kit Gingrich, Newt's mother,
quoted in the *San Francisco Chronicle*

VERBAL ABUSE OF FAT PEOPLE is so pervasive, accepted, and ingrained it is difficult to analyze critically. Verbal abuse is a form of psychological oppression that robs its victims of their dignity. It limits futures by quietly, consistently eroding self-confidence and self-esteem. The damage can last longer than bruises and be more insidious. Verbal abuse does not murder the body, but it can murder the spirit. In addition, while not all verbal abuse escalates into physical violence, all physically abusive relationships begin with verbal abuse and transition to domestic violence.[1]

Most people who suffer verbal abuse receive it from one source, usually an intimate partner, sometimes a parent. When fat people find themselves in an emotionally or physically abusive relationship, they will invariably find their weight a target of the abuse. When a woman is verbally abused and called names like "dumb bitch," she may be able to take comfort from her culture which, at least in part, resists that generalization. When a fat woman is verbally abused and told, "You're a fat slob. Who would want to sleep with you?" the abuse is echoed and reinforced by her culture.

Researcher and author Patricia Evans writes, "Verbal abuse is an issue of control, a means of holding power over another. This abuse may be overt or covert, constant, controlling, and . . . 'crazymaking.' "[2] Normally, verbal abuse is a personal phenomenon that occurs in private, targeted at a specific person. Because there is currently an intense antifat cultural bias, fat people are in an unusual position—they receive verbal abuse outside of the personal sphere. Fat people are the recipients of verbal abuse globally, on a societal level. Not only the culture, but the individual people who agree with the attitudes about fat and fat people are perpetrators of this abuse.

It is impossible to participate in virtually any form of mainstream culture for a twenty-four-hour period and not find several examples of fat prejudice. It may be a stereotypical representation of a fat person in a film, a poorly researched newspaper article about the latest fat-related health concern, or an infomercial model promoting a diet product announcing, "If you hate fat, you'll love our patch/pill/program!" Even progressive organizations like PBS perpetuate negative views about fat people, as when they show Covert Bailey's "Fit or Fat for the '90s." His title alone, in that it states with authority the fallacy that fatness and fitness are mutually exclusive, generates contempt for fat people. Those who watch find that during the program Bailey consistently dehumanizes fat people by calling them names, referring to them as the single word "lazyfatperson" and "El Grosso."

This cultural abuse translates directly into public action. Fat people consistently report strangers calling them names and making negative comments to them as they purchase food in the supermarket. For some, offensive names and comments yelled from passing cars is an almost daily experience.

The phenomenon of public verbal abuse against fat people differs from other forms of aggression like "road rage" in that it is not anonymous. Thin people are so confident of their right to verbally abuse fat people and the total lack of consequences for those acts, that they do it in situations where they are readily identifiable. A woman in her twenties remembers an incident at a local restaurant in California. A young woman in line next to her made a derogatory comment to her about her weight and called her "lard-ass" as they stood together in line waiting for their orders. When her food arrived, the thin woman took her meal with her to her workplace—a bakery only a few stores away. In defining the behaviors that constitute verbal abuse, Evans begins, "Most of us are aware that name calling is verbally abusive. . . . Name calling is the most obvious form of verbal abuse and is not difficult to recognize. Other forms of abuse are less evident."[3]

Besides name calling, how does verbal abuse on the basis of weight manifest itself? Despite clear indications that permanent weight loss is not a possibility for the average fat person, fat people are constantly blamed for and berated about their weight and their failure to reduce. Hostility may be overt or veiled, but its presence is an absolute indication of the abusive nature of weight interactions. This is true even though, as Evans puts it, "Verbally abusive disparagement may be voiced in an extremely sincere and concerned way."[4]

Having traveled more than an hour to see performance artist Karen Finley perform, Prue and her companion stopped for a snack and bath-room break at a McDonald's before making the late drive home. As Prue waited for her friend to finish in the bathroom, she began to eat the burger and fries she had purchased. A fellow fast food patron in the extremely crowded restaurant became very agitated at the sight of her eating and began screaming at her, "Put those down! If you eat those french fries you will DIE!! Do you understand?! *You will die!*"[5] The aggressive patron was ostensibly worried about Prue's health, but the undeserved hostility she displayed makes it clear this was verbal abuse rather than a misguided attempt to express concern over Prue's well-being.

By contrast, the comment from Kit Gingrich at the beginning of the chapter does not demonstrate such overt hostility. The hostility in her words is covert. She seems sincere in her praise of her son's ex-wife, and yet she points to the ex-wife's weight, as opposed to her actions, or Newt's busy schedule or abrasive personality, as the likely stumbling block of the marriage.

Freedom of speech is fundamental to liberty. Many oppressed groups continue to deal with hateful, destructive rhetoric and language because courts may not and should not regulate public speech. Nevertheless, there are some cases where courts take action to curb fatphobic verbal abuse against children, though usually only in passing. In a 1990 child-custody case in Connecticut, the Superior Court used incidents of verbal abuse, both weight-related and not, as evidence of parental unfitness.[6] That court recognized that a mother calling her two-year-old son "fatso" was inappropriate behavior.[7]

The court of appeals of Ohio, in 1992, also recognized that name-calling and taunting a child about weight "could be" detrimental to the child.[8] The court objected to the parents' practice of calling one of their daughters "fatty" and "fatso."[9] (This was one of nineteen reasons given by the social worker and cited by the court when it awarded permanent custody of the children to the Erie County Department of Human Services.) Unfortunately, there were several disturbing aspects of the case. One of the social worker's complaints was that the parents brought nonnutritious snack foods to the supervised visits and seemed to ignore her advice not to feed the children so much of that kind of food.[10] She also complained rather mysteriously that the parents were not able to order restaurant food "in an amount appropriate for a child."[11] Because these complaints lacked specificity it is impossible to be certain, but it seems probable that the social worker was bothered by the availability of what she believed to be "inappropriate food" because of the weight of one of the children.

The parents in the case were both "low IQ"—the father was at a borderline intellectual functioning level and the mother was classified as mildly mentally retarded.[12] It is not clear that the same court would have been as bothered by the name-calling if the parents were of average intelligence. The judge was specifically concerned with the Dixons' ability to understand that the names could be harmful. The judge might be perfectly willing to accept the average parent's determination of whether or not the abusive language was damaging to their children.

Relying on anecdotal evidence, mental abuse on the basis of weight seems very common in various intimate relationships. One mother attributes part of the breakup of her marriage to verbal abuse. Having recently given birth to a daughter and having a young son recovering from orthopedic surgery which left him in a body cast for several months did not slow the tide of verbal abuse from her husband, an attorney. She writes, "Body size was certainly a factor in my decision to leave the children's father, who continually berated me about losing weight when other concerns seemed more important."[13]

In another example from a popular television talk show, a couple describes how the boyfriend controls his girlfriend through regulation of her weight.[14] If she does not constantly and consistently lose weight, he refuses to go out with her. He proudly discussed his "reward/punishment" system in front of millions.

There is always the chance, both for children and for adults, that verbal abuse will cross the line and become physical. According to the National Education Association, between one-fourth and one-fifth of male survey respondents said they were physically assaulted or threatened with violence in junior and senior high school.[15] The survey revealed these acts continued, though to a lesser degree, in college where over 8 percent of the male and 3 percent of the female respondents were threatened or assaulted due to weight.[16] In her research Ann Hill Beuf pinpoints the transition from the verbal arena to the physical one: "There are several instances in which the stigmatizing party went beyond the realm of verbal offense, actually touching the child. Waiting at the train station after school, [a fat child] decided to purchase a candy bar from a vending machine. Just as she was making her selection, a woman she had never seen before grabbed her and dragged her away from the machine, saying, 'You don't need that. You're fat enough already.' "[17]

Adult fat people report similar stories of having food physically snatched away from them or out of their grocery baskets. The anger motivating these acts is apparent in the words of an adult grocery-store worker who has been heavy all her life. She describes her feelings as she watches shoppers check out. With startling vehemence she explains, "I get so angry when I see little girls and boys who are 200 pounds overweight and their parents are buying them garbage. I just want to shake them and say, 'Do you know what you're doing to your child!?' "[18] When people give in to their compulsions to grab food away from people, or to shake people, the physical interaction may technically constitute a criminal assault or battery. Finding an attorney who would be willing to prosecute it is another matter altogether.

When a culture teaches that preventing fat children from eating is acceptable, required, or qualifies as "treatment," parents can become confused. In 1998 David and Jennifer Mayer pleaded innocent to charges that they murdered their son.[19] The boy, almost three years old, died from malnutrition and neglect. By way of explanation, the couple expressed their desire to have a "skinny" child. Many parents restrict the food intake of their children. While the court did act in this extreme case, courts rarely interfere with these limitations and have even required such restrictions without physician approval when making custody determinations.

Abusive attitudes about weight can turn into active violence in both professional and intimate relationships. According to reporter Jaleh Hagigh, in a 1993 malpractice, fraud, and emotional distress lawsuit,[20] Sharon Ryan invoked the courts to get damages for the treatment she received at the hands of Dr. Walter Kempner from the Duke University Rice Diet Clinic.[21] Sharon went to the famous clinic at the age of twenty, in 1970, for help losing weight.[22] Her suit alleged that Dr. Kempner whipped her with a riding crop, dominated her physically and emotion-ally, turned her into a sex slave,[23] and that he convinced her to drop out of college, stop seeing her psychiatrist, move in with Kempner, and work in his clinic.[24] Ryan claims that when she disobeyed Kempner by gaining weight he regularly whipped her bare buttocks with a riding crop.[25] Kempner admits treating Ryan for obesity but denies ever abusing her even though in 1975 Kempner admitted to Duke University officials that he used the whipping technique on several patients, including Ryan. Without admitting wrongdoing, Duke University ordered him to stop using that particular "technique." Duke University continued to defend Kempner as a "respected physician."[26]

The social acceptance of disrespectful, abusive attitudes toward fat people is so ingrained it can even overwhelm notions of common decency toward the dead. Patricia Mullen was discovered dead in her bathroom by two of her three young daughters. The *San Diego Union-Tribune* reports when Chicago police arrived at the downstairs apartment of the thirty-one-year-old single mother, several officers behaved terribly inappropri-ately.[27] They allowed children to gawk at the woman's naked body as she lay in the living room for five hours while making crude comments about their inability to move the body outside for easier viewing. Witnesses claim that, after the officers used their boots to jiggle the body, they dragged the body upstairs by her ankles and across the lawn, exposing her in the process.

Met by a culture that abuses them, fat people respond predictably. Many experience a numbing of the spirit, a lessening of their vitality. A small percentage succeed despite the obstacles. Others opt to leave the abusive relationship. How do you leave an abusive culture? Some create a cultural oasis by participating in the fat-rights community. Some physically leave, uprooting themselves and moving to Santa Cruz, California, one of the few places that offers legal protection from fat discrimination. Others "opt out" by becoming reclusive. They seal themselves in their houses, avoiding the unrelenting abuse by locking the door and staying hidden inside.

NOTES

1. Patricia Evans, *The Verbally Abusive Relationship: How to Recognize It and How to Respond* (Holbrook, Mass: Adams Media Corporation, 1996), 84.

2. Ibid., p. 19.

3. Ibid., p. 23.

4. Ibid., p. 82.

5. This event occurred in a McDonald's in San Jose, California. It is important to note that experiences of this sort severely limit the desire and ability of fat people to use places of public accommodation.

6. *In re Dustin S-F*, 1990 WL 264749, at pp. 1–2.

7. *In re Dustin* at 2.

8. *In the Matter of Anita Dixon*, 1992 WL 277966 at 4.

9. *Dixon*, 4.

10. *Dixon*, 4.

11. *Dixon*, 4.

12. *Dixon*, 2.

13. Jody Savage, "Freeing the Fat Child," speech at the 1994 Association for the Health Enrichment of Large Persons (AHELP) conference.

14. On the *Jerry Springer Show*, as reported in: *Fat!So?* 3 (1995): 14.

15. National Education Association (NEA), "Report on Discrimination Due to Physical Size" (1994): 8.

16. Ibid., p. 9.

17. Ann Hill Beuf, *Beauty Is the Beast: Appearance-Impaired Children in America* (Philadelphia: University of Pennsylvania Press, 1990), 52.

18. The *Tom Lyca Show* in Los Angeles, August 14, 1997, 4 P.M. Quote from a caller identifying herself as "Charlotte."

19. Associated Press (San Diego), Thursday, 14 May, 1998.

20. Jaleh Hagigh, *The News and Observer* (Raleigh, N.C.), 21 October 1994.

21. Jaleh Hagigh, *The News and Observer* (Raleigh, N.C.), 10 November 1993.

22. Associated Press, *The Evening News* (Harrisburg), 12 November 1993, sec. A.

23. Associated Press, *Greensboro News and Record*, 10 July 1994.

24. Associated Press, *The Evening News* (Harrisburg) 12 November 1993, sec. A.

25. Physicians regularly perform what, under other circumstances, would constitute an act of battery when they operate or manipulate the bodies of their patients. With very rare exceptions like boxing competitions or medical acts, consent is not a defense to the crime of battery. A woman's consent is irrelevant if she is beaten. For example, consenting, educated adults participating in sexual consensual power-exchange relationships can face criminal prosecutions for those acts when they involve battery even though there is no complaining victim.

26. Associated Press, *Greensboro News and Record*, 22 October 1994.

27. "Police Abuse of Dead Woman Alleged," *San Diego Union-Tribune*, A5.

CHAPTER 7

JUDGING THE JURY

I'm black and I have a criteria within myself on whether I allow certain black people on a jury. Young, obese black women are really dangerous to me.

—A California prosecutor[1]

WHEN THE ENVELOPE ARRIVES IT is often met with a groan. "Oh no, jury duty." This little notice will often spark a lengthy monologue full of complaints about long waits and inconvenience, peppered with grumblings based on meticulous calculations of lost cost and time. (They are paying me $5, but parking is $6.50! My company only pays me half-time, so I am losing $8.25 each hour. If it goes over four days my company will not pay anything, and I haven't even factored in the cost of gas. . .) Experienced former jury members may add a diatribe about lawyers, big business, and the general ineffectiveness of the prison system. And yet, lurking somewhere deep beneath this layer of mundane misgiving, is recognition that the ability and responsibility to participate in the process of justice has profound meaning.

To be judged not by a king or aristocracy, but instead by one's peers, is fundamental to the concept of freedom and democracy in the United States. The jury system protects the principles of democracy by providing citizens

86

the opportunity to participate in the process of government. In *Powers v. Ohio* the U.S. Supreme Court expresses the importance of jury service through the words of Alexis de Tocqueville:

> [T]he institution of the jury raises the people itself, or at least a class of citizens, to the bench of judicial authority [and] invests the people, or that class of citizens, with the direction of society. . . . The jury . . . invests each citizen with a kind of magistracy; it makes them all feel the duties which they are bound to discharge towards society; and the part which they take in the Government. By obliging men to turn their attention to affairs which are not exclusively their own, it rubs off that individual egotism which is the rust of society.
>
> I do not know whether the jury is useful to those in litigation; but I am certain it is highly beneficial to those who decide the litigation; and I look upon it as one of the most efficacious means for the education of the people which society can employ.[2]

Jurors have significant power. In 1922 Supreme Court Chief Justice William Howard Taft wrote, "The jury system postulates a conscious duty of participation in the machinery of justice. . . . One of its greatest benefits is in the security it gives the people that they, as jurors actual or possible, being part of the judicial system of the country can prevent its arbitrary use or abuse."[3] In criminal trials, jury members ultimately decide whether the accused will walk out of the courtroom free, the community will spend tens of thousands of taxpayer dollars for incarceration, or he will be put to death. The jury's job could not be more important. Jurors must ascertain the truth. They are responsible for determining community standards and preventing gross injustice. Because so much is at stake, the person allowed to compete for a jury seat is a person whose opinion is valued and trusted.

The United States has a lengthy history of excluding groups of citizens from participating in the jury system based on their sex and the color of their skin. White men have always been included. At various times, people of color and white women have been excluded. The methods used to limit juries to white men vary from outright prohibition to subtle discouragement. The strategies used to combat this discrimination, too, have varied as judges disagree about who does and who does not have the right or "standing" to challenge discriminatory jury practices. "Standing" means the person bringing the suit (the plaintiff) is the correct person to take the issue to court. It is an important issue because, unlike most cases of discrimination, legal challenges to juror discrimination tend to share a common characteristic—they are usually brought by a defendant, not by the juror who is being discriminated against.

Individual state constitutions may offer their own protections against discrimination in the jury process. The U.S. Supreme Court has interpreted the Sixth and Fourteenth Amendments to the United States Constitution to guarantee a trial by jury drawn from a representative cross-section of the community.[4] Specifically, it is the Equal Protection Clause which provides, among other things, assurance to the defendant in a trial that the State will neither "exclude members of his race from the jury venire on account of race" nor exclude them due to the "false assumption that members of his race as a group are not qualified to serve as jurors."[5] It has been established for some time, at least theoretically, that the jury pool makeup should represent the community and that racism in jury composition is repugnant. In 1940 Justice Hugo Black wrote for a unanimous court, "For racial discrimination to result in the exclusion from jury service of otherwise qualified groups not only violates our Constitution and the laws enacted under it but is at war with our basic concepts of a democratic society and a representative government."[6] The Equal Protection Clause also speaks to sexism in jury selection.

Today, women may sit on juries in every state.[7] In the past, societal prejudice against women was reflected in jury requirements. At common law, women were simply considered unqualified to be jury members by reason of *propter defectum sexus*—defect of sex.[8] In the 1960s evolving attitudes toward women were slowly mirrored in jury composition. While three states did not allow women to participate on juries at all, some required the same participation from both sexes and others displayed mixed sentiments.[9] In *Hoyt* v. *Florida* the U.S. Supreme Court upheld a Florida law which required women who wanted to serve as jurors to register for jury duty while men were automatically eligible to serve.[10] Though slightly more subtly than in the past, women were systematically excluded. Though the Court acknowledged that the Fourteenth Amendment prevents arbitrary class exclusions from jury service on the basis of race, color, or any unreasonable classification used to "single out" a group, the Court found it reasonable that women be singled out based on prejudicial beliefs about women's roles. It was reasonable for state legislatures to conclude that women "should be relieved from the civic duty of jury service" since women were regarded as the "center of home and family life."[11] And it was reasonable to require all men, even those entitled to exemptions from jury service, to be included in the jury list unless they filed a written claim of exemption. In essence, the Court said the participation of men in the mechanism of justice was so important that it justified and even mandated an infringement on their time and liberty. For women, on the other hand, the duty to bring their experience into the workings of the justice system could be required, tolerated, or prohibited depending on the state in which they lived.

The *Hoyt* method of systematic exclusion of women was finally overruled by the Court fourteen years later, but that did not bring an end to juror discrimination.[12] Women and men of color could be discriminatorily excluded from jury service individually because of their race, gender, or ethnicity, by the use of peremptory challenges.

As they should, courts become concerned with jury discrimination when it affects the defendant's right to a fair trial. The importance of considering the rights of potential jurors has been less straightforward. While the U.S. Constitution prevents an individual citizen from being excluded from the jury pool because of race, it does not guarantee the right of that particular person to serve as a juror. Judges have disagreed over the years about whether juror discrimination affects anyone besides the defendant. In addition, judges have disagreed about which defendants suffer unfairly from juror discrimination, sometimes positing that discrimination against jurors of one race, for example, cannot hurt defendants belonging to a different race. A judge who believed that a black person suffered no wrong by being excluded from jury service and who found that a Hispanic defendant suffered no wrong having black people removed from her jury would find no recourse for that instance of discrimination. These considerations have made lawsuits and procedures for dealing with juror discrimination rather complicated.

In selecting a jury, attorneys may dismiss potential jurors "for cause." A dismissal for cause usually happens when a juror exhibits bias and the reason for the dismissal must be stated or obvious. There is no limit to the number of challenges for cause that can be made, short of trying the patience of the judge and opposing attorney. Peremptory challenges, in contrast, are allotted to lawyers in a limited number per case and, in theory, no reason need be provided with their use. Because peremptory challenges were used by some attorneys to strike minority members from the jury, particularly in criminal cases where black defendants would then face all-white juries, the practice became the subject of litigation and debate.

While certain states already outlawed racist juror exclusions, in the 1986 case *Batson* v. *Kentucky*, the systematic use of peremptory challenges to remove potential jurors on the basis of race was prohibited by the U.S. Supreme Court.[13] The Court reasoned that, if a state was required to employ a race-neutral method for creating juries, it could not later circumvent that requirement by "resorting to discrimination at other stages in the selection process."[14] Four years later, the rationale of *Batson* and cases that followed it was expanded to protect potential jurors who were struck through peremptory challenge based solely on gender in the Ninth Circuit.[15] In that case, *United States* v. *De Gross*, racism and sexism could be viewed as inextricably linked. The court did a good job by outlawing both types of discrimination. The prosecutor was trying a case against a female Hispanic defendant. He attempted to remove the only Hispanic person, a woman, from the group of potential jurors. He claimed that he was motivated not by race, but rather by the desire to achieve a different gender balance on the jury. On appeal the court decided that his reason for excusing her based on her sex was not allowable. The application of the *Batson* rationale of race discrimination to gender discrimination is an important step toward protecting the rights of other excluded individuals to participate in jury deliberations.

Currently, fat people can be dismissed from jury service because of their weight. Though no court has yet acknowledged it, it is indeed wrong to exclude people from jury service simply because they are fat. At first, the concept seems absurd. Why would an attorney want to dismiss someone for being fat? And if they want to, why should they be prevented from using peremptory challenges to do it?

There are many reasons a lawyer might choose to exclude fat people. Attending law school offers no protection against the prejudices that afflict the general population. Acting on stereotypical beliefs, lawyers may deny fat people, for no reason other than their size, the "honor and privilege of jury duty" which for most citizens "is their most significant opportunity to participate in the democratic process."[16] They may mistakenly believe fat people are too stupid to understand their arguments or too lazy to deliberate adequately. The combination of fat and race or fat and gender may spark hidden, compound prejudice. For example, an attorney may be comfortable trying a case before a fat man but not a fat woman. This is a fundamentally different situation than using peremptories to excuse a sloppy dresser or a bleached-blonde. For most fat people, body size is not the result of inattention, but rather is the result of a complicated interaction of genetic, biological, sociological, and undiscovered factors. Fat people cannot choose to become thin the way a sloppy person can choose to wear neat clothes. Style of dress may indicate views outside the mainstream. The only thing fat indicates is a person who has experienced life as a fat person just the way the only thing black skin indicates is a person who has experienced life as a black person. And when the sole evidence about a prospective juror is his body size, the only thing a prosecutor can possibly judge is her own level of prejudice. Whether it is common or not, the practice of excluding people because of an aspect of their appearance which is largely beyond their control violates fundamental tenets of fairness.

Whether or not they hold biases against fat people, lawyers allowed to use peremptory challenges against fat people may use weight as a convenient way to act on other prejudices. Weight might be given as the excuse to legitimize illegal types of racial discrimination since fat is more common in certain racial and ethnic groups than in the white population. When an attorney makes a suspicious peremptory challenge he still possesses a presumption of legitimacy. If the opposing attorney then presents a prima facie case of inappropriate discrimination, the first attorney will have to provide the judge with nondiscriminatory, legal reasons for the use of the peremptory challenge. Because these reasons do not have to rise to the level necessary to sustain a challenge for cause, an inattentive judge may miss the racial aspect of the alleged weight discrimination entirely, or she may simply be unable to determine if it was actually race discrimination because race-neutral, permissible reasons were provided.

The troubling California case *People* v. *Galbert* demonstrates the unfairness, ambiguity, and complexity which accompany peremptory challenges that occur at the intersection between race, weight, and sex discrimination.[17] As in employment discrimination cases, the law can be especially ineffective at dealing with oppression which is the result of compound, interrelated disenfranchisement.

In *Galbert*, the prosecutor used three peremptory challenges to remove three fat, black women from the jury. The jury which was ultimately selected included only one black juror. The defense objected, stating that the prosecutor was dismissing jurors due to their race in violation of *People v. Wheeler*. The prosecutor was then required to elaborate on his reasons for dismissal. To avoid committing Wheeler error he needed to provide a race-neutral explanation for his actions. It is legal to strike potential jurors on the basis of hunches and arbitrary factors, as long as the reasons are not based on impermissible group biases.[18]

Before reviewing the prosecutor's reasons for dismissal to see if they were adequately distinct from race, the court noted the prosecutor's race (black), but did not note the race of the defense attorney or defendant. (Perhaps the court thought it was relevant in determining whether the prosecutor would act in a racist manner, as if people cannot be racist against their own race.)

When questioned, Alameda County Deputy District Attorney William Tingle said he dismissed all three women for two main reasons—because they were young and because of their "appearance and conduct in court."[19] Logically, it makes sense to test whether these jurors were discriminated against because of their race by looking at the way non-black jurors of similar age and appearance were treated. These characteristics, however, are not available in the record. In fact, precedent dictates that judges are not supposed to place an "undue emphasis on comparisons of the stated reasons for the challenged excusals with similar characteristics of nonmembers of the group who were not challenged by the prosecutor" because those comparisons would be "one-sided" and the job would not be "realistic."[20] Recording traits like age, dress, and other subjective factors about potential jurors would be extremely difficult if not impossible. The result is that trial judges, the only consistent witness to juror selection, essentially can end up having the final say about important discrimination issues. In this case, the appellate court ruled that there was no violation of Wheeler because sufficient non-race-related rationale actually was the motivating force behind his use of the peremptory challenges. Nevertheless, the question remains:

Are the assumptions, made by the state of California through their prosecutor, about who is fit to serve on the jury fair or unfair?

Explaining his decision to remove the jurors, Prosecutor Tingle says, "People tell you a lot about what they are, beyond what they say, by the way they dress and how they come into a courtroom and how they look."[21] At first glance, it appears Tingle has identified three separate criteria: entrance style, mode of dress, and "look." Interpreting his later words critically, it appears that "how they come into a courtroom" may not mean whether they enter laughing, or with an apathetic demeanor, or scowling at the police presence. Instead, he is concerned with someone, "Who comes into the courtroom *looking like that*" (emphasis added).[22]

So what does Tingle mean when he says "looking like that"? If he means, looking like a black person or looking like a woman then he is acting unlawfully by discriminating against them as jurors. If he means looking like a fat person, his actions are actually legal in the California courtroom, although fairness demands they should not be. But the great likelihood is that Tingle does not mean any of these things alone. Discrimination is not that straightforward. He is not striking all black people, he is not striking all women, and he is probably not even striking all fat people. His fatphobia seems to apply specially to one particular segment of the fat population—young black women, though his fatphobia could apply to all women or only young women. The *San Francisco Examiner* reports that outside of the courtroom the prosecutor acknowledged, "Young, obese, black women are really dangerous to me. . . . I've never liked young, obese black women and I think they sense that."[23] In court he categorically denies that race played any part or was a determining factor in the decision to use his peremptory challenges against the women. He says that "a person" who is that age, size, and who dresses in that manner is a problem for him, "Whether she's white or . . . black or whatever."[24] Note that, though race is unimportant, sex has not dropped out as a consideration in his statement.

Since the issue of dress keeps coming up as a core element of Tingle's bias against the women, it deserves some scrutiny. Tingle only specifies the clothing two women wore. He complained that one was wearing a "tiny skirt and a sweat shirt."[25] Oddly, the other woman was dressed very differently. She was not wearing a sloppy T-shirt or a leopard miniskirt, but rather "a dark blue pant suit" with large gold buttons.[26] If the prosecution has a problem with both a short skirt paired with a casual sweatshirt and with a conservatively colored pantsuit, one wonders what clothing a young, fat, black woman could possibly wear that would be acceptable.

Mainstream images of the ideal woman as thin and white have diverse, serious ramifications. Just as some companies consider fat inconsistent with a "professional appearance," attorneys may feel that fat people do not seem professional or competent without understanding why they feel that way. Even attorneys who are conscious of the bias against fat people and who are attempting to form their opinions based on a juror's clothes and style, not size, may end up excluding people due to the aftereffects of a fat-oppressive society. Wardrobe often poses a problem for fat people. They are at a huge disadvantage when it comes to clothing, paying more for poorer quality items than their thin counterparts, with a much more limited selection to choose from. Media attitudes define thin people as hip, fashionable, and sexy while reviling a fat person in the same outfit as sloppy and inappropriately dressed. Fat people are not supposed to wear the revealing or suggestive clothing that thin people may wear, so if a fat woman wears a miniskirt, she may be unfairly regarded as making a moral statement rather than a fashion choice.

Tingle objected to the hair of the third woman and to the hair of the woman in the pantsuit. Both women had braided hair. "As a black person," he says, "I've always regarded braided hair as somewhat radical."[27] Here Tingle's race lends credibility to a position which should rightly be seen as intensely hostile toward black women. Braided hair is a common style, with trends and fads affecting braid number, style, thickness, color, and length. Braids may seem radical because they so infrequently grace the covers of familiar, mainstream magazines, just as black women themselves rarely appear on those covers. The texture of most black women's hair lends itself to different styles than the texture of Caucasian hair. Had the women shaved their heads, cropped their hair close, or worn a large "Afro," the prosecution probably would have regarded that as radical as well. Just as fat has become linked with sloppiness, traditional black hairstyles have been linked with radicalism.

Though the court did not agree, it is reasonable to view the prosecutor's acts as instances of discrimination, not because the women are African American, but because their hair is. The hairstyle of braiding, prevalent in the black community, might serve as a proxy for race discrimination. If a prosecutor regards hair braids as radical and thus a cue that the person is inappropriate for jury service, then she will disproportionately exclude black women from jury service. Similarly, if a prosecutor regards fat people as inappropriate for jury service, she will disproportionately exclude certain racial and ethnic minority members from jury service.

Finally, there is one more profoundly disturbing aspect of this case. The woman in the "tiny skirt" was rejected because Tingle was "uncomfortable" trusting her with a case of this "seriousness."[28] Was the reason for his discomfort due to a fear of her sexuality—the sexuality of a fat, black woman? Tingle says, "She's grossly overweight. . . . She's got on a little tiny skirt that doesn't fit her . . . a skirt that's hiked halfway up her thighs when she stands, and then when she sits, you can see everything that God gave the woman."[29] It is precisely her biology, "what God gave her," coupled with the fact that she is fat yet chooses not to dress in an asexual manner, that seems to make him uncomfortable.[30] Would he object to a thin young white woman in the same skirt? What if the same style skirt behaves differently on different body types, riding up more on larger people? Would he object to a male jury pool member who wears his jeans tight so that "what God gave him" was visible under the denim? Or is Tingle's objection not to the juror, but rather to what God actually gave her—a fat, black, female body?

Defense attorney Julia Schumer commented, "I've never had a case involving appearance to this degree. These ladies were black and he is excluding them because they are fat. The fact is he has to state an acceptable reason for excluding these people, and it seems to me that this is not an acceptable reason."[31] Both the trial judge and the appeals judge listened to Tingle's arguments and ruled that his dismissal of the three women was appropriate. The court said, "The prosecutor stated several reasons [for their exclusion] unrelated to race"[32] and thus the dismissals were legal. The courts were not troubled by Tingle's attitude toward or comments about the fat women. According to reporter Tanya Schevitz, John Burris, former president of the black attorneys group called The Charles Houston Bar Association, condemns the decision saying, "There is nothing necessarily about the clothes . . . the physical size of the people that is indicative of a particular bias of any kind, so it is racial stereotyping in its worst form, and I'm disappointed that the judge would affirm something along those lines."[33]

Four and a half months after *Galbert* was decided by the California

Court of Appeals (First District), in a case decided without oral argument, the Ninth Circuit United States Court of Appeals held that the equal protection analysis from *Batson* did not extend to prohibit the use of peremptory strikes against potential jurors based on their obesity.[34] A lawyer may prevent fat people from serving on a jury simply because of their size because attorneys are allowed to use their peremptory challenges against members of groups which are subject only to "rational basis" review.[35] The court notes that even recognition of the class of fat people under and for the purposes of the Americans with Disabilities Act does not grant the group the right to "heightened scrutiny" analysis under the equal protection clause.[36] The opinion ends by noting that the defense concedes that fat is not subject to heightened scrutiny. Judges Goodwin, Farris, and Kleinfeld say flippantly, "We are not surprised, and decline to be the first to hold so."[37]

Marlene Corrigan trusted the opinion of her peers more than the opinion of one judge. She firmly believed what she did was right and she was not afraid to take her story before a representative group of strangers. How representative would her jury have been? Had she exercised her constitutional right to a jury trial, she could expect about 30 percent of her jury to be fat. She could also expect the prosecutor trying her case to use his peremptory challenges to dismiss those jurors. Because fat is strongly genetic, the exclusion of fat people not only limits the direct participation of fat people, but also reduces the likelihood that the remaining jurors will have personal experience with the difficulties of being fat through witnessing the life of a close family member. The U.S. Supreme Court definitively states, "The purpose of a jury is to guard against the exercise of arbitrary power—to make available the commonsense judgment of the community as a hedge against the overzealous or mistaken prosecutor and in preference to the professional or perhaps overconditioned or biased response of a judge. [Citation.] This prophylactic vehicle is not provided if the jury pool is made up of only special segments of the populace or if large, distinctive groups are excluded from the pool. Community participation in the administration of the criminal law, moreover, is not only consistent with our democratic heritage but is also critical to public confidence in the fairness of the criminal justice system. Restricting jury service to only special groups or excluding identifiable segments playing major roles in the community cannot be squared with the constitutional concept of jury trial."[38] Ms. Corrigan believed that she was the victim of overzealous prosecution. She felt strongly that she had done the best she could given the circumstances. Most of all, she felt that the police and district attorney did not understand the level of hostility and inaccessibility her daughter was victim of as a fat person in the world. Had she chosen a jury trial, the prosecutor could exclude the very portion of the population with actual insight into the issues Ms. Corrigan and her daughter faced.

Excluding fat people from juries because of weight is inequitable. It denies fat defendants the Constitution's guarantee of an impartial jury drawn from a cross-section of the community. It prevents fat people from contributing to the important mechanism of justice because of stereotypes and prejudice. It deprives the jury of the perspective of a disadvantaged group. But most important, it belittles the community at large, reducing the promise of democracy to little more than a beauty contest.

NOTES

1. Tanya Schevitz, "Appeals Court Backs Banning of Fat Jurors," *San Francisco Examiner*, 8 February 1995, A1, A12, quoting Prosecutor William Tingle.

2. *Powers* v. *Ohio*, 499 U.S. 400, 406 (1990).

3. *Balzac* v. *Porto Rico*, 258 U.S. 298 (1922) as quoted in *Powers* v. *Ohio*, 499 U.S. 400, 406 (1990).

4. *People* v. *Wheeler*, 22 Cal.3d 258, 271; 148 Cal. Rptr. 890; 583 P.2d 748 (1978).

5. *Powers* v. *Ohio* 499 U.S. 400, 404 (1990).

6. *People* v. *Wheeler*, 22 Cal.3d 258, 267; 148 Cal. Rptr. 890; 583 P.2d 748 (1978), quoting *Smith* v. *Texas* (1940) 311 U.S. 128, 130.

7. While women are not categorically excluded as unqualified today, facially gender-neutral statutes (those which do not specifically exclude women in their actual language) may have the effect of requiring less participation by women on juries. The methods by which juries are selected, for instance, often have differing effects in male/female participation. For an example where an exception from service in federal juries affects more women than men, see *United States* v. *Daly* 573 F.Supp. 788 (D.C. Tex. 1983), affirmed 756 F.2d 1076 (5th Cir. 1985).

8. Claire Sherman Thomas, *Sex Discrimination,* Nutshell, Hornbook, and Black Letter Series (St. Paul: West Publishing Co., 1991), 127.

9. *Hoyt* v. *Florida*, 368 U.S. 57, 82 S.Ct. 159, 7L.Ed.2d 118 (1961).

10. *Hoyt* v. *Florida*, 368 U.S. 57, 82 S.Ct. 159, 7L.Ed.2d 118 (1961).

11. *Hoyt* v. *Florida*, 368 U.S. 57, 82 S.Ct. 159, 7L.Ed.2d 118 (1961).

12. *Taylor* v. *Louisiana*, 419 U.S. 522, 95 S.Ct. 692, 42 2.Ed.2d. 690 (1975).

13. *Batson* v. *Kentucky*, 476 U.S. 79, 106 S.Ct. 1712, 90 L.Ed. 2d 69 (1986). Before *Batson*, individual states may have disallowed race-based peremptory challenges. (E.g.: in California see *People* v. *Wheeler* (1978) 22 Cal.3d. 258.)

14. *Powers* v. *Ohio*, 499 U.S. 400, 409 (1990), quoting *Batson*, 476 U.S., at 88 and *Avery* v. *Georgia*, 345 U.S. 559, 562 (1953).

15. *United States* v. *De Gross* 913 F2d. 1417 (9th Cir. 1990).

16. *Powers* v. *Ohio*, 499 U.S. 400, 407 (1990).

17. *People* v. *Galbert* 1995 WL 108696 (Cal. App. 1 Dist.).

18. *People* v. *Turner* (1994) 8 Cal. 4th 137, 165.

19. *People* v. *Galbert*.

20. *People* v. *Johnson* (1989) 47 Cal.3d 1194, 1220.

21. *Galbert* at 2.

22. *Galbert* at 2.

23. Schevitz, "Appeals Court Backs Banning of Fat Jurors," A1, A12.

24. *Galbert* at 2.

25. *Galbert* at 2.

26. *Galbert* at 2.

27. *Galbert* at 2.

28. *Galbert* at 2. Larry Galbert was charged with attempted premeditated murder.

29. *Galbert* at 2.

30. Tingle again displays an inappropriate readiness to evaluate the woman's looks. He rates the appearance of one woman as "inappropriate but not distasteful" but notes the woman in the blue pantsuit should be dismissed because she is "that big and dresses . . . to draw that kind of attention." *Galbert* at 2.

31. Schevitz, "Appeals Court Backs Banning of Fat Jurors," A1, A12.

32. *Galbert* at 3.

33. Schevitz, "Appeals Court Backs Banning of Fat Jurors," A1, A12.

34. *United States* v. *Santiago-Martinez* 58 F.3d 422 (1995) at 421–22.

35. *Santiago-Martinez* at 423.

36. *Santiago-Martinez* at 423.

37. *Santiago-Martinez* at 423.

38. *Taylor* v. *Louisiana* (1975) 419 U.S. 522, 530.

PROFESSIONAL APPEARANCE REQUIRED

Weight-Based Employment Discrimination

TV demands a certain look, which I've never disputed, and I fit that look more now than I did eighteen or twenty pounds ago.

—Kathleen Sullivan[1]

"I T HAD LASTING EFFECTS—VERY lasting. I was looking for a summer job so I could earn some money for my second year of school, build my resume, gain experience and self-confidence—the same reasons lots of college students get summer work," explains Shawna Deray, a southern California resident.[2] "Well, it started like an ordinary job search. I had some experience—retail, marketing, and performance, good grades from a good school, and my own transportation. I got up early each morning, dressed professionally, and applied to job after job after job. I wasn't doing anything wrong. Other people my age were applying for summer jobs, too, and when we chatted they seemed to be upbeat about it. Nobody seemed to be having the problem I was having, but then again, they weren't fat." Though impossible to prove conclusively, the 230-pound twenty-year-old suspected she was being discriminated against because of her appearance. "No one said anything about my size directly, but there was a look that would cross their faces when I came in. I tried typical

summer jobs like at a local day camp. In particular I remember my experience applying to the nearby theme park. They hired lots of summer help
and even had a special area and system set up for the summer hires. We had
to fill out the application and put it on a pile. We waited in a room and
the interviewers would call us in order. When the woman called me I
smiled and was very friendly, but I saw it in her face as soon as I stood up
to follow her in. She gave me a half-smile and immediately wrote something on my sheet before we spoke. I had been looking at their job openings while I waited and saw that they were looking for people to entertain
the kids in costumes, as well as people to work at the theater. Since I had
lots of theater experience, I thought one of those positions would be per-
fect and I was well qualified for them. I told her what I was interested in.
She did not make eye contact. She told me those positions were not available and that the only thing she had for me was food preparation. When I
left I heard some guys my age outside talking about their interviews—they
had just applied for the costumed-character jobs."

Six grueling weeks later Shawna was finally hired at a different job for
the last few weeks of her summer break. After she was hired she was told
by her manager that she had received the highest score he had seen on the
required standardized test she took as part of the application. Nevertheless, the trying experience left her devastated. "I always knew I could do
the jobs, the problem was I could not get the jobs. I don't think, self-
esteem wise, I ever recovered from that summer. When I started looking
for work I felt like I deserved to be hired as much as anyone else. By the
end, I don't know. I guess I just found out it was going to be really hard
for me to get a job. Those experiences of going day after day and being
politely brushed off over and over, well, they just stick with me even now."

Like Shawna, former president of the National Association to Advance
Fat Acceptance (NAAFA), Frances White, experienced repeated covert
discrimination in the workplace. In 1999 the San Francisco Human
Rights Commission held a hearing to consider supporting the extension
of employment discrimination protection to fat people. Arthur Jackson of
Jackson Personnel, Frances's former temporary agency, raved about her
abilities and performance. Unlike many other temporary agency workers,
Arthur did not let the attitudes of other prevent him from working with
Frances. Nevertheless, she had difficulty conducting her own job search.

Enthusiastic over the phone, as soon as her potential employers met with her face-to-face neither her professional style of dress nor her phenomenal qualifications could prevail over the prejudice. Eventually Frances managed to find a good job, but she had to be better qualified than her fellow applicants and more creative and diligent in her search.

In their paper *"The Relationship Between Obesity, Employment Discrimination, and Employment-Related Victimization,"* Esther Rothblum, Pamela Brand, Carol Miller, and Helen Oetjen confirm that, for fat people, weight has a profound negative effect on self-confidence in applying and interviewing for a job.[3] If Shawna had not been significantly above average in her test score, she might not have been hired. She may be an example of a fat person whose scoring ability compensated for her weight, while the average fat person would not have received the same opportunity for work. Frances had superior skills to rely on. Had she been "average" she too would not have received equal employment opportunities. Once the destructive cycle of employment discrimination starts it is hard to break. If something is not done soon to end the workplace discrimination Shawna and young people like her face, their chances of receiving equal opportunities will fade not only due to active discrimination, but also because they will fall behind their peers in experience and self-confidence.

Although anecdotal evidence abounds, definitive numbers measuring employment discrimination against fat people are difficult to ascertain. Nevertheless, it appears that fat people suffer significant employment discrimination. In the Rothblum/Brand/Miller/Oetjen study of fat discrimination in employment, which involved more than 450 men and women, they effectively used studies about appearance to predict discrimination against fat people. They cite a model of hiring decisions which posits that physical attractiveness elicits positive expectations. This in turn leads employers to perceive attractive applicants to be, among other things, more skillful and intelligent than unattractive applicants, making physical attractiveness one of the factors that influences employment decisions.[4] The Rothblum team relies not only on outside research to conclude that obesity is considered "unattractive" but also on another study conducted by Rothblum, Miller, and Garbutt. Providing photographs of fat women and thin women to college students, the authors instructed the students to rate the pictures on a scale of 1 to 9 with 1 being "very unattractive" and 9 being "very attractive." While the thin women received a mean score of 6.5, the fat women scored a mean of 3.7. None of the fat women scored higher than 4.4.

Fat people share many of the attributes given to unattractive thin people, but also are presumed to be, among other things, lacking in energy, drive, self-discipline, and self-care. Unlike biases against thin people perceived as unattractive, stereotypes of fat people tend to include character shortcomings. These moral flaws are considered to be within the control of the person, meaning fat people tend to be viewed not only as "lacking" but also as "responsible" for the prejudices held against them. Additionally, fat people do not actually have to be seen to trigger antifat employment bias, indicating that fat prejudice easily surpasses ordinary appearance-based discrimination.[5] In another experiment, the Rothblum team simulated an employment setting, passing out resumes to students and asking them to rank the job candidates. Resumes included a written description of either a thin or a fat woman with no description of "attractiveness." Students who received the written description responded conclusively about the employment options available to the fat women, ranking them significantly more negatively on their supervisory potential than the thin candidates.[6]

Another study predicting employment opportunities based on weight was conducted in 1980. The authors Benson, Severs, Tatgenhorst, and Loddenngaard delivered a resume and cover letter to seventy public-health administrators. Some received a picture of a fat woman, some a picture of a thin woman, and some received no picture. The administrators were asked to evaluate the college student's chance of getting into graduate school and securing employment in the health-administration field. They were significantly more pessimistic about the chances of the fat students than about the thin students and the students whose weight was unknown. And, tellingly, the administrators themselves displayed bias in their own response patterns. The recipients of the packets with the pictures of the fat students were less likely to respond to the request for information than the subjects who received the thin and unidentified resumes.[7]

That fat discrimination and prejudice exist is not news to most people. In Britain a 1989 magazine survey showed that as many as 86 percent of participants thought that fat people were discriminated against and 79 percent thought that women were more discriminated against than men. A full 86 percent believed an employer would favor a thin applicant over a fat one in the workplace.[8]

Though several studies predict discrimination, and pervasive negative attitudes toward fat people virtually guarantee discrimination, there are few studies documenting the occurrences of employment discrimination. The leading survey documenting actual reports of experienced weight-based employment discrimination demonstrates a problem worthy of court intervention. The survey was conducted by mailing questionnaires to almost 1,200 members of the National Association to Advance Fat Acceptance. There were approximately 450 responses that were complete and could be tabulated. Respondents were assigned to one of three categories: nonfat (weighing no more than 19 percent above 1983 Metropolitan Life Height and Weight table), moderately fat (20 to 49 percent above Metropolitan Life tables), and fat (50 percent or more above Metropolitan Life tables).[9] The results were significant: 62 percent of fat women, 42 percent of fat men, and 31 percent of moderately fat women were not hired for a job because of their weight. None of the nonfat respondents had ever been denied a job because of their weight. The most common comment made by survey respondents was that they suspected weight discrimination but could not prove it, indicating, "The results on the frequency of job discrimination may actually be underestimating the true incidence."[10]

At first glance, the Rothblum study suggests that protection from employment discrimination for the fattest of fat people is appropriate while protection for moderately fat people is less needed because they receive less discrimination than their heavier counterparts. This conclusion is flawed, however. The suggested guidelines extending ADA coverage only to those fat people 100 percent or more above ideal weight is too narrowly and arbitrarily drawn. The Rothblum study group considered people fat who were 50 percent or more above weight tables, noting the high occurrence of employment discrimination against fat people who weighed considerably less than the ADA recognition, which is based on 100 percent above ideal weight tables. If the medical establishment and public policy position are going to continue to advocate weight loss to this population, it is counterintuitive to reward the rare individuals who manage to lose some weight with the revocation of their protection from discrimination while they still need it. The Rothblum study indicates that someone who transfers from the

100 percent overweight-table group to the 45 percent overweight-table group is still at significant risk of discriminatory treatment.

When compared to discrimination suffered by other stigmatized groups, the prejudice faced by fat people appears even more dramatic. A recent survey of craniofacially "disfigured" adults (disfigurements on the front of the face/head) found that 38 percent had experienced discrimination in employment *or* social settings.[11] Though clearly alarming, this rate is significantly lower than the rates fat women reported in hiring decisions alone. If all employment and social-setting discrimination was also factored in, the rate of weight-based discrimination would climb further.

Joanna Iovino explains what it is like to try to find work as a fat person in *Fat!So?*: "And employers: I don't even want to discuss the trouble I have finding a job. . . . When the ad says, 'Must have professional appearance,' I don't bother to apply."[12] Fat people are correct that they face hiring barriers. The barriers are absolute. One study by Roe and Wickwort reported that 16 percent of employers admitted they would not hire obese women under *any* conditions, while an additional 44 percent would not hire them under certain circumstances.[13] Common sense suggests that many fat people will not even attempt fields of employment like those in the front office or with in-person sales because they know they will never be hired.[14]

Job discrimination has devastating effects on fat people before they secure a job. Shawna's experience of diminished self-confidence after her job search struggle was consistent with the experiences of the tested population in the Rothblum/NAAFA survey. The great majority of "overweight" women reported the same effects. Sixty-four percent of moderately fat women and 73 percent of fat women suffered self-confidence problems in the job interview situation.

A shortcoming with the Rothblum study is the lack of age diversity. The average age of the respondents was approximately forty years. Weight-based discrimination may be more prevalent and have more devastating effects on younger and older populations. Older people may already suffer from age bias and the addition of another prejudice characteristic, especially one often regarded as being a health concern, may trigger greater discriminatory effects. Younger people in general will not have amassed the same work experience and proven track record which may help counteract the effect of fat discrimination in employment for people who have already been in the workforce for some time. A biased manager may believe that fat people will miss more work, convinced they are unhealthy or lazy, for example. When presented with the proven positive attendance record of a forty-year-old worker, their concerns may be allayed. When presented with the unknown quantity of a younger fat person who is new to the workforce, they may choose to rely on their preconceived notions rather than giving the person a chance. Additionally, young fat women may suffer disproportionally more than young fat men. Because women have less leeway in how they are expected to look, their seeming rejection of mainstream norms of appearance and their perceived refusal to conform to the boundaries set for them through cultural objectification may bring them particularly harsh judgment. When women age, appearance expectations of them decrease because they become invisible in the culture. This societal neglect of the importance and beauty of older women is shameful and wrong, but it does mean that the experiences of younger women whose bodies physically reject the size-8 straitjacket of cultural expectations may in fact face more cultural hostility than their older counterparts.

Fat prejudice does not cease once a fat person survives the job search stage and is hired. On the job, fat people receive different treatment than most thin people, which triggers concerns and causes additional stress for the fat working population that few thin people share. Almost 70 percent of the fat men and women in the NAAFA survey were questioned by coworkers about their weight on the job or urged to lose weight. This was true of 30 percent of moderately fat people and 10 percent of nonfat people.[15] Weight-loss pressure at work can be casual or organized, direct or indirect. The NAAFA study reports other types of fat bias including fat people being excluded from office functions and told not to use certain furniture.

The pressure to diet can invade the work environment. Some corporations have created exercise rooms for workers. Providing gyms to encourage fitness for all employees regardless of weight is helpful. Encouraging weight loss as a goal, however, is quite different. Increasingly, commercial diet programs actually enter the business setting (with the companies approval) and hold meetings during lunchtime. Posters for these meetings are displayed publicly to encourage enrollment. Groups form at some workplaces so employees can encourage each other to lose weight. Though generally negative, workplace attitudes toward fat people can be so institutionalized and hostile that these dieting groups can actually be an improvement. A New York police department created an ongoing fitness program to combat the effects of fast food and hours of driving on newly graduated recruits.[16] Despite the fact that the focus seems to be on weight loss, this "supportive" atmosphere is better than constant job fear. Humility and compliance in programs like these can buy fat workers precious compassion, which is essential to workplace survival for the majority of fat people who are sufficiently overweight to be discriminated against, but too thin to have even potential workplace protections under disability statutes. Fat people who dare to reject these programs risk even more alienation or worse—retribution from "concerned" bosses who are no longer sympathetic to employees who seem unwilling to "help themselves."

Fat hatred in employment goes far beyond social stigma, affecting status and finances tangibly. Fat employees are denied benefits that their thin counterparts enjoy, may be charged more for the same health insurance, and are sometimes passed over for promotions because of their weight. In general, heavier people report being employed in jobs with lower prestige.[17] This discrimination is not new. The *New York Times* reported that only 9 percent of top male executives were fat, compared to 40 percent in lower-executive positions, and calculated that fat men pay a salary penalty of $1,000 per year *per pound* they are overweight.[18]

Financial consequences of fat discrimination hit women disproportionately hard. The *New England Journal of Medicine* reports that, on average, fat women have a staggering $6,710 less in income per year than thin women.[19] Because a woman is fat, she is ten to thirty times more likely to live in poverty.[20] Women do not become fat because they are poor, they become poor because they are fat. Statistics about how well fat women fare in the higher salary brackets is hard to gather. Terry Poulton, author of *No Fat Chicks*, reviews a study by Dr. Irene Frieze, professor of psychology at the University of Pittsburgh. Following 1,200 MBA graduates from her university, the study found that male upper-level managers who are 20 percent overweight earn about $4,000 less per year than their thin peers. Meanwhile, similar statistics could not even be calculated for the 350 female graduates because too few of them made it to top management to be statistically significant.[21]

Anytime a group is excluded from the workplace, the effects are not limited to the excluded individuals, but are far-reaching, complicated, and incalculable. In his *Wall Street Journal* column "Managing Your Career," Hal Lancaster explains that women commonly have trouble finding mentors in the workplace because there are few role models. As he recounts the story passed on to him, "Few women hold positions of power. . . . Meanwhile, members of the predominant mentoring class—white males—are too busy seeking clones of themselves."[22]

While women in general have few role models to choose from, fat women have even fewer. Traditionally, biases about women kept women from positions of power. Women were not promoted, because of misconceptions about their ability to do the job, hence there were no examples of women successfully doing the job. The lack of women doing the job and serving as role models reinforced the stereotypes and the cycle continued. In the beginning, not only were women denied options, but men were denied the evidence they needed to correct their prejudices. And just as this early, basic sexism functioned, so, too, does the cycle of fatphobia work to exclude fat people, especially fat women.

Corky Pumilia knows a lot about fighting for what she wants in hostile terrain. The only woman to work in the Glaziers Union in her Texas town, she later became one of only two women in the Carpenter's Union. Corky's unwillingness to let stereotypes dictate her professional life kept her on the job until, while installing glass sheets outside a tall building, a coworker shook the swing in a deliberate attempt to make her lose her balance. After putting up with sexual harassment and sexist attitudes, after striving to be better than the men just to keep her jobs, Corky quit to start her own business with a female electrician.

In addition to being a stand-up comedian, dancer, artist, and art teacher, Corky was actively involved in the Red Cross's water-safety programs. She has taught water-safety classes every year since 1973. In her early forties, at a weight of 280 pounds, Corky decided to pursue her desire to become a Lifeguard Instructor Trainer so she could teach aspiring lifeguards. She had a job teaching lifeguard training lined up for the summer and was taking her Red Cross Instructor class in April of 1998 so she would be certified for the job in time. In her quest for certification she believes she ran head-on into fat prejudice, reminiscent of the sexism she faced in her trade work over a decade before.

That Corky had problems with the Red Cross instructor is particularly disappointing because, unlike many businesses and programs, the Red Cross guidelines and attitude are refreshingly progressive. In their own language the Red Cross recognizes, "The Americans with Disabilities Act has led to an increasing awareness that people with disabilities and other conditions can excel as lifeguards. The skills they need to prevent injury or to save a life may need modification, but the result is the same."[23] Teachers are instructed to focus on the objectives and foster the abilities needed to complete the objectives. The Red Cross manual gives the example that a person with one arm may be physically unable to use the prescribed front crawl or breaststroke as an approach stroke when moving toward a victim. They may be able to perform a modified sidestroke, however. "If the 'objective' is for the lifeguard to reach a victim, the person with one arm will fully satisfy that objective even though he or she has not performed a conventional approach."[24] The book reinforces this message in the section on "Critical Skills," stressing that though the specific skills of the stride jump and compact jump are listed, some trainees may not be able to perform those particular entries. "It is not essential that a rescuer enters the water in a specific manner during a rescue, only that he or she can enter the water safely. Therefore, it is possible that a participant cannot perform the stride jump and compact jump entries, but still meets the critical skill of 'entering the water.' *This participant may continue the course and still receive certification, since he or she is capable of performing that function of a lifeguard during a rescue*" (emphasis added).[25]

Despite the Red Cross's evolved position, Corky feels she encountered a problem rooted in fatphobia. Corky was the only student in the class required to perform the Deep Water Spinal Rescue, which involves stabilizing the breastbone and spine. She claims this rescue caused her great difficulty not because her skills or knowledge were lacking, but because the tube used to help perform the rescue did not work on her body the way it did for men and thinner women. She claims her instructor became hostile, refusing to work with her and humiliating her in the process. The Red Cross says, "We do not agree with Ms. Pumilia's recitation of the facts," but declines to comment further on her case.[26]

Because of her size and her sex, Corky could not use the rescue tube in the traditional manner. While other people perform the rescue with the tube placed around the chest, Corky had to push the tube down below her breasts rather than over them. With the tube across her chest, her breasts float, pushing the tube up under her arms so that she cannot get the correct grip on the drowning victim, which requires having the forearm pressed tight against the victim's breastbone and spine.

According to Corky, the instructor insisted angrily that she move the tube to the traditional position. She explained the problem, "I told him this will not work on my body because my breasts are large and float. He raised his voice to me in an angry manner most every time he spoke to me. This made me very nervous and anxious to be talked to in this way in front of the class. I felt shamed about my body."[27]

When the same issue came up later Corky reports the instructor became irate and demanded everyone get out of the pool. Corky told him she felt ashamed and wanted to leave the class, but he told her to stay through the class, so she did. Later a different rescue scenario became complicated when one of the people on Corky's team became confused and started a rescue too soon. Corky asked to start over but the instructor was angry and would not let her people redo it or finish. She said the instructor made her feel like it was her fault. She describes his attitude toward her as "angry" and "disgusted."

At the end of class the instructor gave everyone but Corky their cards. He told Corky she would have to take the thirty-four-hour lifeguard class and then retest the scenario, the deep water rescue, and the compact jump. On the next business day Corky enrolled in the lifeguard class. After completing the class, she contacted the instructor many times to arrange a time to demonstrate she could perform the skills he required, but was put off repeatedly.

Ironically, Red Cross instructors like Corky was in training to become, are not only allowed to work with the varying needs of the student population, but encouraged to do so. They are told to adapt their teaching to physically challenged individuals. They are supposed to help "participants overcome physical challenges" by increasing the time spent with the person and by "help[ing] participants modify the techniques necessary for skill completion."[28] The examples provided include moving mannequins to tables for those who cannot get to the floor and having one-armed people seal the victim's nose with their chin during rescue breathing. These are certainly more extreme accommodations than the simple one Corky needed—to be allowed to move the rescue tube below rather than above her breasts.

When Corky decided to fight the discrimination she faced, she found herself in a difficult position. After much effort to work quietly and smoothly within the organization, her problems with the instructor were ultimately ignored. People in the organization told Corky that the instructor, who enjoys a good reputation and holds an important position in the water-safety division, was distressed that somebody was unhappy with him. Her disagreement with him was summed up as a simple "personality conflict."

Turning to the law for help resulted in confusion and few options. Many fat people in Corky's position would have to struggle to qualify as a protected person under the Americans with Disabilities Act (ADA), spending time arguing about whether they were fat enough to qualify for protection largely on the basis of weight alone. People who were not fat enough might still be able to use the act depending on why they were fat. They would have to embark on an expensive medical odyssey, trying to pinpoint a recognized underlying condition that caused their weight. These hurdles were not a problem for Corky. Because she suffers from a known underlying condition which affects her weight, she fit easily within the definition of people covered by the ADA. Initial contact with the Equal Employment Opportunities Commission (EEOC) was very promising as they were interested in becoming involved with her case. Unfortunately, though she fit the definition of "disabled," she did not meet the definition of an employee, so the EEOC later declined to work with her.

After telling her story over and over to different Red Cross staff members, Corky received many opinions in passing about where her instructor had gone wrong, but few commitments to fix the problem. Once she had exhausted her own negotiating skills and patience, she found herself in the same position shared by many other people who believe they have suffered from employment-related discrimination. She was informed that her only option was to hire a private attorney with her own money and go to court. With lawyers in her area charging $20,000 to take the case, it was prohibitively expensive and risky to start legal proceedings.

Corky was lucky. Though she was not able to get relief through legal channels, she was able to drive to a neighboring city where she retook the class from another instructor. She had no problem passing the class and was even complimented by the instructor on her skills. Nevertheless, her ordeal affected her self-confidence and cost her a year of anxiety.

WHY ARE WEIGHT-RELATED EMPLOYMENT DISCRIMINATION CASES UNPREDICTABLE?

United States employment discrimination law is a complicated topic. Antidiscrimination laws which regulate employment, and other employment-related laws, can exist on the federal, state, and local levels. In practice, any of the three branches of government can create employment protections which can take the form of executive orders, legislation, or judicial interpretations.

Federal provisions guaranteeing equal employment opportunities include Title VII of the 1964 Civil Rights Act and the 1990 Americans with Disabilities Act (ADA). Title VII makes it illegal for many employers to discriminate on the basis of race, color, sex, national origin, or religion. The ADA makes it illegal to discriminate in employment against people with disabilities by employers who are subject to Title VII.[29] If and when fat is covered under the ADA is a complicated question. As it now stands, the ADA provides protection for some, but not all, fat people depending on their particular physical situation and on the federal district in which they are located.

The Equal Protection Clause of the United States Constitution, or similar clauses in state constitutions, may at times become the centerpiece in protecting fat people from discrimination. The United States' Equal Protection Clause applies to government actions and programs including employment.[30] Its purpose is to regulate governmental group-based discrimination. The U.S. Supreme Court has established a method to enforce this clause which is quite complicated.

Whether or not, and to what extent, a group is protected by the Equal Protection Clause depends on certain characteristics of the group. According to *Frontiero* v. *Richardson* and similar cases, important issues to consider include "whether there has been a history of discrimination against the group at issue, whether the discrimination is unrelated to the individual group member's abilities, and whether members of the group are poorly represented in the political processes such that those processes could not be expected to correct the harm at issue. Some courts have also said that the trait that defines the class must be 'immutable' to be deserving of heightened judicial scrutiny."[31]

When a group sufficiently meets all those characteristics, discrimination against the group should technically receive "strict scrutiny" in the courtroom. Very few types of group classifications qualify for this level of review. Groups that do receive this level of scrutiny include those based on race, religion, and national origin. Discrimination against categories of people according to these characteristics is automatically suspect. The Court will only uphold discrimination based on these characteristics if it is "necessary to promote a compelling government interest."[32] For example, when considering a law which differentiates on the basis of race, the Court looks at the governmental goal to determine if it is indeed important enough to constitute a "compelling" interest that would justify the racial discrimination. The Court also looks at the discriminatory law to determine whether it is "necessary" or whether there is another way to accomplish the goal that does not need to differentiate on the basis of race. Very few cases of discrimination can satisfy these tough standards, so most laws, cases, or practices that receive this type of review are eventually overruled.

Discriminatory practices which do not quite rise to that level are sometimes reviewed using an "intermediate" level of scrutiny. The courts determine whether these types of discrimination "serve important governmental objectives" and "substantially relate" to the achievement of those objectives.[33] Classifications based on sex tend to be reviewed with this level of scrutiny.

The third and least powerful kind of review is called "rational basis" review. When the government makes distinctions based on regular criteria that the Court does not consider suspicious or suspect, the classifications receive this type of review. To satisfy this burden the government need only show that "the classification itself is rationally related to a legitimate governmental interest."[34] It is very hard to win a case that only requires the defendant to prove this. For example, age discrimination cases are reviewed under this basis. Consequently, it is allowable for the government to impose mandatory retirement ages. A case involving zoning laws which prohibited a home for mentally disabled people is one of the rare instances where the Court found no rational basis for the law. With no rational basis behind it, the law was struck down.

Discrimination against fat people as a group shares many characteristics of the types of discrimination protected under "heightened scrutiny" analysis. Stereotypes about fat people affect the whole group and are not based on the abilities of individuals. The prejudice against fat is similar, sometimes more severe, than race-based bias. Young children of different races and sizes identify fat children as lazy, dirty, stupid, cheats, and liars. These stereotypes are identical to many racial stereotypes. Few American prejudices compare in historical foundation or scale to the barbaric treatment of African Americans, Native Americans, and some Asian Americans in the early formative years of the United States. Nevertheless, fat prejudice certainly does compare in history and severity to the continuing treatment of those minority group members as well as to the more recent treatment of other racial minorities. All cases, laws, and practices that discriminate on these bases receive strict scrutiny analysis.

Discrimination based on religious affiliation also invokes heightened protection analysis. W. Charisse Goodman in her book *The Invisible Woman* supports authoritatively her compelling assertion that Nazi beliefs, propaganda, and prejudices against Jewish people "mirror in a number of respects the modern American perception and portrayal of the fat person."[35] "Modern America," she explains, "is as morally bankrupt in its hysterical worship of thinness, and its attendant punishment of large women, as was Nazi Germany in its equally irrational glorification of Nordic/Aryan physical perfection."[36] She points out some of the many repeated stereotypes: "Nazi propaganda consistently represented Jews as fat, ugly, sloppy, dirty, and inherently unwholesome, even diseased. . . . It hardly seems a coincidence . . . that fat people are also commonly thought of as dirty, ugly, sloppy—and as preferring themselves that way. . . . Loudness, vulgarity, greediness, and pushiness are just a few of the qualities typically described as being peculiar to, or exaggerated in, fat people just as anti-Semites have typically foisted these same qualities on Jews."[37] And while courts sometimes hold that only unchangeable characteristics can qualify a group for heightened scrutiny analysis, permanent weight loss seems to be less a matter of volition for the majority of fat people than switching religious affiliation is for the average person.

A just society exists only when all members are seen as equals and treated equally. Nevertheless, it is highly unlikely that a court would currently be willing to extend the blanket of heightened scrutiny to protect fat people. Common sense indicates that courts should be aggressive in attempting to secure civil rights for all groups, encouraging the disenfranchised to step forward and assert their rights, anxious to apply "heightened scrutiny" to any group-based distinctions. Those working for gay, lesbian, and transgender rights have also been fighting this battle. They have been unsuccessful in getting the Court to permanently apply heightened scrutiny in cases of discrimination on the grounds of sexual orientation, although there were several early successes. For various reasons, these rulings were vacated or overturned by higher courts. This history shows a Court desperate not to "give away" civil rights for fear of accidentally granting "special rights."

Because there is no federal law against discrimination on the basis of weight in general, the protection from fat prejudice in the workplace varies from location to location. Laws and rulings differ by state, city, and county. Judicial determinations in one federal jurisdiction can differ from those nearby but in a different federal jurisdiction. Because state and local laws are many and subject to change, it is difficult to get a comprehensive picture of the protection available to fat people. Nevertheless, there are only a few places where fat people are expressly protected from prejudice in the workplace. An employer in one city may be within her legal rights to hire only thin people, while an employer just over the city or state line may be acting illegally when doing the same thing. A fat person in one federal jurisdiction may be protected from size discrimination while his neighbor in the next jurisdiction is not. In many places the law about weight discrimination is unsettled, meaning much is left to the opinions of judges and juries. A fat person may win or lose an employment discrimination case for no reason other than the courtroom and judge assigned to the case.

Though resistance to fat discrimination has been regarded by the media as a novelty, making many headlines recently as the latest diet or weight-related press release comes out, state courts are already acquainted with the problem of weight-based employment discrimination. For decades individual fat people have braved society's ridicule and overcome seemingly insurmountable barriers to demand their rights in the courtroom.

One of the earlier cases of employment discrimination on the basis of weight outlines many of the issues still present in the most recent lawsuits. Only three years after the Civil Rights Act of 1964 was put in place, a woman brought a weight-discrimination case against a board empowered by the city of New York that denied her a license as a substitute teacher because of her weight. In *Application of Nancy Parolisi* v. *Board of Examiners of the City of New York*, the higher court eventually overturned the lower court's decision to deny Parolisi her license.[38]

Parolisi, who weighed 221 pounds, had worked in the city school system for three terms. The court was careful to note that she had an excellent record during the time she was employed. Her superiors agreed and testified to this fact. That she received rave reviews established Ms. Parolisi's competence in the field before the court. When she applied for a substitute teacher license, the Board of Examiners (or the Board of Education) denied her license. They admitted basing the denial solely on the fact that she was overweight.

In its decision, the court looked at the authority granted to the boards by the legislature. Education Law section 2569 provided for the creation of the Board of Examiners whose duty it was to examine all applicants for licensing. The court noted that there was no specific language to suggest that the legislature delegated authority to adopt standards or tests for health and physical fitness in that section, as there was, for example, in the case of police and firefighters. If the boards possessed the authority to do such tests, it was as provided by the Constitution.

Article V Section 6 specified state civil service appointments were to be made "according to merit and fitness."[39] The court interpreted this to mean government agencies were free to adopt health standards as long as they were "reasonably and rationally related to ability to perform."[40] In this case, the court described the skills in question as the ability to both teach and maintain order.

The board's standards dictated that a rating of unsatisfactory would be given in the physical/medical tests if the applicant's condition might endanger the health and safety of the students, cause excessive absenteeism, exert an "unwholesome or disturbing" influence, or interfere with the ability to be effective. Applicants were advised in writing ahead of time that extreme under- or overweight would be looked at with particular reference to the ability to perform. The court conservatively viewed this as a mere indication that overweight people would be tested as the Constitution required. In fact, this statement means more than that. It is a statement which would likely work to discourage applications by people who were not of average weight, whether they were underweight or overweight. It also implies that these applicants should expect to receive a tougher review (without the benefit of the assumption that they are of equal ability).

The court was particularly troubled by the use of "objective standards" (by which it means generalizations about fat people) in particular, individual cases. For example, the court was bothered by the underlying assumption in the board's rule that 40 percent or more deviation from "normal" weight interfered with teacher and student safety. The presumption was that "overweight is inexorably related to agility."[41] This argument, which is a commonly held belief today, was dismissed by the judge without argument. He just pointed out that many football coaches would not agree with that statement.

The court also refused to accept general evidence that all fat people are prone to health problems such as high blood pressure, cardiovascular problems, and diabetes, as evidence that Parolisi in particular was. The court relied on the fact that her record with the school showed she missed only two days, and also on the fact that "a former President and Chief Justice of the United States, also rather obese, rarely missed a day."[42] This is interesting because potential health problems are only being examined in relation to likelihood of missed work, not insurance costs, etc. It also points out the critical need for fat role models, something not common today when President Clinton is constantly being ridiculed about his very modest "excess" weight.

Strangely, while the court insisted that "obesity" is not necessarily connected to fitness in terms of agility and presumption of continued health, it also stated, "Obesity may surely be made a constitutional standard for firemen and policemen. Such a standard is reasonably and rationally related to fitness to perform the duties of such positions."[43] While there may be a portion of fire-fighting work that really does require a person of very low weight (e.g., structurally damaged buildings cannot support heavier people safely), all the other skills for these jobs seem unrelated to weight specifically. Weight does not dictate speed, stamina, negotiating and investigation skills, driving and shooting ability, etc. Perhaps the skills needed to perform the duties of a police officer or firefighter might show that weight maximums may in fact be needed, but the point is that evidence is needed to prove it. Why does the court, rather than saying "agility is not necessarily related to ability to teach," instead say "you may not assume any given fat person is not agile" and then abandon this sensible approach in other professions? Why would the ease of "objective standards" be reasonable for police, but not for teachers?

The court touches on both the areas of fatphobia and sex/weight intersectionality issues. The judge progressively points out that no teacher was ever denied an appointment due to underweight, nor was a male teacher ever denied a position due to overweight. Additionally, it warned, "When an objective standard of obesity, . . . is applied to a female . . . applicant, it can become an aesthetic standard rather than the constitutionally commanded standard of merit and fitness."[44]

Thirty years have passed since Ms. Parolisi successfully fought the governing boards in New York that sought to deny her license, but the fight to keep licenses out of the hands of fat people rages on. This time, New York Transit Authority officials tried to deny a license to Dwayne Richardson, devastating his dream of becoming a subway motorman.[45] The Transit Authority decided that at 450 pounds, the twenty-five-year-old weighed too much to drive subway trains. In the face of great odds, after he lost appeals with the EEOC and Human Rights Commission, Mr. Richardson did not give up. Acting as his own lawyer, he filed a federal lawsuit demanding his civil rights under the Americans with Disabilities Act. This led to a settlement with the Transit Authority and consequently his new position as motorman. Writer James Rutenberg reports Mr. Richardson's positive attitude despite his struggle: "Let bygones be bygones. In the end, everyone wins. I get to operate a train, the TA gets a dedicated worker and the riding public has a competent motorman taking them to work and home."[46]

Until federal legislation is created or expanded to completely prohibit weight discrimination in employment when it is unjustified and unnecessary, fat people will continue to receive a patchwork of protection. Because, in the absence of federal action, people will be forced to rely on state laws, state legislatures must actively pursue protections for fat people. Given that it is the very existence of the prejudice which necessitates legal protection against it, it will be an uphill battle to persuade the public to, in turn, persuade the local governing bodies to institute antidiscrimination policies. Nevertheless, this must happen even as the federal government is simultaneously encouraged to also guarantee that fat people will get the protection they require to ensure they receive equal employment opportunities. The longer the delay in providing equal opportunities for this class of people, the more complicated it will become to compensate for the wrongs committed. Just as years of discrimination against people on the basis of skin color has led to a cycle of oppression which continues to challenge the very foundation of the country's commitment to equality, so, too, will weight discrimination if left unchecked. Discrimination in employment creates a legacy of lost opportunity for some and unfair advantage for others. The reparative policies like affirmative action programs instituted to counteract similar past injustices and to break the cycle of race and sex discrimination in employment have required the nation's continued expenditure of immeasurable effort, time, money, and heartache and at best have only provided partial relief. We must learn from the past and stamp out unjustified weight-based employment discrimination before it does more damage.

NOTES

1. Kathleen Sullivan, interview, *TV Guide*, 11 June 1994.

2. Name changed upon request. Personal interview, March 1999.

3. Esther Rothblum et al. "The Relationship Between Obesity, Employment Discrimination, and Employment-Related Victimization," University of Vermont, *Journal of Vocational Behavior* 37 (1990): 251–66, 262.

4. Ibid., 251–66, 252.

5. Terry Poulton, *No Fat Chicks: How Big Business Profits by Making Women Hate Their Bodies—and How to Fight Back* (N.J.: Birch Lane Press published by Carol Publishing Group, 1997), 121. Poulton reports that Peter Floyd from Per-

sonnel Corporation of America says, "Managers assume that overweight people don't have the energy or drive to operate in the field as salespersons." She cites a study of the effects of fat on service careers by Professor Michael Klassen who found that fat people are thought of as "lazy, unkempt, jolly, lacking self-discipline, lacking self-care, unhealthy, and insecure."

6. Rothblum et al., "The Relationship Between Obesity," 253.

7. Ibid.

8. Shelley Bovey, *The Forbidden Body* (London: Pandora, 1994).

9. Rothblum et al., "The Relationship Between Obesity," 255. The Rothblum paper cites three studies which indicate that self-reported weight corresponds closely to actual weight. See: R. Rzewnicki and D. G. Forgays, "Recidivism and Self-cure of Smoking and Obesity," *American Psychologist* 42 (1987): 97–100; S. Schachter, "Recidivism and Self-cure of Smoking and Obesity," *American Psychologist* 37 (1982): 436–44; and A. J. Stunkard and J. M. Albaum, "The Accuracy of Self-reported Weights," *American Journal of Clinical Nutrition* 34 (1981): 1593–99.

10. The NAAFA Workbook Committee of the National Association to Advance Fat Acceptance, *NAAFA Workbook* (New York and Calif.: NAAFA, circa 1993), 6–13.

11. D. Sarwer et al., "Adult Psychological Functioning of Individuals Born with Craniofacial Anomalies," *Plastic and Reconstructive Surgery* 103, no. 2 (February 1999): 412–18.

12. Marilyn Wann, *Fat!So?* (Berkeley, Calif.: Ten Speed Press, 1998).

13. Charisse Goodman, *The Invisible Woman: Confronting Weight Prejudice in America* (Calif.: Gurze Books, 1995), 143, quoting N. Gustafson, *Lifetime Weight Control* (La Mesa, Calif., Western Schools Press, 1993), 30.

14. See also Naomi Wolf, "Work," *The Beauty Myth* (New York: William Morris and Co., Inc., 1991) for an analysis of the role of beauty specifically in women's ability to secure employment.

15. The NAAFA Workbook Committee of the National Association to Advance Fat Acceptance, *NAAFA Workbook* (New York and Calif.: NAAFA, circa 1993), 6–11 to 6–14.

The survey was created and conducted by Esther Rothblum (associate professor of clinical psychology, University of Vermont), Carol Miller (sssociate professor of social psychology, University of Vermont), Pamela Brand (doctoral student, University of Vermont), and Helen Oetjen (undergraduate research assistant).

The survey found that respondents suffered other forms of job discrimination, as well. For instance, many people reported that their job interviews focused almost entirely on their weight. People who were encouraged strongly to apply over the phone were discouraged in person. They were told they would not have enough energy for the job or that they would not be good role models.

16. Stephanie Young, "Local Police Fight Fat," *Glamour*, August 1994, 41.

17. The Rothblum et al. study measured job prestige using the job title provided by the respondents and census data. The two researchers agreed on 93 percent of the prestige categorizations. They found that there was an overall difference in prestige between the different weight categories with fatter people having lower job prestige in general. (As reported in the *NAAFA Workbook*.)

18. Gina Kolata, *New York Times*, 22 November 1992.

19. Steven L. Gortmaker et al., "Social and Economic Consequences of Overweight in Adolescence and Young Adulthood," *New England Journal of Medicine* 399, no. 14 (30 September, 1993): 1008–12.

20. Ibid. Gortmaker et al. report that women are ten times more likely to live in poverty because of fat. Terry Poulton, in her book *No Fat Chicks,* reports that, "Obesity results in poverty for at least a third of women workers" (118).

21. Poulton, *No Fat Chicks*, 120.

22. Hal Lancaster, "Managing Your Career: How Women Can Find Mentors in a World with Few Role Models," *Wall Street Journal*, 1997.

23. *The American Red Cross Lifeguarding Instructor's Manual* (Mosby-Year Book, Inc., 1995), 17.

24. Ibid., 17.

25. Ibid., 19.

26. Melissa Hurst, Office of the General Counsel, Red Cross, in a letter to Sondra Solovay, 16 April 1999. Because the Red Cross declined to comment, these facts are as told by Corky Pumilia.

27. Corky Pumilia, letter to the Red Cross Board, 7 August 1998.

28. *The American Red Cross Lifeguarding Instructor's Manual*, 18.

29. Mack Player, *Federal Law of Employment Discrimination in a Nutshell* (St. Paul: West Publishing Company, 1992), 16.

30. William Rubenstein, ed., *Lesbians, Gay Men, and the Law* (New York: New Press, 1993), 260–61 generally in relation to the Equal Protection Clause.

31. Ibid., 260–61.

32. Ibid., at 260 quoting *Dunn* v. *Blumstein*, 405 U.S. 330, 342 (1972) and *Shapiro* v. *Thompson*, 394 U.S. 618, 634 (1969).

33. Ibid., at 260, citing *Craig* v. *Boren*, 429 U.S. 190, 197 (1976).

34. Ibid., at 260, quoting *United States Department of Agriculture* v. *Moreno*, 413 U.S. 528, 533 (1973).

35. Goodman, *The Invisible Woman*, 127.

36. Ibid., 128.

37. Ibid.

38. *Application of Nancy Parolisi* v. *Board of Examiners of the City of New York* 285 N.Y.S.2d 936, 55 MISC.2d 546 (Supreme Court, Special Term, Kings County, Part 1) (1967).

39. *Parolisi* at 547, 938.

40. *Parolisi* at 547, 938.

41. *Parolisi* at 548, 939.

42. *Parolisi* at 548, 939. (Referring to William Howard Taft, without mentioning his name.)

43. *Parolisi* at 549, 940.

44. *Parolisi* at 549, 940.

45. See generally James Rutenberg, "It's Full Steam Ahead for a Guy's Big Dream," *New York Daily News*, 31 August 1998, News and Views.

46. Ibid.

CHAPTER 9

INTERSECTIONALITY ISSUES IN WEIGHT DISCRIMINATION

Weight Requirements as Sex Discrimination

JOB REQUIREMENTS SOMETIMES INCORPORATE SPECIFIC "acceptable" weight ranges for applicants and employees. Occasionally, these are illegal in and of themselves. For example, using statistical evidence, the plaintiff in *Mieth* v. *Dothard*[1] was able to make a prima facie case of Title VII sex discrimination. She showed that the weight requirements for the position of correctional counselor in the state prison system were discriminatory because they excluded 41.13 percent of the female population, but less than 1 percent of the male population. (Minimum requirement for the position was a height of 5 feet, 2 inches and a weight of 120 pounds.) While there was a waiver provision for these requirements, the department of public safety never sought a waiver and never informed Mieth that a waiver was possible.

When a weight and height ratio is used which varies according to natural, average weight differences between men and women, then it is not sex discrimination because both sexes are equally burdened.[2] So, for example, Euro-Disney's employment contract which reads, "One of the conditions of your employment consists of maintaining a weight in harmony with your height," would probably not, in and of itself, constitute sex discrimination in the United States.[3] It is an example of weight discrimination.

Sometimes fat people are not discriminated against just because they are fat. They are the victims of discrimination because they are fat *and* something else, like fat and Mexican, or fat and homosexual and Mexican. The multiple layers of prejudice, along with varying degrees of legal protection per category, combine to create special problems when seeking courtroom justice.

SEX AND WEIGHT

Nancy Parolisi was denied her substitute teacher license because she was too fat. No man was refused a position because of his weight. When the court expressed concern about this disparity, it was touching on a complex type of prejudice.

Some discrimination is very obvious, as when women are denied jobs because an employer refuses to hire females. But effective discrimination may be more covert than that.

When employers used otherwise neutral tests against women but not men, lower courts upheld the practice. (For example, marital status might have been a deciding factor in the employment of women but not for men.) Because some women were hired, they ruled that it was not sex discrimination. "Sex" was not the reason for the discrimination, it was "sex plus" another characteristic. If the other characteristic was legal, then there was no problem. The U.S. Supreme Court overturned this holding, ruling that Title VII did not allow one hiring practice for men and a different one for women.

Even if discrimination against Nancy Parolisi because of her weight was legal, the judge seemed to suspect that she was being singled out not just because of her weight, but because of her "sex plus her weight," creating a type of beauty standard that was only required of women. When employers like airlines impose strict weight standards on women, sometimes they may be challenged using this reasoning.

The courts are sometimes willing to recognize that men and women receive differing levels of weight harassment, although they may not consider it strong evidence of discrimination. In *Donoghue* v. *The County of Orange*, the court of the second circuit held that the proof of disparate treatment brought by a fired female deputy sheriff suing under Title VII was sufficient to go to trial.[4]

Donoghue, a deputy sheriff, was terminated for failing training. In addition to being treated more harshly in the training program than her male counterparts, such as being penalized with memoranda, push-ups, and having laps more frequently assigned to her, Donoghue's weight was made more of a problem. Where overweight men were not given negative evaluations because of their weight, Donoghue was. This fact, in combination with many other accusations, was enough to avoid a directed verdict, but the final outcome of her claim is still highly unpredictable.

When the workforce consists only of women, it can be impossible to determine if different weight standards are imposed on women versus men. In the 1982 case *Gerdom v. Continental Airlines*, a court ruled that it was not necessary to show that men and women were treated differently to be unlawful. When stringent weight and grooming requirements were demanded of the all-female workforce *because* the workforce was composed only of women, it constituted illegal sex discrimination.[5]

RACE AND WEIGHT

In *Hill v. Johnson Controls World Services, Inc.*, the plaintiff's suit under the Americans with Disabilities Act failed to survive the defendant's summary judgment motion, meaning the case would not be heard.[6]

Johnson Controls contracted to provide services, including security, to the navy on the Kings Bay Submarine Base. Hill, a Johnson Controls employee, worked there between 1989 and 1992. The defendant implemented a policy of dismissing workers whose body-fat percentages exceeded certain levels, in accordance with its contract with the navy. In 1992 Hill was told he was being fired for his failure to comply with the body-fat standards.

Hill filed a complaint with the Department of Labor alleging racial discrimination. The complaint was forwarded to the EEOC. On the form the only type of discrimination which he checked off was "race-black." In the narrative section his primary point was that he had been treated differently than other overweight workers on the basis of his race. He did not characterize the discrimination as disability discrimination at that time. The EEOC, investigating only the race issue, determined that the evidence did not establish a Title VII violation. Hill subsequently brought this action in federal court under the ADA.

The court held that the claim under the ADA is not sufficiently "like or related" to the race discrimination claim.[7] "Hill's EEOC charge alleged race discrimination. His district court complaint, in contrast, alleged discrimination on the basis of disability. Hill contends that his disability discrimination claim is one that could reasonably be expected to grow out of the allegations of his EEOC charge. The Court cannot agree."[8]

This ruling is consistent with many cases where courts have been extremely rigid regarding EEOC filing requirements. Nevertheless, it illustrates perfectly the problem encountered by many fat people who are also members of other disadvantaged groups. Because fat is stigmatized, because it is neither obvious nor necessarily true that relief may be available under the ADA and because most fat people do not think of themselves as disabled and do not understand the ADA, when intersectionality issues arise like Hill's, the instinct is to look at them only through more traditional classifications of discrimination. In this case, Hill was thinking fairly clearly. He specifically said in his EEOC complaint that there was weight discrimination, and that he was singled out for it because of his race. In other words, Hill said that he was fired for his weight because he is black.

Hill is no longer able to file the necessary EEOC charge to fix the problem because his time to file a claim as allowed by law has expired. Thus, Hill loses his disability discrimination claim as well as his race discrimination claim.

WEIGHT, RACE, AND SEX
(AKA THE "FAT WHITE BITCH" PROBLEM)

Although not a case about weight discrimination per se, *Griffith* v. *State of Colorado, Division of Youth Services*[9] demonstrates the potential for discrimination against one person on numerous grounds. (This case is complicated by the fact that it includes retaliation claims after Griffith's internal grievance and subsequent agreement led to the removal of the supervisor. The focus here will be on the issue of the intersectionality dynamic where multiple, overlapping, or interrelated prejudices result in discrimination.) In *Griffith* a white female employee brought a case of sexual and racial harassment and discrimination against a black male supervisor under Title VII. Although she made no claim about weight discrimination, did she suffer harassment on the basis of her weight?

Griffith worked at the Department of Youth Services for eight years. During the last five years, she was continually subjected to harassment by her supervisor Grier. Grier had allegedly criticized her approach to the kids who were misbehaving on many occasions: he ordered her to cuff and shackle them in contradiction of departmental policy, threatened to write her up, admonished her for hugging the kids and threatened to write her up if she did it again, yelled at her in front of the kids, and used offensive language like "fucking," "shit," etc. Griffith claimed that Grier chose "mostly white females"[10] to pick on in this manner. On at least one occasion he called Griffith a "stupid white woman." He made numerous statements about her physical appearance, referring to her ugliness and her weight.

Dissecting this multifold discrimination to determine how it fits under Title VII, the ADA, or other relevant statutes is tricky. Would Griffith have been ridiculed for her weight if she were a similarly "overweight" black man? If she were a black woman rather than a white woman? If she were a white man? Until weight-based discrimination is outlawed, protection will depend on results of this kind of "discrimination dissection."

While lawyers and judges explore this developing area of employment law to see what sort of legal protections, if any, are available, victims of this sort of discrimination suffer differently than those harassed for their membership in only one group. Attorney Rosezella Canty-Letsome describes residual employment discrimination uncertainty she lives with: "I can tell you about the overt experiences I have had. But as for the covert experiences, I don't know for sure why I didn't get those jobs because I'm an 'FBW.' I'm a fat, black woman. I don't know if it's size; I don't know if it's race; I don't know if it's sex; or a combination of all three why it was I didn't get the job."[11] Prejudice that does not single out only one characteristic, but instead attacks and fragments each aspect of a person's identity, can prove not only more complex to fight, but also a much more devastating, isolating, and alienating experience.

NOTES

1. *Mieth* v. *Dothard* 418 F. Supp. 1169 (M.D. Ala. 1976).

2. See *Craft* v. *Metromedia, Inc.*, 766 F.2d 1205 (8th Cir. 1985).

3. Shelley Bovey, *The Forbidden Body* (London: Pandora Press, 1994), p. 36. (If Disney had a sexist definition of what constituted "weight in harmony with height," then a *Mieth* argument could be made.)

4. *Donoghue* v. *The County of Orange*, 848 F.2d 926 (1987, 1988).

5. Mack Player, *Federal Law of Employment Discrimination*, 3d ed. (Minn.: West Publishing, 1992), 78.

6. *Hill* v. *Johnson Controls World Services, Inc.*, 1994 WL 562583 (S.D.GA.), 3 A.D. Cases 805 (1994). (Case not reported in F.Supp.)

7. *Hill* v. *Johnson Controls World Services, Inc.*, 1994 WL 562583 (S.D.GA.), 3 A.D. Cases 805 (1994), at 2.

8. *Hill* v. *Johnson Controls World Services, Inc.*, 1994 WL 562583 (S.D.GA.), 3 A.D. Cases 805 (1994), at 2.

9. *Griffith* v. *State of Colorado, Division of Youth Services*, 17 F.3d 1323 (1994).

10. *Griffith* v. *State of Colorado, Division of Youth Services*, 17 F.3d 1323 (1994) at 1325.

11. Rosezella Canty-Letsome, Esq., *NAAFA Workbook*, ch. 6 (6–9).

CHAPTER 10

IS AN AMPLE BODY
AN ABLE BODY?

Fat and Disability Law

Historically, society has tended to isolate and segregate individuals with disabilities. . . . Such forms of discrimination . . . continue to be a serious and pervasive social problem. Discrimination against individuals with disabilities persists in such critical areas as employment, housing, public accommodations, education, transportation, communication, recreation, institutionalization, health services, voting, and access to public services. Unlike individuals who have experienced discrimination on the basis of race, color, sex, national origin, religion, or age, individuals who have experienced discrimination on the basis of disability have often had no legal recourse to redress such discrimination. Individuals with disabilities continually encounter various forms of discrimination, including outright intentional exclusion, the discriminatory effects of architectural [and] transportation . . . barriers, . . . segregation, and relegation to lesser services, programs, activities, benefits, jobs, or other opportunities. The continuing existence of unfair and unnecessary discrimination and prejudice denies people with disabilities the opportunity to compete on an equal basis and to pursue those opportunities for which our free society is justifiably famous.

—United States Congress[1]

IT IS THE ISSUE THAT pits activists against activists and experts against experts. It drags to the surface the most unsavory prejudices of already marginalized groups. It is possibly the most controversial topic in the fat-rights community. Is fat a disability? Is weight discrimination the same thing as disability discrimination? Is it appropriate for fat people to seek civil liberties protections under the Americans with Disabilities Act? Should the ADA apply to fat people?

There is no federal law that protects fat people from the effects of fat prejudice specifically, so protection falls to state and local statutes. Only a few places, like Santa Cruz, California, Washington, D.C., and the state of Michigan, have laws to prohibit discrimination against otherwise qualified people on the basis of weight or appearance. Most of the fat plaintiffs who have been successful in court have won because they were able to use either state or federal disability laws to challenge the discrimination they faced. Currently, there are few other legal strategies available to challenge fat-employment and access issues in the courtroom.

Because they can vary, exploring each individual states' disability statutes is beyond the scope of this book. The Americans with Disabilities Act is broad federal legislation that covers all the states and is often similar to the state's own disability provisions. Arguments about weight and the ADA will often also apply to state law and vice versa.

SHOULD FAT PEOPLE USE DISABILITY LAWS?

Various concerns surround the practice of using the Americans with Disabilities Act and other disability laws to secure employment and civil liberty protections for fat people. Some of the most vocal opponents of this strategy are fat people themselves. Having struggled for so long to be accepted and regarded as "normal," this segment of the fat community vehemently rejects what they see as an effort to further stigmatize them. They feel that it is not their bodies that cause problems, but society's treatment of them as unable, different, undeserving, and inferior. They maintain that they can do the same jobs and have the same abilities as thin people despite pervasive stereotypes to the contrary.

The medical imperative to intervene in the lives of "disabled" people in order to "fix" them is repugnant to many fat people. Fat people have been maltreated over the past fifty years by a medical establishment that seeks to eliminate "the obese" and proudly declares a very public "war on fat." Some activists, responding to the biological and genetic root causes of fat, liken such medical efforts to genocide.★ While many parts of the disability community also share mixed or negative views of medical intervention "in their best interest," like outspoken members of the deaf community, few in the fat community are familiar with disability-rights theory and politics. Fat people may choose to hold firm to their own prejudices instead of reevaluating their bias. Some fat people are adamant that viewing fat people as diseased or curable, rather than as afflicted by societal bias, is devastating to their self-esteem and their movement. Others simply want to distance themselves as much as possible from yet another already marginalized group and therefore flatly reject the term "disabled." Fat dieters, on the other hand, may embrace the medical model in their quest for help, but may shy away from disability law because they blame themselves for the weight.

Similarly, some members of the disability community are hostile about including fat people. They, too, have struggled a long time for acceptance and understanding. They have warded off misconceptions about many disabling conditions. They have worked hard to change public response to disability from disgust and pity to respect. Fat-rights activist Bill Fabrey recalls outreaching to work in conjunction with a prominent disabled group on the common goal of making air travel accessible. He was told that some people in the group were uncomfortable doing a joint project with fat people. Some disability rights advocates feel the last thing the movement needs is to be inclusive of a group which engenders such widespread disrespect, especially at a time when many civil rights movements, including the disability rights movement, are experiencing a signficant conservative backlash. (For example, a trio of decisions released June, 1999, substantially undermine the spirit and power of the ADA.) Mainstream attitudes about fat people and the perception of fat as mutable-at-

---

★Coined in 1944, *Webster's New Collegiate Dictionary* defines genocide as "the deliberate, systematic destruction of a racial, political, or cultural group."

will also exist in the disability community. Membership in a traditionally disadvantaged group does not carry with it immunity to this prejudice.

Inspired to action by the writing of Llewellyn Louderback in 1967 as well as the daily difficulties encountered by his fat wife, the thin Bill Fabrey along with eight co-founders gave birth to the National Association to Advance Fat Acceptance (NAAFA).[2] In the beginning they discussed the issue of disability. Fabrey remembers, "Instinctively we felt there were many things in common with other disenfranchised groups, but we felt there were enough problems unique to fatphobia that we should work separately. At the start people felt threatened by feminism and uncomfortable about disability."[3] Whether out of ignorance or simply differing opinions, there exist members of both factions who feel that equating the experiences of fat people with the experiences of disabled people is inappropriate—that they are too disparate. Some believe viewing weight this way belittles the experiences and difficulties of those traditionally disabled people while damaging their rights by appropriating remedies meant for them alone. Others realize that remedies to oppression should be used by those who are oppressed and there is no benefit to acting territorially about laws. More than any other disenfranchised group, the disability community necessarily includes many extremely diverse sub-groups with widely varying experiences, physical and mental difficulties, levels of oppression, and needs.

Some of those in favor of using the ADA for fat people find it as appropriate to consider fat people "disabled" as it is to label any person with that term—they do not shrink away from the stigma. British writer Charlotte Cooper explains in her book *Fat and Proud: The Politics of Size*, "Identifying [fat people] . . . as 'impaired' and 'disabled' requires sensitivity. One disabled friend argues that impaired is too charged a label . . . since it implies . . . the physical ill-health, disease, and low medical status from which fat people are struggling to distance ourselves. I have no such problems with 'impaired'; I regard it without a value judgment."[4]

Many in the disability rights community have long disputed the medicalized view of disability where the goal can be, in the absence of a "cure," to identify the condition genetically and eliminate the disability by selection before birth. Charlotte Cooper describes an alternative view of disability in relation to fat: "The 'social model' redefines disability as less of a problem of one's physical difference compared to able-bodied people, and more as a phenomenon created by cultural attitudes."[5] Rather than referring to a physical shortcoming or difference, "Disability is redefined, so disabled people are not disabled because they cannot walk; a wheelchair user with a mobility impairment is disabled by buildings which do not have ramps; . . . other people are disabled by attitudes which prevent them from becoming one's friend, one's employee, or one's lover."[6]

Segments of the fat community, the medical establishment, and the legal community differentiate between moderately fat people and super-size individuals (usually those the medical establishment terms "morbidly obese.") In determining whose weight is a disability, some argue that only the super-sized should be included under the category "disabled," noting that they often have different health concerns, different access problems, and suffer greater social stigma.

Yet another contingent of civil rights activists and legal experts support using the ADA and similar legislation regardless of the social and moral implications because it is the most expedient, if not the only, current solution to the widespread discrimination faced by fat people. Legal definitions are often far different than lay definitions. If an employer fires a person she believes is a junkie, but who in fact is not a drug user, the ex-employee would be covered as a person with a disability under the Americans with Disabilities Act. The person would also be covered as disabled if he used to be a junkie and was fired for that reason. Because legal definitions and lay definitions are almost never identical, some say that whether weight is a disability under the law does not carry greater social significance—it only addresses the applicability of certain legal remedies in certain legal situations. Legal activists point out that the law is constantly evolving and that much creativity in the practice of law occurs when social justice issues require artful expansion or application of legal arguments to bring about just results. "Truth," they insist, is not what the fat community should seek in the courtroom now—protection is.

The issue of whether or not lawyers and activists should claim disability status for weight cases as a legal strategy is sometimes irrelevant. The court itself can effectively make that decision by approaching a case as a disability case and applying disability laws and policies. This practice was strongly criticized by a dissenting judge in a 1991 case.

Perry DeMarco was suspended from a position in Pennsylvania with the Department of Parks and Recreation because he exceeded the civil service weight limits and failed to lose the 37 extra pounds. The height-weight table requirement was later dropped and DeMarco was called back to his position. Approximately eight days before the city dropped the requirements, DeMarco filed a complaint with the Pennsylvania Human Relations Commission. A full six years after DeMarco filed his complaint, the commission conducted a public hearing and found that the city had unlawfully discriminated against DeMarco due to his weight, awarding him back pay with interest for the two-month period he was suspended.

DeMarco's case was appealed and the Supreme Court of Pennsylvania reversed the decision saying DeMarco's weight was not a disability. They relied on DeMarco's own testimony to draw this conclusion.

"Question: Just to reiterate, just to make sure I am clear; do you feel your weight interferes in any way with any life activities that you do whether it be breathing or doing sports, driving a car, in any way with any conditions?

"Answer: No ma'am, it does not."[7]

In the dissent, Justice Papadakos wrote: "This is not a 'handicap' case. Perry DeMarco filed a complaint with the Human Relations Commission alleging that the City of Pittsburgh's standard of height to weight was a condition of employment, that it was not job related, and that it 'in effect imposes a disqualifying handicap and/or disability for those persons who did not conform to it.'"[8] DeMarco did not consider himself "obese" and said neither he nor his supervisors ever complained that his weight was a problem for him on the job. Rather than pursuing under disability law theory, it is appropriate for him to challenge the weight mandate as having no reasonable relationship to the job. This is essentially how the dissenting judge characterized DeMarco's case. The dissent concludes: "To analyze this claim on whether DeMarco has a handicap is to change the nature of his complaint. He does not allege that he is handicapped. Rather, he argued that the city's weight standard was a discriminatory practice because it is nonjob related and that its effect is to impose an illegal handicap on him. I agree and would affirm the order of the Commonwealth Court."[9] Unfortunately, this court and others like it have been largely unreceptive to this type of legal argument, leaving no practical alternative but disability theory.

THE AMERICANS WITH DISABILITIES ACT

In light of the significant prejudice faced by Americans who have disabilities, the Americans with Disabilities Act was instituted to "remove barriers that prevent qualified individuals with disabilities from enjoying the same employment opportunities that are available to persons without disabilities."[10] Likened to the Civil Rights Act of 1964, the ADA was designed to ensure that merit rather than bias is the measure for judging people with disabilities. Employment hurdles due to disability must be evaluated and reasonable accommodations must be made when possible. The act does not make special allowances for substandard performance and it does not excuse people with disabilities from performing the essential functions of the job. The goal is to guarantee that prejudice, whether social or structural, does not prevent people with disabilities from competing in the work environment. It combats prejudice, demanding employers look to "the same performance standards and requirements" of disabled applicants and employees as they do of everyone else.

WHO IS PROTECTED?

Title I of the ADA essentially requires employers of twenty-five or more not to discriminate against a qualified individual with a disability because of the disability. This covers individuals with a disability who meet the skill, experience, education, and other job-related requirements of a position held or desired, and who, with or without reasonable accommodation, can perform the essential functions of the job.

DISABILITY

The definition of who is disabled under the act is not the same as the lay understanding of who is "disabled," and is at the center of the debate about weight-based protection under the act. According to the ADA, an individual is disabled if she has:

1. a physical or mental impairment that substantially limits one or more of her major life activities;
2. has a record of such an impairment; or
3. is regarded as having such an impairment.

Anyone who meets any one, or more, of these three prongs of the definition is covered as a disabled person, unless they are specifically excluded elsewhere in the ADA. Groups that are specifically not covered are people currently using drugs illegally (when the action by the employer is based on this illegal use and the person is not engaged in rehabilitation), homosexuals, bisexuals, most transgendered people, and people with certain behavior disorders like pyromania and sexual behavior disorders like pedophilia.

IMPAIRMENT

Critical to the definition of "disabled" is the meaning of "physical or mental impairment." What, if any, weight is defined as an "impairment" is determined largely by the particular court(s) in the jurisdiction hearing the case. Currently, "moderate overweight" is not usually considered an impairment while "extreme obesity" (sometimes called "morbid obesity") is generally considered an impairment.[11] "Extreme overweight" is defined as 100 percent above the normal weight, or sometimes 100 pounds over normal weight.[12] Courts make determinations about when fat becomes an impairment based on many factors including: the language of the ADA, ADA and disability interpretive guidelines, their own beliefs, popular culture, other court determinations, academic opinions, and medical views. The ADA itself and the EEOC guidelines are fairly clear about what constitutes physical and mental impairments. A physical impairment is "[a]ny physiological disorder, or condition, cosmetic disfigurement, or anatomical loss affecting one or more of the following body systems: neurological, musculoskeletal, special sense organs, respiratory (including speech organs), cardiovascular, reproductive, digestive, genito-urinary, hemic and lymphatic, skin, and endocrine." A mental impairment is any "mental or psychological disorder, such as . . . emotional or mental illness. . . ." The guidelines differentiate between "disorders" that are covered, and "characteristics" that are not. Simple physical traits that are not considered disorders include "eye or hair color, lefthandedness, or height or weight within a normal range." Physical conditions, like pregnancy, which are not the result of a physiological disorder are not covered.

SUBSTANTIALLY LIMITING

Once a person has been determined to have a covered physical or mental disorder, attention shifts to the next part of the definition. Having an impairment alone does not qualify a person as disabled automatically. That impairment, to be covered, must "substantially limit one or more major life activities," which the average person can engage in easily. These activities include walking, standing, breathing, caring for oneself, or working. The impairment's nature and severity, expected duration, and long-term impact are important to consider in determining if it substantially limits a major activity. Some impairments, like deafness, were considered "by their nature substantially limiting" regardless of what the person with the condition felt or how the condition affected them.

The Supreme Court recently narrowed the reach of the ADA. The 1999 ruling dictates that the determination of whether a person is "substantially limited" should be made "with reference to measures that mitigate the individual's impairment."[13] These measures or devices include eyeglasses, hearing aids, blood pressure medication, and seizure medication. The decision is harshly criticized by disability-rights activists because it may lead to the bizarre situation that a person is disabled enough to be refused a job, but not disabled enough to seek protection under the ADA.[14] The decision will disproportionally erode the rights of many fat people who may face dismissal for high blood pressure, but who successfully control their pressure with drugs. Nevertheless, the decision may not have a direct negative impact on fat-as-disability cases. In fact, it could even help.

In writing about the Supreme Court's recent trio of ADA decisions, many reporters characterized the ruling as "refusing disability status for remediable conditions." Thankfully, this is not an accurate interpretation. Fat is frequently thought to be a mutable, remediable condition despite medical evidence to the contrary, so such a ruling would have almost eliminated disability-law use for fat people.

Instead, the Court writes in *Sutton*, "It is apparent that if a person is taking measures to correct for, or mitigate, a physical or mental impairment, the effects of those measures—both positive and negative—must be taken into account when judging whether that person is 'substantially limited' in a major life activity and thus 'disabled' under the Act."[15] There are two potential benefits for fat people. First, dieters of many sizes who experience side-effects (like diarrhea, memory loss, concentration problems, weakness, or dizziness) from trying to lose weight may suddenly have an argument for coverage under disability law. Second, the court does not *require* the use of mitigating devices, it merely says that *if* mitigating devices are used, their impact must be assessed. When fat people go to court they sometimes face questioning about their efforts to lose weight. Here the court specifically states, "The use *or nonuse* [emphasis added] of a corrective device does not determine whether an individual is disabled; that determination depends on whether the limitations an individual with an impairment *actually* faces are in fact substantially limiting."[16]

Oedipus would be covered under the ADA despite the fact that his condition was the direct result of his own decision and action to blind himself. This is because the events that bring about an impairment are not relevant to the statutory definition of what conditions are covered and when. Whether an impairment stems from risky acts is irrelevant to determining whether it substantially limits a major life activity. As an ADA Information Line Specialist points out, "You cannot be discriminated against on the basis of your disability regardless of how it happened."[17] Similarly, people who engage in dangerous behaviors for their own pleasure or any other reason, like skydivers, daredevils, or storm chasers, are covered under the ADA even if they become disabled due to those choices.

Impairments that are temporary and nonchronic usually are not disabilities. They often do not substantially limit major life activities because of their short duration. A temporary impairment of abnormally long duration or unknown duration probably would qualify for protection. If there were complications surrounding rehabilitation for a broken leg, for example, so that the impairment substantially limited a major life activity, it likely would be covered. Though rare, impairments that are temporary or mutable can be covered. The ADA does not require Herculean efforts be made to overcome an impairment before it is covered. A person using a wheelchair cannot presently be denied the protections of the ADA just because, after years of rehabilitation, they will not, or may not, use the wheelchair in the future.

SOCIETAL ATTITUDES AND PERCEPTIONS

Many fat people do not feel that they are substantially limited because of their weight, but rather because of society's feelings about their weight. This is a common feeling in the disability community. The U.S. Supreme Court and Congress, anticipating the effects of prejudice like this against differently able people, declared, "Society's myths and fears about disability and disease are as handicapping as are the physical limitations that flow from actual impairments."[18] The "regarded as" prong of the ADA exists to counter the discrimination that results from society's biased perceptions of a limitation.

ADA protections under this section apply in either of two situations: First, when there is a mistaken belief that a person has an impairment that substantially limits a major life activity; secondly, when there is an impairment coupled with the mistaken belief that the impairment substantially limits major life activities.[19]

Employers sometimes make negative employment decisions relying on their own bias and stereotypes about the perceived or actual disability. They may be apprehensive about productivity, safety, insurance, liability, attendance, customer and co-worker acceptance, costs of accommodation, accessibility, or worker's compensation costs.[20] According to the EEOC, under the ADA, it is impermissible to make negative decisions based on unfounded fears.

CASE STUDY ON FAT PREJUDICE AND DISABILITY LAW

Cook v. Rhode Island

Cook v. Rhode Island is the single best high-level recent civil case on the topic of weight-based employment discrimination. Although it is only controlling for those courts in its jurisdiction (the first federal circuit), with clear judicial interpretations, few facts in dispute, and a reasonable outcome, it provides a framework to understand the complexities of weight-based disability strategy.[21] The defendant (the Rhode Island Department of Mental Health, Retardation and Hospitals) appealed the United States District Court for the District of Rhode Island's judgment allowing the jury's verdict in favor of Bonnie Cook to stand. The United States Court of Appeals affirmed the lower court's decision, also choosing to stand by the jury's verdict.

Facts[22]

Bonnie Cook worked at the Ladd Center as an institutional attendant for the mentally retarded (IA-MR) from 1978 to 1980 and from 1981 to 1986. Her work record was spotless and even her employer, the defendant, conceded that her past performance met legitimate expectations. At the relevant time, the Ladd Center was operated by the Department of Mental Health, Retardation, and Hospitals (MHRH), which was a subdivision of the Rhode Island state government.

In 1988 Cook reapplied for the IA-MR position she had held before. During the routine prehire physical a department nurse determined that Cook, who was five feet, two inches and weighed approximately 320 pounds, was "morbidly obese" but did not find any limitations that would affect her ability to do the job. Because there were no problems that would interfere with her work duties, Cook passed the physical exam despite her weight.

Although she had passed the physical, the department refused to hire Cook for the vacant IA-MR position, claiming that Cook's weight would compromise her ability to evacuate patients in an emergency, and also that her obesity put her at a greater risk of developing ailments that might promote absenteeism and increase the likelihood of worker's compensation claims. Despite its belief about the jeopardy that would result from hiring Cook, the department offered to hire Cook if she reduced her weight to 300 pounds or less.[23]

The Process

Cook sued under §504 of the Rehabilitation Act in federal district court.[24] The Department of Mental Health, Retardation and Hospitals made a motion to dismiss the case on the grounds that obesity cannot constitute a handicap under the Rehabilitation Act. They lost the motion and the case proceeded. After hearing the law, evidence, and arguments, the jury found that Cook was qualified to hold the position. They also determined that the defendant did not reasonably believe she lacked the necessary qualifications. Cook was awarded $100,000 in compensatory damages by the jury.

The Law

The Rehabilitation Act, Section 504 (in relevant part) provides: "[n]o otherwise qualified individual . . . shall, solely by reason of her or his disability, . . . be subjected to discrimination under any program or activity receiving federal financial assistance."

In a failure-to-hire case, those bringing the complaints (plaintiff) like Bonnie Cook must prove all four of the following separate elements:

1. Plaintiff applied for a position in a covered activity/program,[25]
2. At the time, plaintiff suffered from a cognizable disability,
3. Was, nevertheless, qualified for the position, and
4. Was not hired solely due to her disability.[26]

As under the ADA, a disabled person under §504 is defined as someone who actually has, *or is regarded as having*, a physical or mental impairment which substantially limits one or more of their major life activities.[27]

Discussion

"Perceived-As" Claims

Cook pursued her claim as a "perceived disability" claim. She said that she was in fact a fully capable person but was regarded as being physically impaired by her potential employers. The "perceived as" prong of the definition can be very confusing for courts. Luckily for Cook, the judge in her case understood the plain language of the rule and clearly spelled out the fact that, "The perceived disability model can be satisfied whether or not a person actually has a physical or mental impairment."[28] In general, to satisfy the perceived disability requirement plaintiff must show that she either:

1) does have a physical or mental impairment but it does not substantially limit the ability to perform major life activities[29] or
2) does not actually have a physical or mental impairment;[30] and that the defendant treated the impairment (whether or not it actually existed) as substantially limiting one or more major life activities.[31]

In this case the jury did not specify whether it found that Cook had an impairment or was simply regarded as having one. If, in reviewing the case, the higher court found that either determination could be supported by the evidence, Cook would prevail. Cook acknowledged that she suffered from "morbid obesity" and presented evidence that it was a physiological disorder involving the metabolic and neurological systems which could cause negative effects on the musculoskeletal, respiratory, and cardiovascular systems. MHRH's own stated reasons for its refusal to hire Cook listed her limited mobility and an increased risk of heart disease, treating Cook as though her musculoskeletal and cardiovascular systems were compromised. Because of the evidence about Cook's weight and because her potential employer cited beliefs about Cook's lack of ability and risk of future illness, the court found that both determinations could be supported by the evidence.

Mutability

In its instructions to the jury the lower court incorrectly said, "[A] condition or disorder is not an impairment unless it . . . constitutes an immutable condition that the person affected is powerless to control."[32] Though the jury found for Cook anyway, when the issue of volition is raised by the court it becomes a huge hurdle for fat people fighting discrimination. Common public opinion, informed by billions of diet industry advertising dollars, tends to hold that a individual's weight is within his control. Insightfully, the higher court goes out of its way to state that the lower court's instruction was problematic because "immutability" is not even mentioned in the statute or regulations, let alone listed as a requirement.[33]

To determine if an impairment constitutes a protected disability, disability law generally requires an investigation to discover if the condition in question "substantially limits" major life activities. "Mutability" in a disability case would only be relevant in determining the substantiality of the limitations resulting from the impairment. The court concludes that only if a condition could be "easily and quickly" reversed should it be excluded on the basis of mutability. Additionally, even if immutability were a prerequisite to finding an impairment covered, in a perceived disability case only the defendant's opinion of the impairment as immutable would be required.[34]

Limiting Life Activities

The department contended that the jury could not have properly decided that they regarded Cook's condition as substantially limiting her major life activities. Their testimony contradicted this, though. They said that Cook was incapable of working as an IA–MR because she was limited in her ability to walk, lift, bend, and kneel—all activities the average person can engage in easily. Furthermore, appellants admitted they regarded many areas of employment closed to Cook, and working is itself a major life activity.

Appellants argued that the jury could not find that Cook's major life activity of working was affected because she was only rejected from one job. The inability to work one particular job does not mean the ability to work in general is substantially limited. The court responded strongly to this, stating that the "regarded as" prong of §504 simply does not require Cook to unsuccessfully seek a myriad of jobs before relief may be granted. The court distinguished Cook's situation from other cases where failure to qualify for a job did not constitute a substantial limitation of the life activity of working: when a particular job requires unique qualifications, the lack of those qualifications does not constitute a substantial limitation on working. In an important reflection the court states:

An applicant need not subject herself to a lengthy series of rejections at the hands of an insensitive employer to establish that an employer views her limitations as substantial. If the rationale proffered . . . adequately evinces that the employer treats a particular condition as a disqualifier for a wide range of employment . . . proof of a far-flung pattern of rejections may not be necessary. . . . Denying an applicant even a single job that requires no unique physical skills, due solely to the perception that the applicant suffers from a physical limitations [sic] that would keep her from qualifying for a broad spectrum of jobs, can constitute treating an applicant as if her condition substantially limited a major life activity, viz., working.

While this statement is powerful, it seems that a more savvy employer could have fairly easily attempted to defend the position that this particular job, or even field, had unique requirements of dexterity, and that Cook was free to work in medicine/nursing as a secretary, in-take person, etc., where such skills and abilities were not needed.[35] Of course, if Cook had attempted to get an office-type position, she might then have found herself unqualified for lacking a "professional appearance."

INCONSISTENCY AT ALL LEVELS

Despite success in *Cook* and similar cases, shallow investigation, confusion about the law, court hostility, and employer manipulation have resulted in unfair, muddled, inconsistent decisions in other fat-as-disability cases. In an unpublished 1994 decision, Plaintiff Donna Riehle lost her case before getting a chance to make it in front of a different United States Court of Appeals. (Her challenge was located in the Sixth Circuit which includes Michigan.)[36] In a case more complicated and subtle than Bonnie Cook's, Riehle claimed that the Department of the Army violated her rights under the Rehabilitation Act of 1973 when she was removed from her job, appealing from the district court's summary judgment in favor of the army. To avoid the summary judgment decision, Riehle needed to show evidence on which a jury could reasonably find for her. The court reviewed the allegations according to the standards set forth in 5 U.S.C. §7703.[37]

Riehle claimed that her supervisors harassed her and retaliated against her because of her handicap. She held that the harassment was designed to make it impossible for her to satisfy the requirements of the job, which she claimed were artificially high.

The court reported that Riehle did not present evidence to support her claim that she was handicapped within the meaning of the statute. Riehle asserted that she was a "handicapped person" because she suffered from obesity, diabetes, and carpal tunnel syndrome. The court did not indicate what further evidence she would need to present. Even if the court had been willing to accept her identity as handicapped, her claim would still have failed, according to the court, because she did not present evidence that she was otherwise qualified, or that her firing was based solely on her handicap.

Riehle faces a bit of a Catch-22. She asserted that her inability to do the job was not related to her impairments, but rather to the fact that the job was made particularly difficult. She argued that no normal person could do the job.

This is an interesting case because, if we take Riehle at her word, she was harassed because of her impairment. If the job difficulty was inflated, then she was not fired because she was perceived as being disabled. She would be, in fact, perceived as perfectly able. Too able. Her firing would be the result of discrimination carefully masked to appear to be her own ineptitude. Unlike most of the successful cases, Riehle did not have a stellar work record. Her record showed that, among other things, several meetings were conducted to discuss the revised job standards she would be responsible for, she was sent a letter outlining her deficiencies, and she was given ninety days to demonstrate acceptable performance. The court depended on this record despite the fact that it did not address the real issue: Did the employer unrealistically raise the job standards to be able to eject Riehle because it did not like having a fat person around? As final proof of her inability to perform satisfactorily, the court pointed out that, after all the trouble in her office, she was moved for a thirty-day trial in another office. The court relied on the fact that this move also did not work out in making its determination. This fact is not nearly as compelling as the court believes. There is no discussion about the circumstances of the move or the attitude of the new people toward Riehle. Furthermore, if she was being discriminated against because of her health conditions, the court refuses to recognize the toll the experience can take, expecting her to have unlimited energy. Trying to prove oneself repeatedly for an audience that is never receptive is an unfair burden to heap on anyone, let alone those who may be unjustly discriminated against.

What would acceptable proof of incompetence include? There are many possibilities. In the interest of fairness, the court should have found a way to compare performance. Did the job duties remain the same after she was fired and were they then being adequately performed? If so, was the environment equally friendly or hostile? Were there objective tests that would be relevant, like software-mastery rankings or timed typing, that could show her skill or lack thereof? Instead of pursuing her claims in a neutral manner, the court showed no understanding of the possible effects of prejudice and little sympathy for workplace harassment.

Even with the nearby success of Cook, Riehle's inability to adequately use disability law to fight weight discrimination is not unusual. In another 1994 decision the court reached a similar conclusion. When a female police trooper in Virginia was taken off active duty and put in a dispatcher position because of her weight the court responded, "The case law and the regulations both point unrelentingly to the conclusion that a claim based on obesity is not likely to succeed under the ADA."[38]

WHEN IS FAT A DISABILITY? (AND THE VERY CONTROVERSIAL ASSERTION THAT IT OFTEN IS)

Discrimination on the basis of weight is never trivial. Protecting all otherwise qualified people from fat discrimination is consistent with the stated goals of fairness that give rise to disability rights laws including the Americans with Disabilities Act. Despite judicial refusal to acknowledge it, even slight "overweight," when it forms the basis for disparate treatment in employment or education, meets the expressed statutory definition of "disability." The specific exclusion of "weight within a normal range" from the definition of "impairment" for the purposes of statutory protection is, in and of itself, an example of fat prejudice.

EXTREME WEIGHT

The public school Christina Corrigan was scheduled to attend has a breathtaking view of the bay. In the foggy distance, the skyline of San Francisco is visible rising against the water. But Christina never saw it. She could not make it to the school.

The view is marvelous at the California school because the property is located up a long hill, and the institution itself is constructed on the hillside. For most students, this is not a problem. For Christina, the physical structures of the school, with its endless stairs (some without handrails), steep hillsides, and distant bus stop, were not manageable. Aware that her daughter could not physically handle the environment, Marlene Corrigan called to alert the school that Christina could not navigate the campus and that she would need some assistance. As Marlene remembers, the school said there was nothing they would do because they did not consider fat a disability.

Though not automatically covered by disability law, extreme fat is generally considered an impairment under the law. The Department of Justice explains, "It is generally accepted that morbid obesity, which is defined as body weight 100 percent over normal weight, is an impairment."[39]

In New York the Court of Appeals held that "obesity" itself does meet its statutory definition of disability even if it is mutable. When Xerox said new employee Catherine McDermott was unsuitable for employment due to her weight, the court responded, "There was substantial evidence to support the Commissioner's determination that complainant suffered a disability, and *that the Commissioner's conclusion that obesity itself can constitute an impairment was a reasonable, commonsense interpretation of the statute*" (emphasis added).[40] While many courts try to interpret disability statutes narrowly to exclude fat from coverage, the New York high court, acting before the ADA and accompanying guidelines were released, recognized the fallacy of this practice and rejected the argument. The court railed against the unfounded assertion that fat should be automatically excluded saying, "The court observed that no reason was offered as to why the statute should be construed in such a way as to afford no protection to a person like complainant who suffers from obesity 'but has no other demonstrable impairment.' "[41] So why is the issue of coverage under the ADA so confusing and contentious today?

Modern, mainstream medical science clearly regards the whole range of obesity as a dangerous condition. While credible scientists dispute the statistic attributing 280,000 deaths per year to obesity, this figure has been touted repeatedly by many health and obesity experts including former Surgeon General C. Everett Koop.[42] In direct opposition to the political opinion of most fat-rights activists, obesity expert Dr. Albert Stunkard and others in the field insist that the condition of obesity actually constitutes a "chronic disease" that should be universally recognized and regarded as a "disorder," calling for ongoing treatment.[43] Stunkard and others believe that fat is the result of a complex and only partially understood interaction between genetics, hormones, fat-cell storage and proliferation, metabolism, appetite regulation in the brain and digestive tract, environment, sociocultural factors, behavior, and the rate or energy used in assimilating food and in physical activity.[44] They believe many fat people suffer from metabolic, genetic, and endocrine abnormalities, with the genetic element accounting for 33 to 80 percent of weight variance.[45] Some researchers now believe they have identified a virus that may be related to obesity.[46] Even relatively ordinary events like a chronically stressful environment may affect metabolism in some people and therefore weight gain and weight maintenance.[47]

Authoritative texts recognize obesity as a disorder and it is a settled conclusion that, "Obesity is not simply the result of gluttony and a lack of willpower."[48] Nevertheless, the perception of fat as a dangerous lifestyle choice made out of laziness, nonconformity, or moral and physical shortcomings continues, aided greatly by color of governmental authority. Even in the face of the unparalleled failure of the medical establishment to find a "cure" for the fat "condition," obesity researchers continue to assert that obesity is worrisome enough to warrant continued intervention. The fact that even the best efforts at medically supervised obesity treatment programs have a failure rate as high as 95 to 98 percent has not dissuaded researchers and the medical establishment in general from treating fat as a disorder rather than as a simple "characteristic" or "trait."[49]

While disability law is based in general on a case by case individualized approach, certain conditions are considered inherently disabling like deafness and blindness. When people with these automatically covered disabilities need an accommodation, they do not have to first prove that they have a "disorder or condition which substantially limits a major life activity" because the courts consider it obvious that major life activities are substantially limited. There is nothing inherently limiting about blindness, deafness, or wheelchair usage. These conditions are viewed by the court as limiting because they occur in the context of a society that has constructed structural and communication barriers that restrict people with these conditions from participating in daily activities. The ADA is designed to correct this imbalance and certain building codes and regulations have been implemented toward this end. Structures need to be made to code even if no person in a wheelchair ever rolled up the crosscut curb or no blind person ever paused to hear the intersection signal. These access requirements are not based on individual challenges by disabled people, but rather on general changes that must happen so these groups can participate in the mainstream of American society. Without the help of current codes, people in wheelchairs would encounter absolute structural barriers much more often than they currently do.[50]

A certain segment of the fat population currently encounters an endless barrage of insurmountable physical barriers as real as any uncut curb or stairway. People with "severe obesity," in general referred to as "supersize" in the fat community, account for less than 0.5 percent of the obese population.[51] Just as wheelchair users are unable to enter libraries that only have stair access, supersize people are unable to utilize libraries that do not offer sturdy, armless chairs. Wheelchair users do not have to argue separately for ramp access to places of public accommodation like libraries, first proving their own disability. Neither should this small class of fat people. Though the argument may seem radical at first glance, according to medical and legal experts, severely obese people are, as a class, "impaired." As an impaired group, they are substantially limited in a major life activity that the average person has no difficulty with—navigating all places of public accommodation during the course of an ordinary day. Very large fat people face physical obstacles including but not limited to: seating in public and private means of transportation like buses, subways, and airplanes; certain public restrooms; any establishment with limited seating options like classrooms, stadiums, and theaters; public walkways that lack handrails or accessible periodic rest areas; and public places that are unusually narrow like some hallways and checkout aisles in stores. These problems cause many supersize fat people to live as shut-ins, never venturing out of their homes because the physical world outside refuses to accommodate them. Because everyday structures are, to this subgroup of fat people, physical barriers that substantially limit their lives and activities, this specific minority in the fat population should automatically qualify for the protections and accommodations afforded by the ADA, including building specifications and codes designed to meet the needs of this class of disabled people just as they are designed to meet the general needs of wheelchair users and blind people.

MODERATE FAT

Between "extreme obesity" and "normal deviations in weight" exists a gray area. Modern courts tend to rule that this "moderate" fat is not covered as a disability unless it is accompanied by another disabling impairment. This practice appears to be based on two factors. First, faulty official interpretive guidelines and opinions about the ADA, though they do not carry the force of law, in practice excuse the court from doing its own investigation and decision making. And second, judiciary bias often inserts a lay understanding of disability and "normal weight" where a legal and medical one belongs.[52]

Certainly the prevailing medical view is that "simple obesity" (as opposed to "extreme obesity") also meets the criteria of an impairment under the ADA. According to settled mainstream medical thought, obesity is a physiological condition or disorder that involves and affects the musculoskeletal, respiratory, cardiovascular, digestive, skin, or endocrine systems—the definition of impairment under the ADA. Medical and government tables as well as Body Mass Index guidelines clearly demonstrate the range of weight to height that is defined as "normal." Still, though courts and ADA interpreters are governed by medical definitions of "morbid obesity" (100 pounds or 100 percent over "normal" weight), they consistently fail to abide by those definitions with regard to defining a "normal" weight range.

Usually courts give great deference to the mainstream medical establishment. Nevertheless, weight that is clearly regarded as a "disorder" by medical science resists coverage under the ADA. The confusion may stem from a misunderstanding of Equal Employment Opportunity Commission (EEOC) language stating, "An impairment under the ADA is a physiological or mental disorder; simple physical characteristics, therefore, such as eye or hair color, left-handedness, or height or weight within a normal range, are not impairments." The reference to weight in this comment should be struck because it overlooks the significant distinction between medicosocial views about weight compared to the other examples listed that are clearly regarded as traits.[53]

In the past, left-handedness was misunderstood as an impairment. While the distant past saw lefthanded people as inherently evil and unworthy, more recently lefthanded children were beaten on the hand when learning to write. Happily, there exists now in the medical establishment and the general culture a more rational approach to left-handedness that rejects efforts to change the condition and dispels negative stereotypes of left-handed people.

The modern view of left-handedness is in stark contrast to the current views on fat. In fact, current cultural and governmental approaches to weight are drastically different from present sentiment about height, eye, and hair color. In her book *Fat!So?* prominent author and fat-rights activist Marilyn Wann chronicles the medical establishment's history of pharmaceutical intervention in the lives of fat people. From the use of thyroid extract in the 1800s, to the use of amphetamines and toxic Dinitrophenol in the 1930s, to the disastrous Fenfluramine/Phentermine debacle of the 1990s (American Home Products offered a $4-billion settlement over the heart-valve damage allegedly caused by the diet drug combination[54]), the elimination of even slight fat has long been a focus of medical attention and has served as an excuse for jeopardizing the health of fat people.[55] It is precisely this consistent, continuing medicalization of fat that causes the mistrust and hostility many fat activists hold toward the medical establishment and informs their resistance to coverage under the ADA.

In addition to the medical establishment, the government has had significant influence over the quality of life for fat people, perpetuating stereotypes about fat and fostering a climate of fatphobia. Continued weight-loss research funding, inflammatory antifat public-service announcements, height-to-weight guidelines, discriminatory physical fit-ness standards for high-school students, and former Surgeon General C. Everett Koop's "War on Fat" are only a few examples of the myriad ways government has caused and reinforced the treatment of fat people as second class citizens. Private companies have used and exploited state and federal prejudice against fat for their own goals, amplifying the effects of the government's stance. The gym 24 Hour Fitness®, defending themselves from public protest about an insensitive, inflammatory advertising cam-paign, called on the authority of the government to validate their approach, "Obesity, as we know from the Centers of [sic] Disease Control and the President's Council on Physical Fitness and the Surgeon General, . . . is second only to smoking as the number one cause of preventable dis-ease and death in our society, costing 100 million dollars a year."[56]

Even if, in the abstract, fat should properly be likened to eye color and height as nothing more than a simple trait, as many fat activists insist, this view is inconsistent with the way weight has been treated. Though people suffer discrimination based on height, height is regarded as a trait and not a stigmatizing disorder. In contrast, all gradations of fat, even slight to moderate, have been regarded by government agencies and popular cul-ture as mutable, volitional, and dangerous conditions that are synonymous with physical and moral shortcomings. This is so far from current attitudes toward eye color that the comparison is not only simplistic, but disre-spectful. Classes of people have not been singled out for discrimination due to their eye color. Jobs, education, and other opportunities have not been withheld. Children have not been forced from school, tormented to the point of suicide, or removed from their homes. And the medical estab-lishment has not supplemented their unsuccessful-yet-government-approved life-threatening "treatments" to alter natural eye color with the sale of unregulated, dangerous ocular pills and patches. To specifically define weight "within a normal range" for the purposes of protection from discrimination as a "simple trait" is to be, at best, ignorant of and incon-sistent with other governmental approaches to weight regulation. These government guidelines force people who should be considered within the normal weight range to fear for their well-being and risk their mental and physical health in a potentially expensive pursuit of an illusive slender "norm."

Whether moderate "overweight" qualifies as a disability under the law should be determined the same way other impairments qualify as disabilities—on a case by case basis depending on whether they "substantially limit major life activities." For some fat people weight will not qualify, while for others it will. Yet the class of moderately fat people rarely are given the chance to make their cases because they receive blanket dismissal for failing to meet the threshold "impairment" requirement. This sizable class of "overweight" people are thus refused the privileges of being regarded as "normal," largely due to governmental action, while being simultaneously denied the only regulation that offers protection against the resulting stereotypes and discrimination.

PRIDE OR PITY: DIFFERENT APPROACHES TO THE SAME PROBLEM

Shortly before Bonnie Cook won her employment discrimination case in Rhode Island, a different woman of the same weight filed a remarkably similar case three thousand miles away. Toni Cassista applied for work at Community Foods, a highly regarded, politically progressive collective in Santa Cruz, California. New employees worked all the different positions in the store so they could later enjoy an important benefit of the job— eventually becoming part owners of the business.

Toni had worked with many of the employees before. After hearing about a vacancy from a friend, she applied for it. She was not hired for any of the current openings, but was told she was next in line for the position. When she saw an advertisement a month later she called to say she was still interested. Toni remembers, "I was told they 'did not think I could physically do the work due to my weight.'"[57] In a letter Toni informed the collective that they needed to educate themselves about fatphobia. After receiving her letter she was invited to a meeting called to explain why she was denied employment. She describes the gathering as "adding insult to injury." Telling her they thought she would "appreciate the honesty," Toni reports they questioned her ability to do the full workweek, to stand for eight hours a day, and to fit down the aisles. Members discussed their views about weight and job performance. One woman whose weight had changed remembered, "At the end of the day my feet hurt and my lower back usually hurts, because my stomach is, you know, pulling my back."[58] Toni felt strongly that she could do the job if only given a chance. The attitudes she faced were clear. The personnel coordinator, for example, admitted asking a friend, "If she had a 300-pound worker and a 150-pound worker, how would she decide who to pick?"[59] Toni says, "I felt like someone had hit me with a two-by-four. I was in shock. I felt sick to my stomach, and was shaken for months to come."[60] Making the difficult decision to fight people in the small community that she had known, Toni sued. "I refused to be silent no matter what the cost. . . . I could not bear the thought of one more fat person having to experience what I had to endure."

Toni filed with the California Department of Fair Employment and Housing claiming Community Foods perceived her to be disabled because of her size—that they considered her weight to be disabling, though she was not actually disabled. She argued, "I took offense to anyone thinking just because I am fat—I am disabled." She was angered by the stereotype that, because she was fat, she was unable.

In a terribly confused decision, the California Supreme Court determined that obesity without proof of an underlying physiological condition which caused the obesity was not a handicap under the California Fair Employment and Housing Act. Under this problematic analysis, to logically satisfy the "perceived as" requirement, Cassista would have had to show that the store did not perceive her as unable because of her weight, but rather that they perceived her as unable because an underlying condition was causing her weight. For example, they might perceive her to have a metabolic malfunction which made her unable to do the lifting and climbing that they alleged she would not be able to do, or they might perceive her to have a disabling eating disorder that made her fat. Then, the court's reasoning continues, it would not matter if she had the malfunction or not—as long as the store perceived it, and she in fact could do the work, she would be protected.[61]

This case left a complicated legacy for other California state weight-as–disability cases, forcing plaintiffs into the role of victim. Under state law according to Cassista, plaintiffs who are discriminated against because employers find their weight disabling must show an underlying cause for the weight to be sure to meet the preliminary threshold requirement so they have the opportunity to make their case. The cause may be physical or the result of a mental disorder as long as the weight is the result of a distinct disability. Until it is overruled, the decision suggests that weight alone may never qualify as a disability in California under current California state law. [62]

Only ninety miles away from Santa Cruz, another weight-as-disability case had a drastically different strategy and outcome. John Rossi, who had worked at Kragen Auto Parts in Berkeley and San Francisco for ten years, was fired for being too fat at 400 pounds.[63] Rossi took the position that he was disabled because his weight constituted a physiological disorder and that he needed help from his employers to deal with his condition. He sued for lost compensation and emotional distress due to wrongful dismissal. In contrast to activist Cassista's "capable and proud" attitude which reflected her offense at being presumed disabled, Rossi reported he was seeking weight-reduction treatment. Toni Cassista had a "can-do" attitude and ultimately lost her case. John Rossi was more successful using a "victim" approach. He won $1,000,000.

The Myths of Professional Appearance and Permanent Weight Loss

Police chief Bergstrom had serious concerns about how one of his officers was performing.[64] According to court records, Supervisory Officer Johnson, the second in command, had serious problems doing his job. He had significant absenteeism. He was frequently tardy. On more than one occasion he failed to respond to pages when on duty and could not even be located at certain times. This provided the chief with more than enough evidence to support his decision to demote Officer Johnson, but he did not rely only on this evidence.

Officer Johnson was not just a cop. He was a fat cop. Chief Bergstrom argued that, because Johnson was fat, his appearance alone *engendered disrespect for his rank and for the police department as a whole*.[65] And so Officer Johnson found himself at the center of a uniquely complex area of discrimination.

Fat prejudice is socially acceptable. When it results in discrimination based on inaccurate assumptions about ability, challenging it is straightforward, though not necessarily successful. Often, however, the driving force behind the discrimination is the pervasive stereotype of fat people as inferior due to moral and character flaws. Many of these faulty assumptions are tied to professional characteristics prized in the workplace and include intelligence, energy, stamina, competence, tidiness, ability to follow-through, winning attitude, and drive. Employers seek employees whose appearance conveys these traits, frequently making "professional appearance" a job requirement.[66] Key to a "professional look" in much of the work world is slenderness. The thin component may go without saying, or it may be spelled out with specific weight maximums or phrases like "weight in keeping with height." Either way, people who are not thin may find themselves "unqualified" to hold many jobs regardless of their merit and ability. Caught in a circular argument, they are not hired because they lack a professional appearance. They cannot have a professional appearance since they are fat, and thinness is a common element of the definition of "professional appearance."

Chief Bergstrom had been harassing Officer Johnson about his weight for a number of years. In 1987 he specifically instructed Johnson to lose weight because he believed Johnson was not fit to perform his duties and because his physical appearance was inadequate to represent his position and the department. To satisfy Bergstrom, Johnson enrolled in a program that consisted of a liquid diet of 520 calories/day. Johnson, who went from 383 pounds to 341 pounds, stopped doing the program between May 1988 and January 1989. When he reenrolled, his weight was almost at the level it was before he began. He again got down to 348 pounds, at which point he changed programs. He stopped the new program when he weighed 332 pounds. He had lost and gained well over 100 pounds in the effort to keep his job.

Chief Bergstrom set a goal weight of 200 pounds for Johnson. The police department's weight-loss expert testified that there was no reason that Johnson could not lose weight to achieve this goal weight. Additionally, Johnson's expert said there was no medical reason that Johnson could not lose weight. Based on these statements the court concluded, "Therefore, . . . Petitioner's overweight condition is not due to any disability."[67] No proof was offered about whether anyone has ever managed to lose weight and keep it off through those programs, or any program. The experts would have been unable to provide studies showing that successful weight loss was a realistic possibility if the court had asked for proof. In fact, other judges disagree with this argument, asserting the record of weight lost and then regained may actually prove the opposite proposition—that lasting weight loss is not possible. An Iowa judge reasoned that courts are not entitled to, "Presumptions that obesity is remediable or that an individual's failure to lose weight is 'willful.' The notion that all fat people are self-indulgent souls who eat more than anyone appears to be no more than the baseless prejudice of the intolerant svelte." Writing as early as 1981 the court continued, "Modern studies debunk this myth. See S. Wooley, O. Wooley, and Dyrenforth, 'Theoretical, Practical, and Social Issues in Behavioral Treatments of Obesity.' "[68]

The underlying argument made by Johnson's judge about the possibility of weight loss demonstrates an important bias in fat cases. Weight loss is thought of as an easy, viable choice, or sometimes presented as an option similar to rehabilitation therapy. These comparisons are faulty because the court does not follow through with the analogy. If a person had an impairment that was easily remediable through a simple choice or short-term physical therapy, it probably would not qualify as a disability. In contrast, a person with an impairment that was only mutable through years of life-altering rehabilitation regimens would likely be covered as a disabled individual. If the recommended course of treatment to remedy the condition brought with it dangers to health and if the treatment had a failure rate of 90 percent or more, no judge would consider it a viable treatment. It would be substantial proof that the condition was not mutable. The ADA does not require Herculean efforts to be made by the handicapped individual to cure herself before she receives protection. Whether the impairment was caused by an underlying condition would be irrelevant. And even if the person chose not to pursue the lengthy and risky procedure, they would still be covered under disability law.

Modern studies show that weight loss can pose health risks and that permanent significant weight loss is an unrealistic expectation for most people.[69] Judicial expectations of weight loss as a reasonable possibility are not only unsupported by modern evidence, but by early studies as well. Statistics on the ability to permanently maintain weight loss have always been extremely low. Dr. Robert Rose, himself a diet-book author, estimated a 75 percent failure rate in 1928. In 1940 diet doctor Hugo Rony found that, of his best patients, all had regained the weight they lost within three to five years, and many were heavier than when they started. Yale researchers reported an 80 percent long-term failure rate even in the midst of 1944 wartime food rationing. A 1981 report showed a 95 percent failure rate for those attempting to lose forty pounds or more.[70] More recent figures demonstrate diet failure rates of up to 98 percent, with the National Institutes of Health reporting a 90 percent failure.

Even if some fat people are able to lose weight and keep it off permanently, it does not follow that all fat people can. Diets do not work and the medical establishment does not know why definitively, though documented metabolic changes in the dieting body have shed some light on this area. Weight caused by learned behavior may be mutable while weight caused by nonlearned behavior, genetics, or biology may not be. Most experts cite a complex interaction of various forces including genetics, behavior, biology, and culture, among other things, yet science is largely unable to determine when fat is due to a specific factor or in what proportion, let alone to differentiate between possible classes of fat people.

In determining whether Officer Johnson was disabled, the judge relied on testimony that experts could not offer a reason for Johnson's failure to lose weight. This is reminiscent of the misguided rulings by several courts that weight does not count as a disability or an impairment without the existence of an underlying physiological condition. Even accepting the court's problematic 'mutability' definition of disability, in this case, it appears that Johnson did try very hard to lose weight. Reducing caloric intake to 520 calories is indeed a Herculean effort when a moderately active man's body expects between 2,250 and 2,500 clories per day. Losing upwards of forty pounds only to regain it and then starting the process again is grueling. Given the incredibly high failure rates of all weight-loss programs, it would be correct to shift the burden of proof from Johnson to the defense. It should be up to the police department (the defendants) to show that, contrary to the evidence, Johnson was one of the few fat people capable of losing weight and willfully choosing not to do so.

Defendants would have had a more responsible argument if they had simply insisted that, whether or not Johnson was disabled, he was not qualified for the position.[71] Disability law absolutely requires impaired people to be qualified and capable. The ADA only protects an *otherwise qualified* individual with a disability who can perform the essential functions of the job. The requirements for being qualified in law enforcement, military, and fire fighting are stringent and courts always give great deference to these standards. Officer Johnson's inability to meet those standards should have easily been enough to sustain the demotion.[72]

But Chief Bergstrom made a very different argument. Rather than claiming Johnson's weight hindered his ability to perform physically, he asserted that Officer Johnson's weight resulted in an unacceptable appearance. The department insists that a trim appearance is an essential function of the job of police supervisor. In revealing words the court granted legal legitimacy to bias and stereotypes:

> Chief Bergstrom reasonably felt that Petitioner's weight hindered him in the performance of his duties, and that others in the Police Department and the public may view Petitioner's overweight condition as an indication of his lack of concern or interest in his position, and an absence of willpower and a sense of accountability, and that his appearance could reasonably be expected to engender a lack of respect for him in his position as second in command and for the Police Department.[73]

Imagine Officer Johnson was 350 pounds with an exemplary record and unsurpassed physical abilities. This logic allows him to be demoted as unqualified for his position. Among the legitimate goals of the police department are, "Furthering respect for the department with the community, setting a positive role model and enhancing the pride and morale of employees."[74] These are things the court believes a fat person cannot do because fat people do not, by definition, have a professional, acceptable appearance.[75]

"If a person whose obesity is considered a disability under the ADA is discriminated against on the basis of his or her disability, that individual is covered by the ADA. But an obese individual is not protected by the ADA when that person is discriminated against on some other basis, such as his or her appearance. . . . There is no Federal law that protects obese individuals from discrimination on the basis of appearance," writes the Department of Justice in a nonbinding letter.[76] The overwhelming social acceptability of fat prejudice leads to confusion about where disability ends and appearance begins. For fat people, appearance is not usually about clothes or manicured fingernails. Appearance is about fat.

A form of appearance protection necessarily exists in all antidiscrimination law. If it is illegal to discriminate against a Native American woman, then it is illegal to discriminate against her not only because she *is* Native American, but also because she *looks* Native American. If it is illegal to discriminate against a man in a wheelchair, then it is illegal to discriminate against him because his appearance generally includes a wheelchair. Similarly, if it is illegal to discriminate against a fat person whose weight qualifies for protection, then it is illegal to discriminate against him because of the way his weight makes him appear.[77]

Fat people are denied employment, denied promotions, and segregated in the workforce because of many stereotypes about weight. At the core of these stereotypes is a base prejudice that is as limiting as any impairment. But sometimes this prejudice does not limit itself to those traditionally considered "fat." Even thin people, especially women, can be perceived as being too fat. Once regarded this way, they may find themselves suddenly substantially limited in the major life activity of working. Scores of slender flight attendants have found themselves in this situation.

Weight-control procedures for flight attendants are frequently specific and demanding. For example, if a supervisor suspects an attendant's weight is too high, she may have to get on a scale. If her weight is too high she may get a deadline and a required per week weight loss. If she does not achieve an adequate loss as measured at weekly weigh-ins, she may receive a reprimand or be suspended without pay. When a TWA attendant was fired pursuant to TWA's procedure, she sued the airline in 1989 on behalf of herself and similarly situated workers under New York's Human Rights Law. She used the only available strategy, proceeding with a disability theory.[78]

The TWA manual contained provisions for a weight-reduction program to be implemented for a flight attendant when her weight exceeded stated standards. The program kicked in if and only if she was the subject of a supervisor's determination that the weight detracted from her appearance in uniform.[79] At five feet, four inches and 154 pounds, Underwood was 12 pounds over the goal weight set for her.[80]

The court held that, while obesity was a disability under *State Division* of *Human Rights* v. *Xerox Corp.*,[81] simple "overweight" was not protected as a disability. Thus, the flight attendant's claim failed.

Slender people who are impaired because of their weight are not substantially limited in the ability to care for themselves, walk, hear, or see. They are limited in their ability to work. Since a major component of disability determinations are based on whether a person's impairment substantially limits their ability to work, much attention has been paid to this area and guidelines are quite clear.

Disability law does not consider a person substantially limited just because they cannot hold a particular job with a certain employer or cannot do a specialized job in one field. The EEOC provides some examples: "A person who cannot qualify as a commercial airline pilot because of a minor vision impairment, but who could qualify as a co-pilot or a pilot for a courier service, would not be considered substantially limited in working just because he could not perform a particular job. Similarly, a baseball pitcher who develops a bad elbow and can no longer pitch would not be substantially limited in working because he could no longer perform the specialized job of pitching in baseball."[82] A person is considered substantially limited in the major life activity of working when that person is "significantly restricted" from performing "either a class of jobs or a broad range of jobs in various classes" in comparison to an average person with the same skills and training background.

The TWA regulations seem based on the belief that a "competent professional business look" is not achievable when weight is not "in keeping" with bone structure. This is true despite the fact that there was an exception in the manual for people deemed to look professional even though they did not meet the weight standards. Underwood claimed that the determination about her appearance was made based solely on weight, and not on professional appearance. If, for all practical purposes, "overweight" and professional appearance were regarded as mutually exclusive by TWA, this demonstrates that the airline did not consider slightly overweight attendants to be excluded only from a narrow category of jobs. Instead, they perceived mildly overweight people to be unemployable in a broad range of jobs—all the jobs that require a professional appearance.

The stereotypes about what kind of work a fat person cannot or should not do are broad. Fat people do not have a professional appearance

so they should not be in the front office, sales, or any position that inter-
acts with the public visually. They are not fit so they should not be in any
position that requires strength, speed, stamina, or other significant physical
demands. Flight attendants are not the only relatively slender people who
are perceived as fat and then forced to suffer the consequences of society's
prejudice. Military weight and body-fat standards are notoriously strict.
Exceeding them can result in negative reports, written reprimands, bars to
reenlistment, and discharges. The rationale for these standards is their correlation to health, performance of military duties, and appearance.

A National Academy of Sciences committee studied the army's weight
and fat regulation. Like the "professional appearance" required of flight
attendants, the army requires a trim military appearance. What benefit is
there to a slim look for military personnel? The report discovered, "A relationship between trim military appearance and military performance could
not be identified."[83] Furthermore, the scientists discovered there was no
consistent correlation between body-fat content and physical performance.[84] Many people have been discharged from the military for
exceeding these arbitrary weight limits. A former military lawyer's assistant
remembers doing hundreds of weight discharges. He explained that he
was eager to contribute his experiences to this book to ease his conscience.
"I ruined a lot of people's lives. Once put out [of the military] employers
would discriminate. People came back and told me." Here the military's
bias started a chain of discrimination.[85] An active member of the military
corroborates the overwhelming soldiers' fear of becoming fat. According
to him, people who are at all over the weight guidelines are tormented by
the threat of discovery, reprimand, and expulsion.[86] Even more disturbing,
the National Academy of Sciences' committee identified serious problems
in the procedure used to calculate body-fat levels, including racism in the
standards: "Many investigators have recognized that the methods currently
used do not accurately predict body composition in blacks, and their
applicability to other racial and ethnic groups, such as Asians, Hispanics,
and Native Americans is uncertain."[87]

Most mildly overweight people do not consider themselves substantially limited or impaired because of their weight. EEOC guidelines explain, "The legislative history of the ADA indicates that Congress intended
. . . to protect people from a range of discriminatory actions based on

'myths, fears and stereotypes' about disability, which occur even when a person does not have a substantially limiting impairment."[88] When a person is perceived as being fat though he is not, and then suffers discrimination that prevents him from working in a broad range of jobs, like all military jobs or all jobs needing a professional appearance, he should receive protection from disability statutes. It is in keeping with the fundamental tenets of this group of laws that a person who is capable not be denied employment based on faulty perceptions of disability.

SUMMARY

The Americans with Disabilities Act is broad federal legislation which provides much needed legal recourse for people with current or past disabilities as well as those who are perceived as disabled. Such recourse is needed because this highly diverse group is united by the existence of barriers that prevent them from participating up to their capabilities in mainstream society. These barriers range from inaccessible physical architecture to pervasive prejudice which frequently takes the form of employment discrimination.

While the actual discrimination encountered by fat people is undisputed, the strategy of using disability law to fight fat discrimination is the subject of continuing debate. Coverage under the ADA and other disability laws for fat people is inconsistent, with protection varying by federal district, state, city, and county. Even the same case in the same state may have different outcomes depending on which side of a town line the discrimination occurs.

Looking to the ADA as a legislative model, people experiencing fat discrimination should fit one of three basic legal categories: people with extreme "overweight," people with weight outside the "normal" range, or people within the "normal" weight range.

The subgroup of fat people whose weight is extreme should automatically be covered by the ADA where "access" is involved. They have a physiological condition or disorder affecting major, covered, body systems. Statistics show the vast majority of fat people cannot become thin through the use of any known method including drugs and diets. Given the abysmal failure rate of even medically supervised programs, and given the starting weight of a supersize person, the process of reducing is sufficiently lengthy and the outcome sufficiently unpredictable to automatically qualify the person as "impaired." Because of their size, supersize people are as a class substantially limited in the major life activity of accessing places of public accommodation during the course of an average day. Because of these two factors, the small segment of fat people who are "morbidly obese" or supersize should always qualify for coverage under the ADA because they meet the threshold "impairment" requirement as well as the disability definition.

Most courts interpret the ADA as offering no protection to fat people unless their weight reaches the point of "morbid obesity" or is the result of another separately qualifying disability. The majority of fat people, those who are moderately fat, are usually barred from making their case under the ADA because courts make a blanket determination that they do not meet the threshold definition of a "person with an impairment." This practice seems to stem from fat prejudice and faulty, nonbinding ADA interpretive opinions and guidelines. This current policy is inconsistent with mainstream medical opinion and is internally inconsistent with regard to other government policy. While one segment of government (the surgeon general, for example) labels all fat people as having a dangerous, abnormal physiological condition and fosters a pervasive climate of hostility toward them, another branch (the judiciary) says that most of these people (those who are moderately fat) have no recourse against discrimination because they are not "abnormal" enough. The current judicial approach is also highly inconsistent with the government's stated goals of improving public health through weight loss. Because fat people are often protected from discrimination at extreme weights, but lose that coverage if they manage to successfully reduce to a moderate weight, there is an incentive not to lose weight. Moderately fat people still face significant employment discrimination, so losing the potential of recourse under the ADA is a dangerous prospect.

Moderately fat people should rightly be able to use the ADA. Moderate fat can be an "impairment" as defined by the ADA. Moderately fat people may have a disabling impairment or may be perceived as having one. They should be allowed to make their case to determine if their impairment rises to the level protected under the law. This should be decided on a case by case basis just the way the ADA prescribes such rulings be made. Some moderately fat people will be covered and some will not, depending on their situation.

Surprisingly, people whose weight is within a "normal" range are sometimes the victims of fat discrimination because current "ideals" are so much thinner than "normal" weights. Though not actually fat, they may be perceived as being fat in such a way that they qualify for protection under the ADA. Moderately fat people may not actually be disabled due to their weight, but may be protected nonetheless because they are perceived as being disabled by it. Occasionally, thin people find themselves in the same situation and they, too, should be eligible for protection under the ADA when that happens.

"Normal" weight and moderately fat people are rightly protected from discrimination on the basis of weight when it stems from an employer's belief, perception, or articulated thoughts that they are substantially limited in their ability to work. Ironically, they are not generally protected from pure prejudice. So, many times, employers may not be able to refuse employment to an otherwise qualified fat person just because they think the person cannot physically handle the job, but they may refuse to hire the person because they do not want to have a fat person around. This counterintuitive result happens because fat people are not protected from discrimination in general, only discrimination based on their weight, and then only if it meets the criteria of being a disability. Since disability law only speaks to weight-based discrimination in certain circumstances, to achieve the goal of outlawing all discrimination based on fat prejudice, additional legislation is necessary. This type of law is warranted and can be made at the local or national level.

NOTES

1. Excerpts from the *Americans with Disabilities Act*, Findings and Purposes, 42 USC 12101 sec. 2 (a) (2), (3), (4), (5), and (9).

2. The name was changed from the National Association to Aid Fat Americans to the current one.

3. Bill Fabrey, interview, 16 February 1999.

4. Charlotte Cooper, *Fat and Proud: The Politics of Size* (London: Women's Press, 1998), 123.

5. Ibid., 121–22.

6. Ibid., 121. See also generally 117–24.

7. *Civil Service Commission of City of Pittsburgh* v. *Commonwealth of Pennsylvania, Pennsylvania Human Relations Commission*, 591 A.2d 281, 284 (Supreme Court of Pennsylvania, May 1991.)

8. *Civil Service Commission of City of Pittsburgh* v. *Commonwealth of Pennsylvania, Pennsylvania Human Relations Commission*, 591 A.2d 281, 285

9. Ibid.

10. Equal Employment Opportunity Commission, *Technical Assistance Manual to the ADA* (Web version, March 1999).

11. Deval Patrick, Assistant Attorney General, Civil Rights Division, letter to Congressman Souder, U.S. House of Representatives, 14 March 1996 (01–04154; n:\udd\milton\congress\obesity.sou\sc. young—parran).

12. Deval Patrick, Assistant Attorney General, Civil Rights Division, Letter to Congressman Souder, U.S. House of Representatives, 14 March 1996 (01–04154; n:\udd\milton\congress\obesity.sou\sc.young—parran) and letter to Congresswoman Eleanor Holmes Norton, U.S. House of Representatives (01–03650).

13. *Sutton and Hinton* v. *United Airlines, Inc.*, Supreme Court of the United States (No. 97-1943) (June 22, 1999), lines 5–6.

14. For example, a marathon runner with a leg prosthesis could be fired from work because of bias about his missing limb. When he tries to sue, he may find that his hard work to thrive with his disability is used against him—he is not substantially limited in his ability to walk, run, work (in other jobs without bigoted employers), etc., so he does not qualify to sue under the ADA.

15. *Sutton and Hinton* at sec. III.

16. *Sutton and Hinton* at sec. III.

17. ADA Information Line Specialist, phone interview, 19 February 1999 (ADA Information line [800] 514–0301).

18. Equal Employment Opportunity Commission, *Technical Assistance Manual to the ADA.*

19. *Sutton and Hinton.* See sec. IV.

20. Equal Employment Opportunity Commission, *Technical Assistance Manual to the ADA.* (Web version, March 1999.)

21. *Bonnie Cook* v. *Rhode Island, Department of Mental Health, Retardation, and Hospitals*, 10 F.3d 17 (United States Court of Appeals, 1st Cir.1993).

22. *Cook* at 20–21.

23. *Bonnie Cook* v. *State of Rhode Island, Department of Mental Health, Retardation and Hospitals*, 783 F.Supp. 1569, 1576 (United States District Court, D. Rhode Island, February 19, 1992). Note: This is not the final determination on the Cook case.

24. She also sued under Rhode Island Fair Employment Practices Act, Rhode Island General Laws § 28-5-1 to 28-5-40 (1992 Supp.), and under Rhode Island Civil Rights of Individuals with Handicaps Act, Rhode Island General Laws § 42-87-1 to 42-87-4 (1992 Supp.) but for the purposes of this discussion, the federal law and Rhode Island law are identical.

25. MHRH concedes this element.

26. *Cook* at 21.

27. *Cook* at 22, from 29 U.S.C. § 706(8)(B)

28. *Cook* at 22.

29. 45 C.F.R. § 84.3(j)(2)(iv)(A)

30. 45 C.F.R. § 84.3(j)(2)(iv)(C).

31. 45 C.F.R. § 84.3(j)(2)(iv)(A),(C).

32. *Cook* at 23.

33. *Cook* at 24. (The discussion of the mutability issue occurs in footnote 7.)

34. *Cook* at 24. Since the defendant's witness testified that a dieter should not lose more than 20 percent of his/her total body weight in a year, it would have taken Cook two years to get to a "normal" weight. A jury could find that this was evidence of the defendant's view that the "obesity" was immutable. Sometimes fat is viewed as a symptom of an impairment. In these cases, losing weight does not mean the underlying impairment has been eradicated.

35. *Welsh* v. *City of Tulsa*, 977 F.2d 1415, 1419 (10th Cir. 1992). Three factors to consider when determining if the impairment is substantially limiting include (a) the number and type of jobs from which the individual is disqualified, (b) the geographical area to which the individual has reasonable access, and (c) the individual's job expectations and training.

36. *Riehle* v. *Stone, Secretary of the Army*, 41 F.3d 1507, 1994 WL 659156 (6th Cir.[Mich.]). Unpublished.

37. 5 U.S.C. §7703 permits the overturning of the Merit Systems Protection Board's decision only if the action, findings, or conclusions are: (1) arbitrary, capricious, an abuse of discretion, or not in accordance with the law; (2) obtained without procedures required by law, rule, or regulation having been followed; or (3) unsupported by substantial evidence.

38. *Doretha Smaw v. Commonwealth of Virginia Department of State Police*, United States District Court, 862 F.Supp. 1469, 1475 (1994).

39. Merrily A. Friedlander, Acting Chief, Coordination and Review Section, Civil Rights Division, Department of Justice, departmental correspondence in response to letter from Saint Paul, Minnesota (01–03560, 01–03557, 171–39–0): "The ADA authorizes the Department of Justice to provide technical assistance to individuals and entities with rights or obligations under the Act. This letter provides informal guidance to assist you in understanding the requirements of the ADA. It does not, however, constitute a legal interpretation and is not binding on the Department."

40. *State Division of Human Rights, on Complaint of Catherine McDermott v. Xerox Corporation*; 491 N.Y.S.2d 106, 108; 65 N.Y.2D 213, 217 (Court of Appeals of New York, May 1985).

41. *State Division of Human Rights, on Complaint of Catherine McDermott v. Xerox Corporation*; 491 N.Y.S.2d 106, 108; 65 N.Y.2D 213, 217 (Court of Appeals of New York, May 1985).

42. The *New England Journal of Medicine* editorial, January 1998, stated that the 300,000 figure is "derived from weak or incomplete data" which contain methodological flaws.

43. Albert Stunkard, "Current Views on Obesity," *American Journal of Medicine* 100 (February 1996): 230, 231.

44. Ibid., and Frances Berg, *Health Risks of Weight Loss*, 3d ed. (N.Dak.: Healthy Weight Journal, 1995), 9.

45. Stunkard, "Current Views on Obesity," 231.

46. A. Astrup et al., "Is Obesity Contagious?" *International Journal of Obesity* 22 (1998): 375–76, as reported in Frances Berg, ed., *Healthy Weight Journal* 12, no. 4 (July/August 1998): 50. University of Wisconsin Medical School researchers found that a particular adenovirus, which causes upper-respiratory infections in people, could cause obesity when injected in chickens. They found that 15 percent of the 154 fat subjects had antibodies in their blood while none of the 45 thin control group did. They also identified another virus which may be related to fat and found 19 percent of the 52 fat subjects they tested had antibodies for that virus.

47. Louis Aronne, "Obesity," *Medical Clinics of North America, Women's Health Issues, Part I* (January 1998): 161. The author explains that environmental factors can trigger weight gain in those with genetic predispositions to it. Additionally, chronic stress may increase cortisol secretions and affect metabolism.

48. Ibid.

49. F. Kramer et al., "Long-Term Followup of Behavioral Treatment of Obesity," *International Journal of Obesity* 13, no. 2 (1989): 123–26.

50. It is important to note that, despite existing code, many structures are still not accessible.

51. This data is based on the 1992 *Merck Manual of Diagnosis and Treatment*, 16th ed. The recent federal redefinition of cutoff points for "overweight" and "obesity" may alter this statistic.

52. Contagious diseases like HIV infection may not meet the lay definition of impairment, yet they fall solidly within the definition of impairment for statutory purposes under the ADA.

53. Equal Employment Opportunity Commission, *Technical Assistance Manual to the ADA.*

54. David Morrow, "$4 Billion Offered for Fen-Phen Suits," *San Diego Union Tribune,* 19 September 1999, A2.

55. Marilyn Wann, *Fat!So?* (Berkeley: Ten Speed Press, 1998), 71–73.

56. Craig Pepin-Donat, Divisional President of 24 Hour Fitness, interview on the *Leeza Show,* 19 February 1999. The exercise-club chain's billboard, erected in San Francisco, depicted a thin alien with the caption, "When they come, they'll eat the fat ones first."

57. Toni Cassista, private interview, February 1999.

58. *Cassista v. Community Foods,* 5 Cal 4th 1050 (1993) at 1054.

59. *Cassista* at 1054.

60. Toni Cassista, from "Lesbian Resistance," *Sinister Wisdom,* no. 48.

61. Note that the *Cook* decision occurred just after the *Cassista* decision and before the *Rossi* case.

62. *Cassista v. Community Foods,* 5 Cal. 4th 1050 (1993). Even if the Cassista decision in California stands, plaintiffs in that state still have rights under federal law.

63. Marilyn Wann, ed., "Fired for Fat," *Fat!So?* no. 4 (1995): 19.

64. See generally *B.F. Johnson v. City of Tarpon Springs,* 758 F.Supp. 1473 (1991).

65. *Johnson* at 1478.

66. Dress and grooming are part of a professional appearance, but the parameters are changing. In many companies workers maintain their professional appearance even though they "dress down" on certain days, for example. It may be that this trend shifts even more focus on weight. Most people look professional

in a tidy blue suit. On the other hand, a thin person in a clean shirt tucked into blue jeans may present as perfectly professional, while a fat person in the same outfit may not.

67. *Johnson* at 1479.

68. *Stone v. Harris, Secretary of Health, Education, and Welfare*, 657 F.2d 210, 212. (United States Court of Appeals, 8th Cir., 1981). *Journal of Applied Behavior Analysis* 3, no. 5 (1979).

69. Risks associated with weight loss and the failure rate of weight-loss methods are available in many studies. For a good overview see generally: Berg, *Health Risks of Weight Loss*.

70. Hillel Schwartz, *Never Satisfied: A Cultural History of Diets, Fantasies, and Fat* (New York: Free Press, 1986): 228–30.

71. Even this line of reasoning could be somewhat suspect, though. One of the major complaints about Johnson's job performance was that he did not come to the scene of a hostage situation, but called in by phone. He claims that he was unable to be there because he was suffering from severe diarrhea. This could easily have been a side-effect of the diet he was ordered to follow. (Diarrhea is a common side-effect of very-low-calorie diets. See, for example, *Toward Safe Weight Loss*, Michigan Department of Public Health, 1991.)

72. This case is complicated by the fact that the plaintiff also suffers from Pickwickian syndrome, which a medical doctor described as causing sudden sleepiness during the day. Apparently the only cure is weight loss. (*Johnson* at 479). This condition may be the cause of Johnson's naps while on duty. Nevertheless, defendants do not claim that this makes him unable to perform his duties, a potentially compelling argument.

73. *Johnson* at 1479.

74. *Johnson* at 1481.

75. Note the existence of different standards for what constitutes "fat-enough-to-be-unprofessional" for men and women. (A male police chief is unprofessional at 400 pounds, a female flight attendant at less than 150.)

76. Merrily A. Friedlander, Acting Chief, Coordination and Review Section, Civil Rights Division, Department of Justice, 23 December 1994. Correspondence in response to a letter from Saint Paul, Minnesota, April 5, 1993. (01–03560, 01–03557, 171–39–0).

77. People whose appearance is protected in part are not protected from all appearance discrimination. Grooming standards apply to people of all races and abilities. There are fascinating cases exploring the border area between protected

categories and their relation to appearance. For example, it is illegal to discriminate against black people, but is it illegal to discriminate against "black" hairstyles?

78. *Underwood, individually and on behalf of all other persons similarly situated* v. *Trans World Airlines, INC.*, 710 F.Supp. 78 (United States District Court, S.D. New York, 1989).

79. It is important to note that this policy legitimizes the examination of bodies of flight attendants, mostly female, by supervisors, mostly male, and creates an atmosphere where harassment can easily be fostered. *Underwood* at 80.

80. Goal weight is determined by increasing the weight at hire by 12 percent. Plaintiff was hired by TWA twenty-one years earlier. *Underwood* at 81, footnotes 3 and 4.

81. *State Div. of Human Rights* v. *Xerox Corp.* 65 N.Y.2d 213, 491 N.Y.S.2d 106, 109, 480 N.E.2d 695, 698 (1985). In Xerox "disability" includes clinical diagnosis of disease of active gross obesity.

82. Equal Employment Opportunity Commission, *Technical Assistance Manual to the ADA.*

83. Institute of Medicine, National Academy of Sciences, *Body Composition and Physical Performance* (Washington, D.C.: National Academy Press, 1992).

84. June 1993 Army Law 49, Department of the Army Pamphlet 27–50–247, *Weight Control*, The Judge Advocate General's School, Major Peterson (1993).

85. Personal interview, name withheld. Orinda, CA. October, 1999.

86. Personal interview, name withheld. Moraga, CA, October, 1999.

87. *Weight Control*, The Judge Advocate General's School, Major Peterson (1993), quoting Institute of Medicine, National Academy of Sciences, *Body Composition and Physical Performance* (Washington, D.C.: National Academy Press, 1992), 9.

88. Equal Employment Opportunity Commission, *Technical Assistance Manual to the ADA.*

CHAPTER 11

THE BRAND NEW, EAT-ALL-YOU-WANT, SAFE, EFFECTIVE, IMMEDIATE, FOREVER WEIGHT-LOSS PLAN

Truth in Advertising

"I lost 80 pounds fast without dieting!" Medically proven and guaranteed to work for you too. . . . WARNING: Since Panasol so is [sic] effective at removing fat and cellulite . . . people can lose weight too fast. Don't allow yourself to become too thin. [1]

The weight-loss industry generates over $30 billion annually. Because the vast majority of weight is regained, it is the rare purchaser who really gets what they wanted. Usually, the money spent is wasted. Author Marilyn Wann points out that money spent on the diet industry *each* year could instead buy four-year college educations for one-third of the country's high-school graduates, provide each of the country's 2.5 million homeless people with two homes of their own (with money left over), or fund the National Endowment for the Arts for 250 years. [2]

In their quest for dieting dollars, much of the weight-loss industry incorporates sales strategies that are destructive to fat people. The industry creates and reinforces stereotypes of the fat condition as easily mutable through willpower and of fat people as flawed, pathetic, and deficient. Simultaneously, the industry builds a more hostile cultural environment for fat people. For example, advertisements frequently claim that lack of energy is due to being fat and promise that losing any amount of weight will bring about renewed energy and enthusiasm. Painting a picture of fat people as lazy and lacking in energy, the industry harms the self-esteem of fat people while deepening the prejudice against them. Bombarded with the idea that fat people are energy-deficient, employers are less likely to choose fat workers, schools are less likely to select fat students, and on and on. The worse the environment toward fat, the greater the fear of becoming fat. Fear of getting fat or getting fatter expands the industry's potential customer base to include thin people, especially thin women.

The desperation to shed pounds in combination with the fact that there is no effective weight-loss program to turn to invites unscrupulous advertising and dieting schemes. People of all sizes believe the government has enough control over advertising to prevent blatantly dishonest practices. This is untrue. Unethical companies bilk millions of customers of their money, their hopes, their efforts, and sometimes their health through fraudulent and misleading advertisements.

Because diet programs and centers do not tend to provide lasting weight loss for their clients, they must rely primarily on advertisements rather than reputation and word of mouth, to generate business. Ethically and legally businesses are forbidden from engaging in false or deceptive advertising practices. This mandate means companies must refrain from claiming that a product for sale can accomplish a task unless it actually can.

The growth of the diet industry with its internal competitiveness has resulted in several decades of absurd cure-all claims reminiscent of the snake-oil sales of the last century. Eager companies and their endorsers have inundated popular culture, especially women's culture, with promises that weight loss will solve loneliness, depression, poverty, and disease. Often these claims go unchallenged by the courts and our legal system. Even when they are challenged individually, companies frequently "reinvent" themselves using a different name, or new companies enter to fill the void left by those whose claims have been questioned. Often these new companies simply offer more deceptive and fraudulent claims.

The Federal Trade Commission (FTC) oversees the area of fraudulent advertising, both at the national and local level. The FTC prides itself on "play[ing] a key role in protecting the consumer"[3] and has significant, but not unlimited, power to regulate and create remedies when companies engage in false advertising. While the First Amendment does not protect false or deceptive commercial speech from government regulation, it does limit the government's control to no more than that which is necessary to protect the public. For example, the Federal Trade Commission may not be able to ban particular phrases from a misleading advertising campaign, but may be able to insist that the phrases are used in a way which does not mislead the audience. Sometimes the court will interpret the First Amendment as limiting the FTC's remedial powers quite substantially when it comes to clarifying misleading advertising that has already run. Usually the FTC either cannot or chooses not to order a company to publicly correct misinformation from a previous advertising campaign. This practice of failing to insist on corrective advertising allows contemporary diet companies to continue to benefit from old claims they made that are completely unfounded and patently untrue, like "you will lose weight on this program," even though they are no longer legally allowed to make such claims. Without corrective advertising, weight-loss companies rarely suffer the injury to their reputation that they deserve. Furthermore, because they are often only admonished to be careful in the future, there is little incentive for new weight-loss companies to be honest about their product.

The FTC's Division of Advertising Practices may choose to direct its attention to a suspect weight-loss company upon receipt of numerous consumer complaints, competitor complaints, or when their own internal advertisement-monitoring division notes a potentially deceptive campaign. The FTC can be less than enthusiastic about the initial information-gathering stage. Two different advertisements for two separate weight-loss products each of which shows the identical before and after pictures in conjunction with their product are described to an FTC attorney. He admits that it could be deceptive, but shows no interest in securing copies of the ads for review. To effectively combat the myriad scam diet companies, an attitude is needed that more accurately matches the aggressiveness with which the diet companies proceed.

Recently the FTC demonstrated more enthusiasm for pursuing faulty diet-industry claims. In the wake of the 1990 House Subcommittee on Small Business's hearings about weight loss programs, the FTC began investigating advertising practices of major commercial weight-loss programs. The FTC has filed approximately 150 cases challenging weight-loss advertising claims since 1927. Of those cases, 75 were filed since 1990. Choosing overwhelmingly to pursue the conflicts administratively, not even a dozen of them were actually filed in federal district court as cases. Addressing "unsubstantiated weight loss and weight-loss maintenance claims, atypical consumer testimonials, and misleading staff credentials and endorsements," the investigation did produce more than twenty consent orders.[4]

The policies of the FTC dictate a fairly isolated approach to regulation. Once the FTC commences an action regarding a company, the commission will not issue any comment. It will not even confirm or deny whether an action has been initiated. This means that activists and consumer rights groups that organize to fight deceptive practices through utilization of the FTC are kept completely uninformed of whether or not there is any progress at all being made with the complaint they lodged. Furthermore, the Federal Trade Commission refuses to comment on how it decides which instances of deceptive advertising to pursue. This leaves consumer advocates at a total loss about how to proceed when they have found a faulty advertisement. It also makes it almost impossible for consumer groups to effectively critique the commission because they cannot secure information that would let them know if the FTC is inappropriately ignoring a particular company or fraudulent practice while taking action against others.

Many weight-loss companies sell diet pills of some sort. When the claims made about weight loss involve a drug, supplement, or medical device, the Food and Drug Administration may have power and responsibility over the product. The FDA thoroughly regulates prescription drugs and medications. Dietary-supplement regulation is different, however. Officially, dietary supplements are regulated by the FDA, but diet pills do not need any preapproval before being marketed. Under the Dietary Supplement Act it is now the responsibility of the FDA to prove that the supplement does not do what it is supposed to do. Of course, the FDA does not have the resources to do this on the scale needed to protect the modern consumer. There are so many diet pills and patches for sale that the FDA focuses primarily on the ones that do physical harm to the body, not the ones that only cause economic harm to the misled purchaser. As an FDA representative put it, "There are so many hoaxes out there, we just concentrate on the dangerous ones."[5] The priority products the FDA directs effort and attention toward are generally serious ones associated with deaths, like herbal, over-the-counter products including ephedra/ma huang.

With its remaining resources, the FDA seeks to educate the over-whelmingly naive general public about "miracle pills" and "magic vita-mins."[6] To this end, there are a few helpful but not widely distributed booklets available that provide guidelines for recognizing suspect products. One pamphlet produced in cooperation with the FTC warns the con-sumer to beware of diet patches, "fat-blockers," "starch-blockers," "magnet" diet pills, glucomannan, bulk producers and filler, spirulina, electrical muscle stimulators, appetite-suppressing sunglasses, and weight-loss earrings. Another pamphlet called *The Big Quack Attack: Medical Devices* is eerily accurate and appropriate despite the fact that it was written in 1980 and used materials published in 1978. The booklet warns that gov-ernment resources are limited so the consumer should remember "If it sounds too good to be true, it probably is."[7]

Unfortunately, this government campaign is too little, too late. If the FDA and FTC's educational outreach program has not worked yet, there is as much reason to believe it will miraculously start working now as there is to believe that those miracle diet pills will suddenly start taking off thirty pounds in thirty days. Weight loss is big business and consumers need more from their government than a twenty-year-old pamphlet available upon request. Rather than spending money to print a glossy booklet, why not institute a toll-free hotline number where consumers can get information about the weight-loss product they are considering buying before they purchase it? The line could list suspect programs and devices, and make it clear to the consumer that the effectiveness of other products has not been proven. Policies that provide more substantial fines for false claims and dangerous products would help expand the ability of the agency to increase awareness. And again, working in conjunction with other agencies to insist that deceptive companies pub-licly correct their misleading advertising in the same way they advertised falsely would help greatly at no cost to the taxpayer.

Recognizing the need to educate the public on a large scale, the Center for Science in the Public Interest along with other supporters urged the FTC to adopt stricter trade regulations for the weight loss industry. Following a year-long study sponsored by the National Academy of Sciences, the Institute of Medicine's Food and Nutrition Board rec-ommended diet program disclosures to aid the consumer. Publishing their findings in *Weighing the Options*, the report calls for:

- Disclosure of the program's goals and approaches,
- Staff credentials in summary form, with more details available on request,
- A statement of client population and experience over a period of nine months,
- The full disclosure of costs, and
- Publication of preprogram recommendations like physician monitoring.[8]

Requiring companies to set out the risks, average weight loss and maintenance, and other information would help consumers be informed and have reasonable expectations. Citing advances made by its case-by-case investigations and enforcement in truth in advertising, as well as concern that the benefits would not outweigh the costs, the commission declined to adopt the petition.

Diet-scam creators and marketers are aware that, even without these program-warning requirements, some consumers will be savvy about the efficacy of the product the weight-loss company offers. They know that one of the FDA's recommendations is to check the product out with a doctor or organization in the appropriate medical field. Perhaps in response to this concern, many of the advertisements for diet regimens, whether on television or in print, are endorsed by "medical experts." It may be the authority of the endorsing doctor that causes consumers to trust and then purchase the diet product. That medically trained personnel support a weight-loss program inspires consumer confidence both in the effectiveness of the program and in its safety. Diet companies' exploitation of both consumer naiveté and public trust in the medical profession is a common strategy in the industry. Just as a con artist dresses to play a part, some weight-loss companies have been known to clothe their employees in white lab coats. *Caveat emptor!* The buyer should beware, but sometimes the buyers are just confused. Is it reasonable to expect the woman walking into the diet office desperate to lose weight, assured by various strands of propaganda echoing through her head ("trained weight-loss professionals," "scientifically formulated to help you lose weight"), to fully realize that the people parading by her looking like medical staff are not particularly experienced in anything except sales?

Members of the diet industry will frequently manipulate medical professionals and use their status to sell diet products. They do this by building their advertising campaign on the paid endorsement of doctors, nurses, and nutritionists. This part of the marketing strategy is often so central that there may not even be a formal product or company until they secure the medical endorsement. Once an endorsement agreement between a company and a medical professional is made, no matter how disreputable the business, it may be financially risky for even a well-meaning endorser to retract her support, even though she suddenly realizes she does not believe in the product.

To understand the magnitude of the ethical and legal problems involved in many weight-loss businesses and direct marketing methods, consider the 1994 case of *Source Direct, Inc. v. Mantell, M.D.* According to court records, Source Direct typically operates by getting vitamin pills and creating a weight-loss program that centers around their use. Then they find and contract with a doctor willing to endorse the program and give him an advance to create a file of people who benefited from the diet. They form a new corporation to market the system, buying advertising in tabloids and on television. After the round of advertising stops being lucrative (generally about two years) the diet plan is "reborn"! It is renamed, a new corporation is created to market it, and a new physician is hired to endorse it. The shareholders of Source Direct, Inc., also own at least six other enterprises which do "direct marketing of 'miracle' diet products."[9]

How do Source Direct and other similar companies manage to effectively secure voices of medical authority? Who are the doctors willing to sell their reputations for the right price and what standards do the weight-loss marketers use in their selection process? If a physician wants to enter the endorsement market, one approach is to contact an appropriate talent agency. And that is exactly what Dr. Donald Mantell did. In 1988 Morton Walker, medical talent agent and sole proprietor of the Connecticut-based Freelance Communications Talent Agency, and Dr. Mantell signed an agency agreement together.

There may be serious questions regarding the professionalism of the endorser that, barring legal action or journalistic disclosure, rarely come to light. Sometimes the misrepresentation is mild, sometimes it is outrageous. In a 1975 advertisement for a weight-loss program, lawyer Mike

Freeman appeared using the false name Robert Ridgefield. When his father was running for the office of treasurer a newspaper printed a letter to the editor saying, "Mike Freeman himself once appeared in such an ad for a diet, in which his picture was identified as the famous Dr. something or other. When I asked him why he, a lawyer, was appearing as a doctor, he said it wasn't unusual to use a 'pen name' in advertising."[10] Freeman unsuccessfully sued for libel and emotional distress. Had the newspaper not run the letter and had Freeman not sued, the important information that some people, anxious to lose weight, were likely tricked into relying on a product endorsed by a person they thought was a medical professional, would have gone completely undocumented. It would have been just another little diet swindle, like so many others, swallowed up by time.

If Source Direct had walked away from Mantell when he broke their endorsement agreement as many suspect companies would, another even more problematic diet industry practice might have been lost to history. Dr. Mantell's questionable medical background would have gone unnoticed had he not been involved in the lawsuit over the breach of their endorsement agreement. Mantell claimed to be a doctor of homeopathic medicine and a member of over thirty professional societies. In reality, the court found his degree in homeopathic medicine was awarded after a brief correspondence course from the defunct International University in Los Altos, California and few, if any, of the professional societies he claimed membership in actually existed at all.[11]

Walker brought six diet product projects to Mantell including Cal-Block 3000, whose advertisements contained a number of false representations that Mantell knew about but did not object to; and Finnslim, which Mantell falsely stated he had reviewed. In fact, the endorsement letter for Finnslim was created entirely by Walker with no input and no objection by Mantell. In Mantell's advertisements for Metabozene/3X, false representations were made and a phony Kansas City office was listed. Another endorsement letter allegedly written by Mantell praised LiquidTrim and listed a Kansas business address. Mantell's clinic is actually located in Evans City, Pennsylvania.

When sales for LazyTrim (endorsed at that time by Dr. Kirk) dropped, Source Direct decided to dump Dr. Kirk, selecting a different doctor to advertise the program. They settled on Mantell for the endorsement. For a five-thousand-dollar advance and royalties to come, Source Direct bought Mantell's name, photo, and reputation for use with their product. Mantell gave preliminary approval to the advertisement but requested to see the final copy before it ran. Source Direct started its LazyTrim campaign in the *Los Angeles Times* in April 1991. Mantell testified that the start of the advertising campaign brought with it several threatening phone calls to his office by people who had seen the advertisement and were unhappy with it. He also said that his father was disturbed by his association with the product. As a result, he withdrew his endorsement, and the advertising was pulled. Source Direct sued Mantell and was awarded $41,823. Mantell won on appeal and did not have to pay, but the potential judgment against endorsers can prevent physicians from pulling out of these questionable arrangments. Mantell was successful because, when he canceled his endorsement, Source Direct immediately contacted Walker again and hired yet another physician, Dr. Robert Rogers, to endorse the product. They had very little, if any, loss of revenue because they simply substituted Dr. Rogers' name and picture in the advertisements. At the time of trial in 1994, Source Direct was still doing business marketing LazyTrim with Rogers' endorsement. During that time sales of LazyTrim had exceeded $3 million.

Losing weight is difficult. Keeping weight off is almost impossible. Most fat people know this. Diet companies know this, too. They know what a difficult program they are marketing. They also know marketing is critical to their financial success. Diet companies are completely invested in creating and maintaining a social order that only accepts and rewards thin people. To this end, they create advertisements designed to play on the fears and emotions of fat people. While all advertising seeks to use emotions to some extent, diet company advertising is usually much more sinister. Far from simple bandwagon appeals, the advertisements threaten ostracism, many times basing their appeals on fear. For example, they may play on fears of workplace and interpersonal discrimination. In so doing, they foster the notion that ostracism is appropriate and prejudice is not only acceptable, but deserved because thinness is shown as completely volitional—a simple choice.

In an effort to combat misleading advertising, much of which attempts to manipulate medical and scientific authority, many lawsuits against diet companies have been initiated by individual states' attorneys general. The Missouri attorney general's office has instigated several such suits. San Diego-based Meditrend International, Inc. (also known as Bokkie International) has been challenged for deceptive marketing practices related to its sale of subliminal weight-loss tapes. Meditrend's claims that the diet patches it sells have been tested in hospitals and universities for safety and effectiveness, and that their patches are approved by the FDA were also in dispute. The Missouri attorney general challenged California-based New Source, Ltd.'s Le Patch. Le Patch was promoted as having been clinically tested for weight-loss effectiveness and having received FDA approval. It was accused of being sold through an illegal pyramid scheme. When Twin Star Productions, Inc. from Arizona started marketing Am Euro Sciences International, Inc.'s "Eurotrim Diet Patch" through the *Michael Reagen Show*, the attorney general accused the show of misleading consumers. Missouri claimed that the show was a paid advertisement yet appeared to be a regular talk show.

Both the Missouri and the Texas attorneys general have initiated lawsuits against Nevada-based Allied International Corporation (which does business as Fat Magnet and United States Corporation of Carson City) seeking civil penalties, restitution, and injunctions. Allied made several fantastic claims that earned it legal attention. It said its product was an "amazing new weight loss pill developed and perfected by two prominent doctors at a world famous hospital in Los Angeles," which would cause weight loss without dieting or changing normal eating habits. It promised to back its pills with an unconditional money-back guarantee, but the attorneys general allege that Allied would not honor requests for refunds and sometimes would accept payment for the product and simply never deliver it. Allied was also accused of not seeking needed FDA approval and of trying to deceive the public by making its newspaper advertisements appear to be news text instead of paid product promotions.

Other states have also attempted to combat weight-loss scams and misinformation. The California attorney general has charged Nutrition for Life, Inc., with deceptive and unlawful business practices with respect to allegedly unsubstantiated weight-loss claims. The Vermont attorney general charged California Concepts, Inc. with violations of the Vermont Consumer Fraud

Act for its claims of FDA approval in the marketing of the Derma Trim diet patch. Ohio's Consumer Direct, Inc., was sued by that state's attorney general for making fraudulent claims—specifically that its diet plan was a "surefire way to lose 20, 40, [or] 60 pounds in record time," with some results within hours. Consumer Direct also got in trouble for using numerous testimonials without disclosing that the endorsers were paid.

The attempt to legitimate suspect diet programs by associating them with or claiming for them medical or scientific authority is common, though some lawsuits are challenging the practice. In Iowa, Merlin Pharmaceuticals' claimed that its Absorbitol/2000 Diet Pill Plan would turn consumers' bodies into fat-burning frenzies and the result would be that unwanted fat would melt off was challenged in a lawsuit by the attorney general. Merlin Pharmaceuticals played specifically to the public's belief in scientific authority by stating that Absorbitol/2000 was the "fastest and most effective way to lose weight modern science has ever invented." Iowa challenged National Dietary Research, Inc., of Washington, D.C., and Florida, when it claimed that its diet pill, FS-1, would decrease the absorption of calorie-rich dietary fats. The Iowa attorney general also attacked Florida-based Health Care Products, Inc., which sells Cal-Ban 3000. Iowa says there is no reasonable basis for Cal-Ban's claim that it will bond with food thus preventing absorption of calories. Further, the motivation behind the company's warning included in the promotions ("Cal-Ban is so effective . . . some people tend to overdo it. Do not allow yourself to become too thin. If you start to lose weight too rapidly, reduce your tablet intake or skip a day or two") is called into question by the attorney general. The weight-loss company named Board of Medical Advisors (part of the Amerdream Corporation of Nevada) was hit with a deceptive advertising lawsuit by the Wisconsin attorney general. Board of Medical Advisors promises $1,000 to those who agree to test their diet product and participate in a survey. In fact, to qualify the consumer was required to purchase a two-month supply of the product for $229. The $1,000 the company gives is a savings bond which matures in twenty-seven years.

Despite the number of lawsuits alleging fraud and misleading advertising, the diet companies emerge fairly unscathed, ready to reinvent themselves and make the same claims in a different state or under a different name. In every state, in almost every newspaper, on some TV channel, in many magazines, weight-loss companies make claims that are patently untrue. They are everywhere and they are easy to spot—after all, if they were not visible they would not make money because they could not entice the consumer. The penalties must be more severe and those who are in the position to protect consumers must become more vigilant. Consider Arizona's success in challenging Health and Nutrition Laboratories' claim that its product, Berry Trim, would convert food into energy rather than fat. Health and Nutrition entered an agreement with the Arizona attorney general that required it to cease its claims, refund consumer purchases, and pay a thousand-dollar fine. That constitutes a victory. Or does it? It is true the company is no longer going to be able to make these claims in Arizona. But the company should never have been able to make them at all. The company will have to refund money. But the money it will be refunding is money it should never have been able to collect. What punishment does it receive for its unscrupulous behavior? What penalty looms for companies who are considering similar schemes? Fines of a thousand dollars are absolutely nothing to these companies. And it provides very little to defray the attorney general office's investigation costs. When the full muscle of the state can only threaten a small fine, and the potential profits on the diet scam are several million dollars, marketing a miracle weight loss product seems like a savvy business move. After all, even if one state catches you, there are forty-nine others to try.

With the exception of a possible state consumer protection suit, fly-by-night diet companies are fairly safe from threat. Individuals are unlikely to sue when their injuries are purely financial because of the high expense of initiating a lawsuit compared to the much more minor loss of money they suffered. When diet companies get larger, however, they may get investors and franchisees. For this group, a lawsuit may be financially viable when the parent company acts incorrectly. In 1991 a group of shareholders unsuccessfully sued, arguing that the prospectus which they relied on when deciding to invest in Nutri/System was misleading.

By the middle of 1990, rumors were well underway that some weight-loss regimens were causing gallbladder problems. The Nutri/System diet, created in 1971 by businessman Harold Katz to help his mother lose weight, centers around prepackaged meals made by the company and sold to clients. Short weekly meetings with Nutri/System staff individually and in groups are included. The cost is approximately $75 per pound for a thirty-pound weight loss.[12]

Several people in Florida had started a suit against Nutri/System claiming gallbladder injuries from following the program and Congress called for diet-safety hearings. Only months before, however, Keegan Management, Nutri/System's largest franchisee which operated sixty-four Nutri/System weight-loss centers, decided to sell stock. Selling the stock to their broker, Keegan Management received $8,750,000.

The negative publicity about potential gallbladder problems affected customer enrollment in the diet program and Keegan Management was named as a defendant in the suits alleging problems with the Nutri/System program. Profits sagged. In April, Keegan disclosed the negative effects the bad public opinion was having on the business. In May, Keegan sold thirty-one of its Nutri/System centers. By August stock had dropped $10 per share. Suffering major financial losses, two investors filed class action suits against Keegan Management. They claimed that Keegan Management either knew or was reckless in not knowing that there was information that called into question the safety of the Nutri/System diet program at the time when they invested. They charged that such information about the potential for health problems should have been disclosed in the prospectus, as well as the resulting risk of personal injury litigation against the company.

The plaintiffs claimed that one statement in particular made an affirmative misrepresentation that the weight-loss program was safe. The prospectus read, "The Nutri/System Program combines the three key areas to safe, fast, and effective weight loss: nutrition counseling, exercise and behavior education, and a structured weight maintenance plan. Together, these three elements make up a comprehensive weight-loss program."[13] The judge first interpreted this statement to mean that the plan contained elements found in safe weight-loss programs, not that the plan itself was safe. Somewhat grudgingly he says that it is ambiguous and certainly implies that the diet program is safe. In order to avoid being thrown out of court, the plaintiffs now had to produce evidence showing that the diet plan was not safe.

The plaintiffs brought in a doctor who testified that he believed that any amount of weight loss may lead to gallbladder disease, including weight loss on the Nutri/System program. Because the doctor came to this conclusion in May of 1990 and the stock was offered five months earlier, the judge ruled the opinion irrelevant. The doctor described many studies (authored prior to the stock issuance date) that showed a correlation between weight loss and gallbladder problems, but the judge also dismissed these because the caloric intake was 500/day of liquid. The defendants' doctors stated that Nutri/System posed no health risks at all. The judge was extremely impressed with their point that there had never been a medical study linking solid-food diet programs of 1,000 to 1,200 calories/day with gallbladder problems—he mentioned this fact twice in his discussion.

The judge's behavior shows a profound but common lack of understanding of the way fatphobia plays out in the medical research setting. Of course there is no study linking those factors—who would have funded it? Not the weight-loss companies. Not the obesity clinic directors. The question should not be whether there was a study linking it, but whether a reputable study could be devised that would have noticed such a link if it existed. Then again, this judge was asking the wrong questions consistently. He said that it was absurd to think that the 500-calorie liquid-diet problems could imply a similar problem with the 1,000 solid-food diet. Expressing his logic with an anecdote he says, "Based on such reasoning, a car manufacturer would be required to warn that a car is unsafe at 50 miles per hour based solely on studies which showed it to be unsafe at 100 miles per hour."[14] His analogy, which fits the situation well, betrays his argument. The question he asks is incorrect. The question is not whether the car manufacturer should warn the consumer. The question is whether the car manufacturer is able to make the affirmative statement that the car is safe at 50 miles per hour. If there is no study that proves the car to be safe at 50 miles per hour but there is a study that demonstrates that the car is definitely dangerous at 100 miles per hour, what should be expected of the maker? Can the manufacturer say the car is safe at 50 mph? He should not because he does not have enough information. He is put on notice, however, that the car may well be dangerous. The judge ignored this warning entirely. To do otherwise, to call into question the safety of dieting in general, while appropriate, would be far too radical. He dismissed this allegation entirely, granting summary judgment for the defendants on this issue, nearly ending the case.

The plaintiffs had one more chance. They had also charged that the prospectus omitted entirely the prior existence of serious allegations that put the program at heightened risk of future lawsuits and negative publicity. As evidence they pointed to: declarations by several former clients of the Nutri/Systems owned by Keegan who stated that they suffered from gallbladder problems while on the program; records that listed refunds given for unspecified "medical reasons" at Keegan's centers; other Nutri/System franchisees' records written before the stock issuance where many clients informed the companies of gallbladder problems; a doctor's testimony that there was a lot of information, including various studies, which showed that weight loss put people at risk for developing gallbladder problems; testimony that Keegan himself may have seen an advertisement seeking information about the correlation between Nutri/System's plan and gallbladder problems in a legal newspaper; a three-part television show documenting a potential link between diet programs and gallbladder problems; legal proof of a 1987 lawsuit against Nutri/System alleging a connection between the diet program and gallbladder disease; and finally, the statement of the Nutri/System national medical director, Stuart Shapiro, admitting he began collecting articles related to weight loss and gallbladder problems approximately one year before the issuance of the stock.

For the case to proceed, these omitted facts must be material. In other words, if the disclosure of the facts (or inferences drawn from them) would have deterred or tended to deter the average prudent investor from purchasing the stock, then the plaintiffs could survive the defendants' motion for summary judgment and the case could proceed through the court. If not, then the case would be dismissed.

Basing his decision on the lack of medicoscientific proof that there was a connection between 1,000–1,200 calorie/day solid-food diets and gallbladder disease, the judge simply dismissed almost all of the plaintiffs' evidence. Inexplicably, he said that without such a study the remaining information did not need to be disclosed. He pointed out that, since the lawsuit for gallbladder problems was settled out of court, there was "no indication whether the client's allegations had any basis in fact."[15] The judge stated that the fact that Keegan knew that a lawyer was seeking clients who had gallbladder difficulties would be of no concern for a prudent investor. Such an investor's confidence in the diet program's impermeability to attack could be "reinforced" by the very fact that the attorney was "forced to advertise nationally" the judge reasoned.[16] With a final flourish, the judge negated the three-part television investigation of the connection between gallbladder disease and the diet plan by saying, "It is common knowledge that the content of television programs is based more on ratings than on truth."[17] With that, the judge dismissed one of the few cases with enough money at stake to make it into the justice system.

This case ended disastrously. The judge accused the plaintiffs of pursuing the case on the off chance of finding damaging information in discovery (during discovery parties may get access to all relevant, nonprivileged information that could reasonably lead to evidence to be used in the trial). Many poor decisions were made by the judge along the way. Perhaps other cases, in other states, will have more luck. While it may be too expensive for individuals to sue diet companies, and too difficult for class actions to proceed, franchisees and investors who lose money as the public slowly grows tired of paying for weight-loss programs that do not work may have a good chance of bankrupting the diet industry from the inside. After all, Nutri/System promised to combine "the areas of safe, fast, and effective weight loss." Even if these plaintiffs could not prove that the weight loss was unsafe, they should have been able to prove that it was ineffective. And certainly the prudent investor would shy away from an opportunity to buy stock in a product that made claims it cannot back up.

To effectively combat fraud in the diet industry, it is important to pursue strategies that come at the problem from a new direction, like the Nutri/System investor case. Similarly innovative, the FTC's Operation Waistline, under the guidance of the Bureau of Consumer Protection Director Jodie Bernstein, has embarked on a clever approach to the problem. Recognizing the part publications play in helping deceptive diet advertisements reach their audience, she has issued letters to over one hundred of the publications that ran advertising from groups challenged by the commission. It calls for them to be more responsible about reviewing advertisements to prevent blatantly deceptive copy from reaching the public. If companies are met not only with educated consumers, but demanding business buyers and skeptical advertising departments, they will be forced to clean up their promotion strategies and substantiate their claims.

Unfortunately, even if it does become unprofitable for diet companies to advertise deceptively, it may only increase the emotional volatility in the ads that fill the airways and Sunday newspaper supplements. These advertisements take advantage of and perpetuate the fat person's very real experiences with discrimination. They do not condemn employment discrimination against fat people, they revel in it, proudly producing testimonials from people who got or kept jobs after their weight loss. They do not condemn verbal abuse, they use it for their own purposes as they make fat jokes and belittle fat people. And while companies may have no moral obligation to do good, these practices actually inflame existing prejudices. While it is difficult to scientifically measure the psychological harm done to fat people by this advertising, it is not hard to understand that seeing representations of fat bodies over and over in such a hate-filled context can do permanent damage to self-esteem and spirit. The repetition of the stereotypes also amplifies the prejudice fat people face in the culture. The Svelt-PATCH promises to "speed up the body's metabolism and burn up fat!" pointing to the ability of "fucus" to "absorb fat and to trigger the 'combustion' of fat" for "long-lasting results." With use of the Svelte-PATCH Plan, "You will have greater self-confidence. . . . Your love life will be more interesting. . . . Your entire life will improve. Your spouse, your family, and your friends will find you more attractive."[18] Making weight-loss companies accurately represent their products should be the easy part. Changing society so the rest of the advertisement is inaccurate—that should be the challenge.

NOTES

1. Glossy circular from *Oakland Examiner* coupon section advertising Panasol, Dept. P6, 645 Vermont St., Box 7060, Lawrence, KS 66044-7060, 1995.

2. Marilyn Wann, *Fat!So?* (Berkeley, Calif.: Ten Speed Press, 1998), 92–93.

3. FTC, telephone recording describing the role of the agency. Washington, D.C., October 1996.

4. Report of the Presiding Panel, "Commercial Weight Loss Products and Programs: What Consumers Stand to Gain and Lose," A Public Conference on the Information Consumers Need to Evaluate Weight Loss Products and Programs; October 16–17, 1997, Washington, D.C., FTC. As reported on the FTC Web site,

1999. See 1D (1–2) and "Federal Trade Commission Addresses Deceptive and Misleading Advertising of Weight Loss Products and Programs."

5. Mary Ellen Taylor, FDA, interview, October 1996, Oakland, California.

6. It may be unfair to categorize the public as "naive." Most people are under the impression that these departments of the federal government offer more product testing and product control than they do, so they do not adopt a skeptical approach to product claims. The FDA's booklet *The Big Quack Attack: Medical Devices* printed in 1980 acknowledges, "A recent national poll indicated that more than 50 million adult Americans agreed with this statement: 'Advertisements about medications and health aids must be true or they wouldn't be allowed to print them'" (2).

7. *The Big Quack Attack: Medical Devices* (U.S. Department of Health and Human Services, Public Health Service, FDA, January 1980).

8. Report of the Presiding Panel, "Commercial Weight Loss Products and Programs: What Consumers Stand to Gain and Lose," 1(D)4.

9. *Source Direct, Inc.* v. *Mantell*, Court of Appeals of Kansas, March 18, 1994; 870 P.2d 686, 689. (19 Kan. App. 2d 399).

10. *Freeman* v. *Hanke*, 1989 WL 66279 (Court of Appeals of Ohio, Stark County), May 15, 1989.

11. *Source Direct* at 689.

12. Deralee Scanlon with Larry Straus, *Diets That Work* (Los Angeles: Lowell House, 1992), 34–37. (Price per pound of weight loss calculated from statistics given on page 37.)

13. This claim appears on page 2 of the prospectus filed on Form S-1 with the Securities and Exchange Commission.

14. *Keegan Management Co.* v. *Keegan Management Co.* 794 F. Supp. 939, 943, United States District Court, N.D. CA (May 29, 1992)

15. *Keegan* at 946.

16. *Keegan* at 946.

17. *Keegan* at 946.

18. Advertisement from coupon section in Sunday paper from United Research Center, 1414 Place Bonaventure, Montreal, Quebec, Canada, copyright 1995.

CHAPTER 12

THE MEDICAL PROFESSION

Assumptions Before Science

The position of weight loss in medicine today can be compared to bloodletting 150 years ago. . . . Bloodletting improved the symptoms of sick patients. Of course, we now know that blood loss creates a state of shock that lowers body temperature but ultimately increases the risk of death. Similarly, weight loss produces short-term improvements in symptoms, but may not be ultimately beneficial. Before weight loss can be removed from its exalted status as a therapy, a revolution in medicine may be required, comparable to the one that brought an end to the practice of bloodletting.

—Paul Ernsberger, Ph.D.[1]

THERE ARE THREE FUNDAMENTAL BELIEFS about fat held by the medical establishment all of which have profound implications not only for the health and well-being of fat people, but also for the law. These rarely challenged assumptions are: that weight is mutable, that weight loss is a benign procedure, and that fat is unhealthy. Medicine's failure to examine these basic assumptions critically has resulted in the development of a field riddled by bias. The surprisingly unscientific absence of critical analysis in the science of "obesity" medicine derives from a combination of social prejudice and the pronounced conflict of interest in the area of obesity research. Sometimes the product of greed, sometimes the natural consequence of market forces, this conflict of interest leads to the antifat bias in medicine. The bias in the field of medicine, in turn, contributes to the cycle of negative attitudes toward fat people held by healthcare providers. These attitudes spiral into poor care, mistrust, delay, and avoidance of health treatment, and worsening of health problems.

MUTABILITY

Like racial minorities and women of all ethnicities, fat people suffer discrimination; unlike these groups, fat people have very limited recourse through the legal system. The justification for this treatment is that being fat is viewed as volitional—a choice made out of laziness, hostility, social disdain, or other moral shortcomings like lack of willpower, failure of motivation, greed and dependence.

The law and the public rationalize their apathy toward the prejudice fat people endure on the grounds that fat is a mutable condition. It is a settled tenet of antidiscrimination law that people should not unnecessarily be prevented from participating in and contributing to society because of a characteristic that is not in their control. If weight is an immutable condition, most forms of discrimination against fat people become legally indefensible and invalid.

Zero. This is the most compelling statistic in the debate over whether fat is a volitional state. Despite the tens of billions of dollars per year spent on weight-loss products and procedures, despite the substantial money invested in "obesity" research and the pressure those researchers are under, despite the absolute desperation of countless fat people, there are no programs, no diets, no doctors, no surgeries, no amount of willpower, no drugs, no lifestyle changes, no "treatments" that have been able to produce safe, lasting, significant weight loss for the average fat person.[2]

The American Heart Association classifies obesity as a "modifiable" risk factor for heart disease, yet according to the National Institutes of Health, diets fail 90 percent of the time. Like the dangers of dieting, the failure rates of weight-reduction efforts are startling, but they are not news. In 1992 the National Institutes of Health convened a panel of neutral experts to analyze weight-loss practices, calling for presentations from weight and obesity researchers. According to Laura Fraser, author of *Losing It: False Hopes and Fat Profits in the Diet Industry*, "The list of speakers was a Who's Who of prominent obesity researchers."[3] She points out that many of those chosen to speak "were advocates of very-low-calorie-diets, diet pills, behavior modification, and other short-term weight-loss methods" while similarly renowned antidieting researchers were not invited to speak to the panel. Even though the panel did not hear from those opposed to focusing on weight loss as a goal, the testimony and studies that were presented led the panel to conclude that diets do not work, and actually can cause serious harm. The NIH noted that while almost all have regained lost weight within five years, two-thirds regain the weight within one year.

Other reliable sources have found the NIH's figures too generous. A study published in the *International Journal of Obesity* puts the weight-loss failure rate at 95 percent. Other studies put the rate higher still, at 98 percent. Past studies also confirm the overwhelming lack of success in weight-loss attempts. Occasionally, university-based programs have claimed a higher weight-loss success rate than the studies. One reported 15 percent of participants maintaining weight loss at the three-year mark, an improvement, but still a failure rate of 85 percent.[4] In "Obesity Control" David Sharp recently reported that some Duke University clients had achieved some small but lasting weight loss. They had not gained back 15 to 20 pounds, which constituted only about 5 percent of their body weight, over the course of five years.[5] When private research is funded by the weight-loss industry, negative study results can easily be swallowed up by the companies and never published, killed as soon as their lack of success becomes evident.

In fact, the study numbers were so dismal, with many people gaining what they had lost plus some extra weight, that researchers chose not to study any specific program, knowing most people in it would fail. Instead they developed a Registry and put a call out to find those rare people, the 2 to 10 percent, who had been able to lose a moderately significant amount of weight and keep it off for a reasonable amount of time. The experts decided to focus on them, instead, in the hopes of discovering some common key to their "success."

A 500-pound person could reduce to a weight of 150 pounds, and then steadily gain the weight back. If the person weighed 470 pounds at the one-year mark, he would count as a weight-loss success and qualify for placement in the registry. With a required minimum of a 30-pound loss maintained for at least one year, the 1993 National Weight Control Registry's definition of "success" is modest.[6]

The registry is not a scientifically compelling or careful compilation, but it is of interest because it is the only project of its kind and it has been held out as proof that weight loss is a practical possibility for people. Though reported registry procedures do not include any process for checking on any of the claims made by participants, entry to the registry was supposed to be granted only to those who could provide documentation of the weight loss they claimed (a wise safety mechanism since the diet industry has both an interest in proving weight loss is a practical option and a track record of improper behavior). Documentation requirements were less than rigorous. Participants only needed to provide photographs at the higher and lower weights or the names of an individual who could verify the weight loss. Nevertheless, a full 19 percent of the participants were "unable to provide any source of documentation."[7] These individuals were included in the registry anyway because the researchers felt their answers fit the pattern of answers provided by the other subjects who could provide verification.

Each year there are approximately 70 million Americans on diets. The National Weight Control Registry recruited people through local and national media coverage, mailings sent by several commercial weight-loss companies to clients, and articles in newsletters and magazines. The registry could find fewer than 800 people who met their definition of "success," even including the nearly 20 percent who could provide no documentation for their claims.

Though registry press material sounds upbeat about their findings, actually, the survey reveals little. Registry members were divided about weight-loss methods, with 55 percent using outside assistance like a commercial program or counselor while 45 percent did it on their own. In a press release clearly designed to go directly into popular print, researchers write, "For Immediate Release—Trigger Prompts Obese to Become Highly Successful at Weight Loss."[8] Implying that weight-based unkindness by a spouse can have positive results, they relate a woman's trigger: "My husband left me and my lawyer told me it was because I was too fat."[9] The emphasis on "triggers" can be dangerous because it can be used as a license for abuse, an excuse to perpetuate hostility against fat people. Even before the registry, an antifat article in a woman's magazine advocated being cruel to fat people and encouraged discrimination against them as a method to motivate them to lose weight. That people are motivated by triggers is an unimportant observation and a strange basis for a newspaper report. Most unsuccessful dieters probably also would cite a trigger for their weight-loss efforts, making it unlikely that this characteristic differentiates successful from unsuccessful dieters. The registry has no control group that could prove the relevance of "trigger events."

The news of the registry results brought another wave of antifat sentiment, with newspaper headlines again proclaiming the possibility of general weight-loss success if fat people would just "do it." For legal purposes, however, the registry data suggests that not only are there no identifiable similarities between weight losers that indicate lasting weight loss could be attainable by the average person, but also that the number of people for whom weight is mutable is minuscule. Furthermore, people who easily qualify as "successes" for purposes of the registry or the press can still be in dire need of legal protection from discrimination because maintenance of a 30-pound weight loss for one year is not the equivalent of being thin. A person could be a "successful" weight loser and still suffer workplace discrimination for being too fat. Finally, there seems to be a quality of life trade-off with maintained weight loss. Those who manage to lose weight and keep it off need to devote a great amount of time and energy to that pursuit, sometimes "to the point of seeming obsessive or neurotic."[10] People should be free to pick the path that leads to the best quality of life for them. Discrimination protection should not hinge on this choice.

The regulation of fat and the mechanisms of weight loss are not well understood. Part of the reason weight loss is so illusory may lie in biology more than behavior. Studying twins, researchers have concluded that genetics may account for up to 80 percent of weight, as opposed to willpower or environment. Rockefeller University researchers explained that the body defends against weight loss by adjusting the regulatory systems. They found that a 10 percent weight loss triggered a 15 percent reduction in metabolism. (They also discovered that the body defends against unnatural weight gain the same way, increasing the metabolic rate with a weight gain of 10 percent.) Leptin, a substance that helps regulate the body's "set point" and can be affected by genetic irregularities, or defects in the hypothalamus are examples of other biological factors that also have implications for weight. Laura Fraser writes, "The likelihood is that there are many other types of fat genes—as many as sixty, some researchers guess—and the cure for one type of genetic obesity won't work for the others."[11]

Sharp reports, "Experts at the forefront of obesity treatment have concluded that the traditional definition of weight-loss success—helping a patient slim down to an ideal weight—is simply too unattainable even to attempt."[12] Even zealous weight-loss advocates realize prescribing programs that have not worked does not make sense. This sensible approach has been ignored for decades. As applicable today as it was when written in 1978, researchers implore the medical establishment to "discontinue the routine application of treatments already proven impotent."[13] These weight-loss advocates recognized, "It makes little sense . . . to prescribe low-calorie diets and anorectic drugs . . . and expect that weight loss will occur."[14] A recent New England Journal of Medicine editorial contradicts the popular belief that fat people would lose weight if they just stopped eating so much: "Why is it that people cannot seem to lose weight, despite the social pressures, the urging of their doctors, and the investment of staggering amounts of time, energy, and money? The old view that body weight is a function of only two variables—the intake of calories and the expenditure of energy—has given way to a much more complex formulation involving a fairly stable set point for a person's weight that is resistant . . . to either gain or loss.[15] Fat is caused by complex and varied factors, so identifying the reason or the way for one fat person to lose weight will not necessarily work for other fat people. While the causes and mechanisms of fat are not always clear, there is no question that most fat people who try to lose weight will be unsuccessful. Furthermore, even fat people who maximize the weight they can lose and keep off will probably still be classified as "fat" in American culture and therefore still vulnerable to social oppression and stigma.

That some formerly fat people have managed to defy the odds and keep weight off only addresses their individual situation—perhaps they were fat because they suffered from an eating disorder, for example, which was cured through diet or counseling. The vast majority of fat people will remain fat no matter what effort they apply to losing weight. Though the statistics are well-settled, they appear counterintuitive because people do go on diets and they do lose weight. People are very adept at reducing. Some courts have tried to use as evidence of the mutability of weight the fact that plaintiffs had been able to lose weight in the past.

Losing weight and becoming a thin person may prove to be two very different things. How is this possible? Imagine telling a person to squat or duck down. They can function like that, walking and moving around while hunched over, for quite some time. But most people cannot hold this posture indefinitely. Eventually, the body and mind will exert increasing pressure on them signaling the time to return to a more natural upright position. Inspired not by comfort but by survival, these commands to the dieting (starving) body are overwhelming. And just as physical problems may develop from keeping the body bent over, physical problems can develop from weight reduction.

The law cannot continue to ignore the statistics that diets do not work and that temporary weight reduction is not without danger. At a minimum, in court cases there should be a presumption that a plaintiff in a discrimination suit is part of the up-to-98-percent of dieters who cannot lose weight, not part of the 2 percent who can.

If fat is not mutable then discrimination against fat people mirrors discrimination on the basis of sex or race. Not only would fat people clearly be eligible for protection under disability laws, but, as an oppressed biological minority, they would have a compelling case for strict protections under constitutional law.

For some fat people, weight is mutable. Even though it seems to be a very small class of fat people, critics would argue that all fat people looking toward the courts for help should first be forced to try dieting. This would identify those who can lose weight and thus would not necessarily be eligible to receive workplace protection. Those who can lose weight but choose not to would not deserve to be covered under antidiscrimination law, the argument would hold.

THE CONSEQUENCES OF WEIGHT LOSS

Whether or not it is possible for a fat person to become thin, it is unfair for the courts to compel fat people to try to reduce before receiving legal protection. Despite the silence of mainstream obesity researchers on the topic, significant evidence exists that weight loss is not a benign treatment. Either in the course of losing weight or as a consequence of losing weight, people suffer serious side-effects that do harm to physical and mental health and have implications for future weight gain. It is not simply that diets do not work, but also that diets cause damage. Neither the medical establishment nor the justice system have any right to direct people on a course that may jeopardize their health. Most fat people will accept any risk for a chance to lose weight, but they should make these decisions of their own free will; their civil rights should not be held hostage to their choice.

Christina Corrigan's pediatrician, like hundreds of others, recommended that her mother put her on low-fat milk when she was a baby. Noted University of California endocrinologist Dr. Dianne Budd explains that calorie restriction can have serious, long-lasting repercussions. When children are put on diets their ability to recognize satiety may never develop or recover. Doctors who prescribe diets and give other weight-related advice without actually researching the consequences can cause physical and psychological harm to their patients.

Perhaps the most commonly offered medical advice is to lose weight through diet and exercise. Over fifty years ago a study on human starvation was conducted by Ancel Keys at the University of Minnesota, which involved diet and physical activity. This effort probably could not be duplicated now because of current ethical standards for studies involving human subjects. Nevertheless, the project offers a helpful window for modern medicine. Unlike much of the other data about weight loss, the Keys study, which fills two volumes, used scientifically sound methods and provides important information about the results of weight loss and calorie-restrictive diets.

Of the more than one hundred men who volunteered for Keys's 1944 study, thirty-six were selected to participate.[16] The group was largely composed of men who opposed military service on religious grounds.

Responding to the call "Will You Starve That They Be Better Fed?" Laura Fraser writes, "[The men] were highly motivated to participate in a study that they believed would help their fellow citizens. Like most dieters, they were determined to be good."[17]

The chosen men were young, had higher than average intelligence, were the most psychologically and physically healthy of the one hundred volunteers, and were the most committed to the study's objectives. Though the study was conducted in a reasonable manner, toward its conclusion personality changes were so severe that one previously healthy man, anxious to leave the study, chopped off three of his own fingers. He wrote, "There was only one thing that would pull me out of the doldrums, that is release [from the experiment] . . . I decided to get rid of some fingers."[18]

The study began with a three-month period of detailed observation. As a group the men demonstrated an active sense of humor and responsive nature—participants were in good spirits. They ate normally, got exercise, and performed chores.

Over the next six months the men were put on a semi-starvation diet. Eating about half of their normal amount, the men were fed an average of 1,570 calories each day. David Garner, Ph.D., points out that this coincides with a "conservative" weight-reduction diet. It is a significantly more generous diet than many people engage in when trying to lose weight. The final three months consisted of rehabilitation and refeeding. During the first half of the third period, the men were divided into groups and refed at a rate of 1,877 to 4,158 calories per day depending on the group. The men lost weight during the food restriction phase, but the effects of the experiment were devastating.

Food Obsession. The men became preoccupied with thoughts of food. They talked about food. They collected recipes. They became fascinated with cookbooks, menus, and bulletins about food production, even in the absence of any such interests before the experiment. They made plans about how they would eat their food. Some smuggled food out of the dining hall and brought it back to the room to eat on their bunks. They became emotional about food, becoming possessive of their own food and angry about wasted food. Every crumb was eaten and plates were licked clean. Nail-biting and gum chewing became common, with one participant chewing forty packs a day. Some started collecting kitchen gadgets and utensils. Some of the volunteers even changed their future career plans. Three chose to become professional cooks after the study.

Attitude and Personality Differences. Selected for emotional and physical stamina, members of the group were more endowed in these areas than a randomly selected sample would be. Nevertheless, the participants manifested extensive emotional distress, 20 percent being so severe it interfered with their ability to function.[19] The men experienced depression, mood swings, irritability, anger, anxiety, restlessness, sensitivity to noise, and apathy. They lost sexual desire and neglected normal grooming like shaving and toothbrushing. They became more solitary and egocentric. Some engaged in pack-rat behavior, collecting strange items they did not want; by contrast, others started squirreling money away. The men became distracted and felt their judgment was impaired. Their work suffered and they described feelings of inadequacy in the normal tasks of daily living. Profiles showed an average increase in neurosis and hysteria. Six men reacted with severe character neurosis and two bordered on psychosis. One man whose Minnesota Multiphasic Personality Inventory score was firmly in the normal range initially developed gross personality disturbances after ten weeks on the weight-loss regimen despite the fact that he only lost 10 pounds. Refeeding did not alleviate these disturbances, with some symptoms actually growing worse.

Eating and Food Problems. Hunger was experienced by all the men, but the sensation took different tolls on different people. Several volunteers broke their diets and binged, with one even stealing candy. They then experienced feelings of guilt, disgust at themselves, and self-recrimination. After the extreme calorie-restriction phase of the experiment ended, the men continued to have problems. Irritability and depression became even worse for some while concerns previously expressed for the health of starving people evaporated. One man, who was expelled from the study, kept eating until he became sick and then would repeat the process. Emotional crisis and near refusal resulted when another week of controlled refeeding was proposed. The subjects argued and questioned the researchers. They remained extremely concerned about their rations and continued licking their plates, with some table manners becoming even worse. Some of the men ate constantly. They had serious problems identifying when they were full. After large meals the men still complained of hunger, consuming five to ten thousand calories a day, others eating as much as they could. As they gained weight back, muscle was replaced with fat.

The experiment radically affected the men's emotional stability, social interactions, and futures. The calorie restriction lasted for six months. Afterward, the men gained back what they had lost plus about 10 percent. At the end of the follow-up period their weights were headed down, but still generally in excess of their starting weights.

Keys's study also documented some important physical changes. With particular implications for continued or lasting weight loss, after the calorie-restrictive period, the researchers found that basal metabolism had fallen approximately 40 percent. Frances Berg of the *Healthy Weight Journal* reports that other studies indicate these rates fall even more significantly for women.[20]

The men's heart volume, pulse, and body temperature decreased. They had fluid accumulation (edema) at some joints. Their hair fell out and they commonly felt cold, even during the summer. They became weak and less energetic. They could not walk, stand, or work as much and lost about 30 percent of their strength.

Weight loss and weight-reduction diets have been tied to all of the Keys's symptoms as well as others including: decreased growth in children, decreased mental performance (equivalent in degree to consumption of two alcoholic beverages), gallstones, cardiac disorders, fainting, psychological trauma from weight-loss failure, anemia, stroke, nausea, gouty arthritis, poor nutrition, aches and abdominal pain, elevated uric-acid levels, delayed healing and scar development, changes in liver function, cardiac problems, and death.[21] Experts claim that eating disorders, which exist in epidemic proportions and can cause severe problems including death, are borne of diets.[22]

Fat people have been bombarded with "treatments" for their weight for decades. Whether backed by lay people or the medical industry, one after another these recommendations have proved to carry risks which can easily outweigh the risks of living at a higher weight. As soon as one "treatment" gives way due to deaths or negative side-effects, another is waiting to take its place. No matter how risky the procedure or plan, most fat people will gain back the lost weight and may add some extra.

In the face of the near complete failure of dieting, the medical establishment has contributed two options: surgery and the lifestyle-change/drug combination. Weight-loss surgery has become popular even with its $20,000 to $30,000 price tag. The pitch is smooth and compelling, promising a new life to people 100 pounds or more overweight. It sells. Between 15,000 and 25,000 weight-reduction surgeries are performed each year in the United States. Older techniques, like inserting a balloon into the stomach to replicate a feeling of fullness, sometimes performed in-office by poorly trained physicians, have largely given way to a more modern approach. The two most common types performed today are: *gastroplasty* (stomach stapling), where the stomach is reduced in size often by use of a band so it can hold only a tiny amount of food, and *gastric bypass*, which involves stomach stapling in combination with reconfiguration of the intestines to bypass areas where food can be absorbed. Immediate mortality associated with gastric surgery is about one in 100. It is hard to get accurate statistics about dieting deaths because they are not tracked, but one study found sudden death for women in the general population to occur at 1.6 in 100,000.[23] Tracking supersize fat people who underwent surgery by obesity surgeons, the rate of death within two years was forty times higher. Dr. Paul Ernsberger explains that the typical surgery patient is a woman in her thirties.[24] A supersize woman can expect to live five years less than her thinner counterpart, according to the world's biggest ten-year epidemiologic study, which included 1.8 million Norwegians. The typical surgery patient still has four decades of life left, therefore the surgery risks must be evaluated over the long term. Ernsberger points out that complications from these surgeries are not adequately recorded and that weight regain is common, with up to 76 percent of patients failing to maintain the loss after only thirty months.

According to members of the National Association to Advance Fat Acceptance, concern over the complications caused by these procedures is well warranted, which has led the organization to call for an end to weight-loss surgery. Laura Fraser reports that 10 percent of NAAFA members have had weight-reduction surgery. Many have had negative experiences and belong to the organization's Weight-Loss Surgery Survivor's Group. Complications can include aggressive vomiting, digestion difficulties, bowel movements up to twenty times per day, extreme diarrhea, excessive flatulence and foul odors, infections, peritonitis, stomach perforation, dehydration, malnutrition, kidney stones, and liver failure. Even when the side-effects are not life-threatening, they can significantly diminish the quality of life. A woman interviewed about her surgery by Fraser explains that not only has she regained weight, but her surgery-related health conditions prevent her from being able to engage in the activities that kept her healthy before the surgery.[25] She must carry a change of clothes in case she cannot make it to a bathroom in time, her hair has fallen out from nutrition problems, and she avoids social situations because of all her health complications. Sometimes the patient must undergo additional surgeries to correct problems or to reverse the procedure. Decrying the lack of animal-based and independent trials, Dr. Ernsberger writes, "When the risks of surgery and long-term complications are taken into account, the net outcome for the patient who regains weight becomes highly negative."[26]

For fat people with less than 100 pounds to lose, those who have heeded the warnings of NAAFA against surgery, or who cannot raise the $25,000, may turn to physicians for pharmaceutalogical assistance with their weight-loss desires. Available drug options are limited and of questionable merit. Fat-rights activists are adamant in their rejection of these drugs, based on the medical profession's earned reputation for undervaluing the well-being of fat people.

The industry has an uninterrupted history of peddling dangerous and ineffective weight-loss pills to fat people. Author Marilyn Wann chronicles "substances that our very own doctors told us were safe and effective but which were, all too often, neither."[27] The late 1800s saw thyroid extract which resulted in osteoporosis, chest pain, and sudden death. This was followed by Dinitrophenol which caused neuropathy, cataracts, and death through high fever resulting from sharp increases in metabolism. Amphetamines were introduced in 1937 causing addictions and deaths. Phenylpropanolamine became popular in the 1970s and brought side-effects of insomnia, disorientation, stroke, and heart problems. Even liposuction, a cosmetic surgery to remove fat, has resulted in death. The most recent large-scale example of the medical profession endangering people all sizes of large is demonstrated by the fen-phen debacle—a health crisis whose magnitude dwarfs even the recall of silicon breast implants.

In early 1996 Lynn McAfee, director of the Council on Size and Weight Discrimination, attended the FDA hearings on dexfenfluramine with Dr. Ernsberger. A year and a half before its recall she resolved, "We're determined that we're not going to pay again for drugs that harm us rather than help us," blaming the cultural hostility toward fat for the approval of dangerous drugs.[28] Blazed by fat-rights activists, antidiet medical professionals, and a few astute reporters, there is a paper trail leading directly from FDA approval of Redux (dexfenfluramine) to its recall, warning repeatedly of the health dangers it posed. The public did not listen. Fat people were assured that, though taking the drug over three months increased their risk of developing the rare, deadly, and debilitating condition Primary Pulmonary Hypertension (PPH) by thirty-fold, it was worth it because, "Obesity itself is even more dangerous, and is now the second largest cause of preventable death."[29] (This is a widely quoted but disputed figure. Read more about it in chapter 13.) Redux was approved in April 1996. By June 2.5 million prescriptions had been written at a cost in excess of $70 per month for a medication that caused an average extra 5.5 pounds of weight loss (per year while continuing with the drug) compared to dieting alone.[30] Then reports of women disabled or dying started making their way to the papers. The drugs caused valvular heart disease, neurotoxicity, and PPH. Before they were recalled, somewhere between 14 million and 27 million prescriptions for the drugs phentermine, Redux, and fenfluramine had been issued, most of them to women.[31] Checkups and echocardiograms, which cost about $800 to $1,000, were recommended to screen for deadly health problems for everyone who used Redux and fen-phen.

Now Lynn McAfee again finds herself on the front page of the NAAFA newsletter, explaining the details of another potentially dangerous new diet drug, Meridia (sibutramine). Meridia increases blood pressure in 12 to 17 percent of healthy patients and heart rates in a quarter of those tested.[32] The FDA's own advisors voted 5 to 4 *not* to approve the drug.[33] NAAFA reports that half of the drug-test subjects did not complete the one-year test. Of those who had the highest doses, the weight loss was a mere 14 pounds (only seven to 11 more than the control group) and is regained if the drug is discontinued. Using these statistics, the drug annually costs users $100 per pound of weight lost. Fat people are pressured to lose weight usually out of concern for their blood pressure and heart. Fat people who have these problems cannot safely take Meridia. It is not to be taken if there is a history of stroke, hypertension, or heart problems. Because of the dangers of the medication, it is not supposed to be given to moderately fat people, but reserved for those with more extreme weight. Ironically, the fat people who can safely take the drug do not need to—they are the fat people who are healthy!

Obesity researcher and diet advocate Dr. Jules Hirsch is not optimistic about drug therapy. He explains that since the varying causes of fat are not understood, drug treatments will not be specifically tailored to the particular cause of the weight. The expected result is that the hazards will be high compared to the benefits, making the risks inappropriate "except in those with severe obesity that is immediately life-threatening."[34]

Comparing hazards to benefits is a helpful approach to employ in crafting medical recommendations for fat people, and it is a tactic that has been slow in coming. Dieting and weight loss are not benign procedures; there are hazards. For the overwhelming majority of dieters who will regain the weight, the benefits are few. Weight loss is commonly prescribed without thought to the consequences because fat is presumed to inherently carry health risks. As we have seen, this assumption is currently under attack.

Many researchers believe the dangers of moderate fat have been exaggerated and misinterpreted while the dangers of underweight have been ignored. Cornell professor David Levitsky analyzed nineteen studies involving 357,000 men and 249,000 women. He concluded that being 20 to 30 pounds "overweight" resulted in no increased mortality.[35] A ten-year study of nearly two million Norwegians showed that the fattest women, with Body Mass Index (BMI) of 45 ("morbid obesity" begins at a BMI of 35) still outlived the longest-lived men. The difference in longevity between the fattest people and the longest-lived people is only five years, with the thinnest people having about the same or shorter life expectancies.[36] While these studies are valid and do challenge the status quo approach to fat and disease, other researchers disagree and promote their own numbers. The NIH recently lowered its definition of "overweight" and "obese," causing 29 million Americans to become fat overnight, bringing the total of fat Americans up to 97 million.

Many researchers criticize the "treatments" for fat because they do not work and are dangerous. Other researchers challenge the concept that fat is unhealthy, believing studies have not adequately separated "fatness" from other factors that can accompany the weight. The health problems that are associated with fat are precisely the health problems present in people who are out of shape.

It is the level of fitness, researchers have found, that predicts health problems, not fat. The Cooper Institute for Aerobics Research in Dallas, Texas, has conducted a continuing study of over 25,000 people, measuring not just weight but also fitness. Fat men who exercised regularly were almost three times more likely to avoid premature death than thin men who did not. Furthermore, when fat and thin people were matched for fitness levels, it turned out their longevity was comparable. According to Laura Fraser, no researchers have been able to contradict this view.[37]

Even if evidence disproved the Cooper Institute analysis, it is illogical to assume that losing weight would even out the health risks of fat and thin. This illustrates the important difference between correlation and causation. There is simply no reason to believe that a person who loses weight will now gain the health advantages of someone who started and remained at that weight. According to the *New England Journal of Medicine's* editorial on weight loss, "The few studies of mortality among people who voluntarily lost weight produced inconsistent results; some even suggested that weight loss increased mortality."[38]

Others feel results from studies about increased mortality are clear. Though ignored by the mass media, several large, impressive studies have shown a clear connection between weight loss and death. According to Glenn Gaesser, exercise physiologist and professor at the University of Virginia, fifteen studies conducted on moderately fat people between 1983 and 1993 show that weight loss increases the risk of premature death by up to 260 percent.[39] Only two studies during that time period showed contradictory conclusions, one of which posited only an eleven-hour increase in longevity per pound lost. A 1969 study by the American Cancer Society tracking 800,000 men and women found weight loss increased the risk of death due to stroke or heart disease up to 176 percent while weight gain had no effect on the rates.[40] In their thorough review of obesity research, Ernsberger and Haskew find prevailing views to be unbalanced: "Much medical literature has documented elevated risk factors in heavy people, but these risk factors fail to translate into high mortality rates. In fact, many studies show maximum longevity is associated with above average weight. . . . These findings pose a paradox . . . we review the evidence that adiposity protects against several diseases and is associated with more favorable prognosis in others. . . . The hazards of obesity which are associated with fatness . . . may themselves be due to the ill effects of treatment for obesity. . . . Weight-loss methods [are] frequently unsafe [and] are almost always only temporarily effective."[41] How is it that weight loss improves risk factors for disease, like high blood pressure but simultaneously endangers health?

The answer may lie in the dangers of weight cycling, also known as "yo-yo dieting." Data from the American Cancer Society showed that otherwise healthy women who intentionally lost up to 19 pounds increased their risk of premature death by up to 40 to 70 percent as compared to their fat but weight-steady counterparts.

While the Keys's study men were in the refeeding stage of the study, Gaesser reports that several of the men seemed to be "on the verge" of experiencing congestive heart failure while one actually had to be hospitalized for his heart problems.[42] The *Healthy Weight Journal* summarizes the existing studies: "Research consistently shows an increase in mortality from all causes and from coronary heart disease with weight cycling."[43] The Framingham Heart Study followed data about the weight fluctuations of 3,000 people for over thirty years. Publishing in the *New England Journal of Medicine*, researchers discovered that subjects who either experienced many changes in weight or a big change increased their risk of heart disease and death by 25 to 100 percent over weight-stable subjects. In a different study, Centers for Disease Control epidemiologist Elsie Pamuk, Ph.D., found that weight loss of 15 percent or more was related to higher death rates for all people no matter what they weighed and any weight loss for women in any of the weight groups increased their mortality.[44] Laura Fraser reports on a review article in the *Archives of Internal Medicine* by Brownell and Rodin who confirm the increases in risk of death and heart disease, as well as eating disorders and the advent of dangerous fat placement during the weight-regain phase of weight cycling.[45]

The infamous siege of Leningrad in 1941 provides unintentional but similar weight-cycling data. Food was unavailable to the citizens, who lost weight. After food became available again, researchers found blood pressure had risen from 100 to 400 percent and the incidence of hypertension increased from 6 percent during the food restriction to 55 percent once food was again available.[46]

Dr. Paul Ernsberger and Douglas Nelson have found consistent results in animal studies they have conducted. Dividing rats into three feeding groups—one that got plain rat chow, one that got a sweetened higher-calorie food, and one that was dieted—they matched the triplets of rats and then studied blood pressure changes. The dieted rats displayed extremes of blood pressure. The fed rats' pressure was consistent; ranging from 115 to 125, they never had drastic changes. The calorie-restricted animals had pressures that jumped throughout the study from 105 to 145 to 118 to 140, indicating dangers for humans on food restriction.

These studies are representative of an even larger body of evidence that suggests serious health repercussions for yo-yo dieters. The process of dieting itself appears not only to have emotional consequences, as demonstrated dramatically in Keys's study, but also important physical health risks. There is some controversy in the medical field about the meaning of weight-cycling studies, which indicate the need for more investigation. Nevertheless, the data is compelling enough that it cannot be ignored and scientifically sound enough that it cannot be dismissed.

This research should have affected the American public greatly, changing the standards of practice. Because doctors are sworn to "first do no harm" this information should have given every physician pause. Suddenly, doctors would have to seriously reconsider advising their patients to diet. Specifically, a doctor should only advise 2 to 10 percent of their fat patients to diet because the rest could not be expected to succeed at losing weight and maintaining the loss. The risks were known and widely reported. Doctors who did not have reason to believe that their patient would be in the minority of dieters who were successful at maintaining their weight loss, would be prevented ethically from recommending weight loss because weight cycling would increase their risk of death 25 to 100 percent. Doctors who routinely promoted dieting or who did not inform their patients of the risks would not only have an ethics problem, they would have incurred legal liability.

It would have been a revolution in medical care. Instead, shortly after newspapers proclaimed the dangers of yo-yo dieting, the story changed. The influential *Journal of the American Medical Association* printed a review of weight-cycling studies that looked at over forty studies. While many studies demonstrated the dangers of weight cycling, others did not confirm the findings. More research was needed to clear up the questions and contradictions, but the researchers ignored the risks and advised fat people to keep dieting. This message was aggressively marketed to the media. Laura Fraser reports that the abstract read, "Weight cycling does not appear to have adverse health effects."[47] By the time it got to the media, the opinion was understood and reported as having the authority of the NIH. It translated into a barrage of conservative articles claiming yo-yo dieting was perfectly safe.

How did so many studies suggesting serious risks get overlooked? The answer to that question caused an ugly controversy which played out in the pages of *JAMA*.

NOTES

1. Paul Ernsberger, "Exploding the Myth: Weight Loss Makes You Healthier," *Healthy Weight Journal* 13, no. 1 (January–February 1999): 6.

2. For a detailed investigation of the "obesity research" field, see "Thinking Disorders: Obesity Researchers" in Laura Fraser's informative *Losing It: False Hopes and Fat Profits in the Diet Industry* (New York: Plume, 1998). According to Fraser, grants from the National Institutes of Health for obesity research in 1995 totaled 87 million dollars. The majority of funding for this research, she points out, actually comes from the diet industry businesses (214).

3. Ibid., 218.

4. Marilyn Wann, *Fat!So?* (Berkeley: Ten Speed Press, 1998), 40.

5. David Sharp, "Obesity Control," *Hippocrates* (October 1998): 36.

6. "What It Takes to Take Off Weight (And Keep It Off)," *Tufts University Health and Nutrition Letter* January (1998): 4. Actually, participants in the registry averaged a more impressive, 5.5 pounds per year loss maintenance. The average person lost 66 pounds and maintained a minimum of 30-pound loss over the five-year period.

7. Mary Klem et al., "A Descriptive Study of Individuals Successful at Long-term Maintenance and Substantial Weight Loss," *American Journal of Clinical Nutrition* 66 (1997): 239, 239–46 generally.

8. Press release from the University of Pittsburgh Medical Center News Bureau to the *San Francisco Examiner*. Release dated 6 August, 1997; sent to the *Examiner*, 30 September, 1997.

9. Ibid.

10. "What It Takes to Take Off Weight," 5.

11. Fraser, *Losing It*, 234.

12. Sharp, "Obesity Control," 36.

13. Thomas Coates and Carl Thorenson, "Treating Obesity in Children and Adolescents: A Review," *American Journal of Public Health* 68, no. 2 (1978): 148.

14. Ibid.

15. Jerome Kassirer and Marcia Angell, "Losing Weight—An Ill-Fated New Year's Resolution," *New England Journal of Medicine* (January 1998): 53.

16. Information from this section derived from: David Garner, "The Effects of Starvation on Behavior: Implications for Dieting and Eating Disorders," *Healthy Weight Journal* (September–October 1998): 68–72; Fraser, *Losing It*, 238–40; and Frances Berg, *Health Risks of Weight Loss*, 3d ed. (N.Dak.: Healthy Weight Journal, 1995), 29–31, 66–69.

17. Fraser, *Losing It*, 238.

18. Garner, "The Effects of Starvation," 70 (quoting Keys study, 894–95).

19. Ibid.

20. Berg, *Health Risks of Weight Loss*, 30.

21. Andy Coghlan "Dieting Makes You Forget," *New Scientist* 148 (1999):5 (October 1995); Berg, *Health Risks of Weight Loss*, 18; "Low-Fat Diet May Be Related to Stroke," *Nutrition and the M.D.* 24, No. 3 (March 1998): 7, citing *JAMA* 278 (1997): 2145; and "Wound Healing in Vegetarians and Dieters," *Dr. Alexander Grant's Health Gazette* 18, no. 5 (May 1995), citing *JAMA* 273 (1995): 910.

22. For more information on this observation, see generally chapter 8 in Fraser, *Losing It*.

23. Berg, *Health Risks of Weight Loss*, 23, citing E. J. Drenick and J. S. Fisler, *American Journal of Surgery* 155 (1988): 720–26.

24. Ernsberger, "Surgery Risks Outweigh Its Benefits," *Obesity & Health*, March/April (1991): 25.

25. Fraser, *Losing It*, 207.

26. Ernsberger, "Surgery Risks Outweigh Its Benefits," 24.

27. Wann, *Fat!So?* 71, and generally 71–73. Also generally, George Bray, "Drug Treatment of Obesity: Don't Throw the Baby Out With the Bathwater," *Journal of Clinical Nutrition* 67 (1998): 1.

28. "Amphetamine Redux?: The Scary Spectre of New Diet Drugs," *NAAFA Newsletter* 26, no. 1 (1996): cover.

29. "New Weight-Loss Pills," *Dr. Alexander Grant's Health Gazette*, 19, no. 9 (1996), citing *NEJM* 335 (1996): 609, 659, and *Science News* 150 (1996): 134.

30. Frederic Golden et al., "Who's to Blame for Redux and Fenfluramine?" *Time*, 29 September 1997, 79; Wann, *Fat!So?* 72–73; and Jane Brody, "Obesity Drugs: Weighing the Risks to Health Against the Small Victories," *New York Times*, 3 September 1997, C9.

31. Tara Meyer, "Redux, Fen-Phen Users Urged to Get Check-Ups," *Contra Costa Times* (Associated Press), 11 November 1997, cover, A18.

32. "Knoll Launches Meridia," *NAAFA Newsletter* 27, no. 5 (1998): cover, 9.

33. "FDA Approves Meridia as New Diet Drug," *Healthy Weight Journal* 12, no. 2 (1998): 18.

34. Jules Hirsch, "The Treatment of Obesity With Drugs," *American Journal of Clinical Nutrition* 67 (1998): 4.

35. Scripps Howard News Service, "Study Debunks Danger of Excess Weight," *Oakland Tribune*, 25 September 1995.

36. Ernsberger, "Surgery Risks Outweigh Its Benefits," 25.

37. Fraser, *Losing It*, 255.

38. Kassirer and Angell, "Losing Weight," 52.

39. Gaesser, *Big Fat Lies: The Truth About Your Health and Your Weight* (New York: Fawcett Columbine, 1996), 155. Also, 153–80 generally.

40. Ibid., 158.

41. Paul Ernsberger and Paul Haskew, "Health Implications of Obesity: An Alternative View," *Journal of Obesity and Weight Regulation* 6, no. 2 (Summer 1987): 258–359.

42. Gaesser, *Big Fat Lies*, 167.

43. Berg, *Health Risks of Weight Loss*, 70, also 70–88 generally.

44. Ibid., 81.

45. Fraser, *Losing It*, 226.

46. Gaesser, *Big Fat Lies*, 168–69.

47. Fraser, *Losing It*, 229.

CHAPTER 13

THE MEDICAL PROFESSION

Conflicts of Interest

*Money is the reason I became a Nutri/System franchisee. And now I have
more money than I ever dreamed I could make in a lifetime.*

—Dr. Richard Gordon[1]

THAT PHYSICIANS "HAVE BEEN THE most conspicuous promoters" of the
"diet hustle" in recent years is not news.[2] With an unending history of
trendy diets like *Dr. Schiff's Miracle Weight-Loss Guide*, Dr. Joyce Bockar's
The Last Best Diet, and Dr. Barbara Edelstein's *The Woman Doctor's Diet for
Women*, it should come as no surprise that doctors are willing to exploit
their medical degrees in the hope of cashing in on the weight-loss frenzy.
Court records are full of cases against physicians concerning misconduct
over diet-drug prescriptions.[3] As W. Charisse Goodman says, "Advanced
degrees or no, some members of the medical and psychiatric professions
are more than happy to put their prejudices on display and make money
at the same time."[4]

Nowhere is the conflict of interest more palpable, more insidious, and
more accepted than in the composition of the higher tier of obesity
"experts." To examine a list of the leading medical obesity authorities is to
examine a list of the university diet-clinic leaders and commercial diet-
center consultants. The problem is straightforward. The conflict of interest

is manifested by the physicians' personal, professional, emotional, and financial stakes in the determination that obesity is an evil. Laura Fraser has done marvelous investigation into this conflict, pointing out that "almost everyone who funds their work is in the diet business."[5] She explains that the presence of weight-loss companies and drug manufacturers is a pervasive one. It can be felt from their purchase of advertising that keeps medical journals functioning to drug company-sponsored continuing medical education credits to sponsorship of conferences. For example, the conference "Women and Obesity . . . The Risks, the Reasons, Resolutions for Empowerment" was sponsored by Weight Watchers®.[6] Outside the conference, the message delivered to the public via the media was that obesity in women had reached epidemic proportions and the result was a major damaging effect on women's health. Inside the conference, scientists from the NIH mingled with often-biased "obesity experts."

Sometimes the conflicts are even more blatant, and they occur at all degrees of importance. Examples include:

- The researcher whose company owned the patent to dexfenfluramine was often quoted as an expert about the drug without disclosure of his obvious financial interest.
- An editorial in the *New England Journal of Medicine* addressed the question, "Given the benefits of weight loss among the obese, how is the small risk of primary pulmonary hypertension . . . to be interpreted?" minimizing the risks of Redux. It was written by two people who had been paid by the drug company.[7]
- Doctors who sit on the board of directors of products like Slim Patch are often paid and own stock in the company.
- The *JAMA*-published conclusion that very-low-calorie diets are safe was written by a panel whose members had been paid or supported by Sandoz Nutrition Corporation, makers of the low-calorie Optifast liquid diet drink. The paper claimed to give a "balanced" understanding of the issue, while no mention of the financial conflicts of interest were to be found.[8]
- *Obesity Research Update*, a clinically oriented newsletter summarizing "obesity" news for healthcare workers, gives away free 5-HTP and DHEA with subscriptions.

- Two of the three articles in *Science* about the discovery of a gene that makes mice fat are authored by drug companies.
- When "obesity" researchers at Rockefeller University isolated an "obesity" gene, the drug company Amgen paid them $20 million for the patent and "many times that amount if the protein proves useful in treating fat people."[9]
- A study in the *Journal of the American Medical Association* found almost 20 percent of researchers said their paper publication had been postponed for "six months or longer to allow time for patent applications, to protect the proprietary value of results, to slow dissemination of undesired findings, or to resolve disputes over intellectual property."[10]

Obesity studies that appear neutral may not be. They may be created or interpreted in an unscientific and biased manner, crafted by people whose livelihoods depend on pathologizing fat to secure more study grants or consulting fees.

The weight-cycling debate suffered from a heated debate about conflict of interest. Several authoritative studies showed (and still show) that weight cycling is hazardous to health.[11] The national media picked up the story. Soon thereafter, a review was published in the influential *Journal of the American Medical Association*. The NIH's advisory group, the National Task Force on the Prevention and Treatment of Obesity, reviewed many studies on weight cycling. They found that changing weight was associated with death from all causes including heart disease, but determined that more studies were needed to settle some issues.[12] The response to their findings—a media blitz reassuring people that losing and regaining weight was not dangerous! When this opinion was reported in the media it was erroneously referred to as an independent government panel study of the National Institute of Health because an NIH employee was involved either with the group or with media contacts.[13]

Many researchers who voiced concerns about yo-yo dieting dangers were dismissed irresponsibly. Some believed the reason was not so much a difference in interpretation as a consequence of a conflict of interest. The nine-person National Task Force for the Treatment and Prevention of Obesity included seven people affiliated with weight-loss clinics, like members of the advisory board to Weight Watchers and Calorie Control Council.[14] They also get "research support" and "consulting fees" from weight-reduction drug makers as well as others with a financial stake in the weight-loss industry.[15] In a letter to *JAMA* Paul Ernsberger wrote, "*JAMA*'s Editorial Policy requires full disclosure of any affiliations . . . that might constitute or appear to constitute a financial conflict of interest. We strongly believe . . . that a significant financial incentive existed for minimizing the hazard imposed by unsuccessful treatments of obesity."[16] The *Healthy Weight Journal* had similar concerns about Task Force financial interests. They twice requested financial information on the group under the Freedom of Information Act.[17] The concept that diet cycling is not harmful is crucial for the survival of weight-loss companies and clinics because the services they provide will almost always end up with the client regaining or cycling. Pat Lyons, RN MA, also had strong words for the Task Force, "The course they are on at present . . . advocate[s] weight loss at any cost in a social climate that perpetuates discrimination against fat people."[18]

Task Force members are not the only ones to nurture bias against fat people. Former Surgeon General C. Everett Koop declared a very public war on fat. His crusade to promote weight loss and exercise is called *Shape Up America!* Preaching about what he claims are the dangers and financial costs of fat at every opportunity, he is well aware of the credibility he carries, both in the eyes of the general public and at the legislative level. "I think people believe me. That's why it's important that I'm the figurehead for this campaign."[19] Using his credibility, Koop circulates statistics that become widely quoted in the media. His claim of 300,000 deaths due to fat per year is very controversial. The *New England Journal of Medicine* explains, "That figure is by no means well established. Not only is it derived from weak or incomplete data, but it is also called into question by the methodological difficulties of determining which of many factors contribute to premature death."[20] Nevertheless, "The 300,000 figure has been used by many, including the FDA, pharmaceutical companies, and the American Obesity Association, to justify approvals of antiobesity drugs that cause serious side-effects and to justify greater funding for obesity research, according to the *Wall Street Journal*."[21] Similar controversy surrounds Koop's claim of fat-related costs and his assertion that fat is the country's number two cause of preventable death. A look at the composition and financial interests of the program sheds some light on the motivation to promote those disputed statistics.

Shape Up America! is backed by sixty medical groups and thirty corporations, which include, for example, Jenny Craig® and WeightWatchers®. Some of the companies contribute as much as one million dollars.[22] *Time* magazine's 17-page Shape Up America advertisement starts with a photo of two fat men's stomachs. The second page is a full-page ad for Slim Fast®. The Shape Up America text reads, "The campaign is the result of a unique coalition of *three complementary groups*: major corporations with an interest in health and fitness; leading medical and public health organizations; and the top medical and scientific experts in the fields of nutrition, exercise, and disease related to overweight" [emphasis added].[23] Public health messages might well conflict with the message of companies like Slim Fast®, making this a less than "complementary" alliance. When Heinz, owner of Weight-Watchers®, gifts Koop with the $250,000 Heinz Award for "his work on behalf of advancing public health," there is a sense of impropriety.[24]

The flood of publicity surrounding the Shape Up America campaign generates publicity that benefits other ventures. Taking advantage of the media attention, Koop launched a $25 six-issue newsletter and a line of medical videos backed by Time-Life and Tucker/Green, Inc. The videos would be priced at approximately $19.95 and were expected to generate sales of $50 million by 1998. Although Koop's specific yearly salary for recruiting medical advisors for the tapes and then reviewing the tapes was not disclosed, the company confirmed it would exceed $90,934.[25]

Koop is also involved in other projects. For example, the C. Everett Koop National Health Awards recognize and promote employers with effective wellness programs who share their strategies with other companies. These so-called wellness programs often do not treat fat people well at all. They can perpetuate the prejudice and social inequality faced by fat people in the workforce by including financial and other bonuses for employees who are thin or lose weight, using the number on the scale as a convenient proxy for health.

Complaining about bias in the field of obesity research, Dr. Paul Ernsberger points out, "The major problem is an employment conflict of interest. That is, almost everyone considered an authority on obesity runs a clinic that proposes to eradicate it. This is not going to lead to a balanced picture of obesity. Obviously, people first decide that obesity is terrible, go to work for a clinic, and then start to do some research."[26] The field of obesity research is essentially synonymous with the field of weight-loss research. No medical expert has any financial stake in weight maintenance, and most have a social aversion to it. Numerous dangers result from allowing an entire field to proceed with such unrelenting bias. The creation, validation, and perpetuation of social dangers, like stigma and discrimination against fat people, are to be expected. But there are other more subtle dangers, too.

The legal implications of this unchecked imbalance are awesome. Judges making life-altering custody and adult commitment decisions are eager to rely on the advice of the medical profession in ordering placements. With most of the medical profession espousing the view that obesity is a mutable condition within the control of the individual, protection under the Americans with Disabilities Act is elusive. Lawyers have even tried to win various legal arguments based on the common medical opinion that fat people are necessarily in worse physical condition than thin people.

A fifty-four-year-old mother and her twenty-three-year-old son were aboard a vessel that collided and sank. Lawyers argued that the mother would have been the first to die not only because her son was younger and a good swimmer, but because the mother was fat and suffered from shortness of breath. Survival advantages of fat in a water crash could include increased bouyancy and more protection from the cold, but people are not currently accustomed to associating fat with advantages. Attorneys focused on who outlived whom in the accident because of the significant ramifications on the distribution of the estate.[27]

It is important to challenge the medical profession to approach weight regulation with scientific neutrality. Dangers and difficulties of weight loss have been documented for decades, but have long gone ignored by the profession. Negative views of fat are deeply entrenched in the medical field because they are backed by prejudice and by financial interests. Situations where logic and scientific accuracy succumbs to financial profit and social bias are generally good candidates for court intervention.

NOTES

1. Dr. Richard Gordon (owner of forty centers in eight states), from Nutri/System franchise literature.

2. Donald Dale Jackson, "The Art of Wishful Shrinking," *Smithsonian* (November 1994): 147.

3. See, for example, *State of Texas* v. *Bachynsky, M.D.* 770 S.W.2d 563 (Supreme Court of Texas) 1989. Appeal from judgment of physician and clinic fine of $50,000 under the Texas Deceptive Trade Practices-Consumer Protection Act for allegedly, after a permanent injunction, continuing to represent the drug Dinitrophenol (DNP) as being safe for weight loss despite the fact that DNP is a toxic herbicide, advertising for patients with the intent to distribute/prescribe DNP, and failing to advise prospective patients that DNP is not generally recognized as safe for the treatment of obesity.

4. Charisse Goodman, *The Invisible Woman: Confronting Weight Prejudice in America* (Carlsbad, Calif.: Gurze Books, 1995), 32, 33–34.

5. Laura Fraser, *Losing It: False Hopes and Fat Profits in the Diet Industry* (New York: Plume, 1998), 214, ch. 7 generally.

6. "Women and Obesity: The Rising Epidemic," PR Newswire, 7 February 1992.

7. JoAnn Manson and Gerald Faich, "Pharmacotherapy for Obesity: Do the Benefits Outweigh the Risks?" *NEJM* 335, no. 9 (1996): 659.

8. Fraser, *Losing It*, 217.

9. Gina Kolata, "Researchers Find Hormone Causes a Loss of Weight: Drug Bonanza Expected," *New York Times*, 27 July 1995, A1.

10. David Perlman, "Drug Firm's War on UCSF Study Ends: Company Fought to Hide Findings on Thyroid Pill," *San Francisco Chronicle*, 16 April 1997, A13.

11. See: "Weight Cycling and Mortality: Support From Animal Studies," *JAMA* 269 (1993): 1116; "Refeeding Hypertension in Obese SHR," *Hypertension* 24 (1994): 699–705; "Weight Cycling," *JAMA* 273 (1995): 998–99; "Weight Cycling in Obese SHR Exacerbates Hypertension," *FASEB Journal* 6 (1992): A1674.

12. Berg, *Health Risks of Weight Loss*, 78.

13. Zee Starns, "Rethinking Body Size: The Other Side of the Fat-Is-Bad Research (From an interview with Paul Ernsberger, Ph.D.)," *BBW* (*Big Beautiful Woman*) (Spring 1996): 52; and Fraser, *Losing It*, 229.

14. Starns, "Rethinking Body Size," 52.

15. *Boston Globe*, "Measuring Effects of Obesity Drugs: Short-term Use Doesn't Keep the Weight Off, Doctors Find," *San Francisco Chronicle*, 18 December 1996, A12.

16. Paul Ernsberger and Richard Koletsky, Letter to George Lundberg, Editor, *JAMA*, 11 November 1994.

17. Berg, *Health Risks of Weight Loss*, 79.

18. Ibid.

19. Mike McNamee and Geoffrey Smith, "Now It's C. Everett Koop Inc.," *Business Week*, 19 December 1994, 36.

20. Jerome Kassirer and Marcia Angell, "Losing Weight—An Ill-Fated New Year's Resolution," *NEJM* (January 1998): 52. For a more detailed discussion of the source of this figure, see Laura Fraser's investigation in her book *Losing It*, 174–78.

21. "Is Obesity a Disease?" *Nutrition and the M.D.* (April 1998): 7.

22. McNamee and Smith, "Now It's C. Everett Koop Inc.," 36.

23. "Shape Up America! Special Advertising Feature," *Time*, 8 May 1995.

24. Terry Poulton, *No Fat Chicks: How Big Business Profits by Making Women Hate Their Bodies—And How to Fight Back* (N.J.: Birch Lane Press, 1997), 13–14.

25. McNamee and Smith, "Now It's C. Everett Koop Inc.," 36.

26. Paul Ernsberger, Correspondence sent to Sondra Solovay, 13 July 1995.

27. *Young Women's Christian Home* v. *French* 187 U.S. 401, 23 S.Ct. 184, 186 47 L.Ed. 233. Lawyers unsuccessfully argued that the mother would have perished first.

CHAPTER 14

HOW THE MEDICAL PROFESSION TREATS FAT PEOPLE

My sister had cervical cancer. She didn't go back for her postop checkup for over 10 years. I asked her, "Why? Don't you know this is dangerous stuff?" She said, "They're just going to tell me I'm too fat. I don't want to hear it. If I die, I die." My sister works in a hospital.[1]

THE REFUSAL TO REQUIRE MORE neutral practices regarding weight-related research and studies contributes directly to the spiraling civil rights problem for fat people seeking medical assistance. Ignoring the bias present in the medical data offends the scientific professionalism of the medical community and compounds the culturally learned bigotry of individual care providers. This apathy prevents fat people from receiving the same quality of health care that thin people receive; fat people are consistently denied basic respect and needed treatment by healthcare workers. Prejudice against fat people in the industry is blatant and condoned by codes of medical ethics.

Members of the medical profession harbor bias against fat people. Unlike other personal prejudices they may hold, the attitudes toward fat people are reinforced by bias in the field. Many times prejudice is hard to prove. People are ashamed of their bias, so it is expressed covertly. Antifat sentiment, however, is so socially accepted that it is not hidden. When Terry

Poulton, author of *No Fat Chicks: How Big Business Profits by Making Women Hate Their Bodies—And How to Fight Back*, appeared on a Canadian talk show she was joined by Dr. Kenneth Walker, author of a newspaper column that circulates nationally. He repeated the opinion he had earlier published in his column: For the good of the country's finances as well as for their own good, fat people should be locked up in prison camps.[2]

In addition to extensive anecdotal evidence, several studies have documented these biased feelings in the profession. One physician survey showed that doctors saw their own obese patients as "weak-willed, ugly, and awkward."[3] In a study conducted on medical students, volunteers were videotaped in their normal slim appearance and then disguised with padding to look fat. The doctors-to-be described the "fat" people as "more defensive, cold, nervous, incompetent, insincere, depressed, and unlikable."[4] Similar attitudes have been found in nutritionists and public health administrators.[5]

A study of 120 mental-health professionals demonstrates how easily these negative, stereotypical beliefs can influence professional opinion and diagnosis.[6] A picture of a middle-aged woman and copies of a case history were distributed for evaluation. The picture was altered by a photographic process in some cases to make her appear 40 percent overweight while others left her appearing thin. When the woman was fat she was ranked higher in sexual dysfunction than when she appeared thin. More alarming, in the category of Total Psychological Dysfunction on a scale of 0 (no dysfunction present) to 100 (all dysfunctions present), the identical "thin" woman received a score of 42.55 while her fat counterpart received a score of 54.77—a very significant increase.[7]

Prejudice in the medical field affects fat people two ways. It affects the way medical professionals treat fat people, both in the office and in research. It also affects fat people themselves and the way they treat their own health concerns.

Tufts University Health and Nutrition Newsletter exposes that nurses admit, "They would rather not care for or touch an obese patient."[8] Jaclyn Packer surveyed 150 fat women, who weighed in the low 200-pound range, about their medical treatment.[9] Every single woman reported having her weight commented on by a physician and almost all disliked being in situations where they had to discuss their weight with a physician.[10] They disliked discussing their weight with doctors because they were insulted and made to feel embarrassed. Often, they felt the condition they were seeking treatment for was being overlooked because of excessive, misplaced concern about their weight. Of the people who reported they were treated disrespectfully by the doctors, illustrations of that harassment and disrespect include being yelled at, called names, and slapped. In particular, gynecological exams were troubling, with many women experiencing cruel comments from doctors who had trouble believing they were sexually active.

One woman brought in after surviving a rape was harassed about her weight by the physician examining her for legal evidence.[11] Hers is just one in a long list of complaints concerning incompetent gynecological care for fat women. One woman describes her pregnancy examination: "My doctor said I couldn't get pregnant, I was fat, who would want to make me pregnant?" She was pregnant.[12]

Consider the medical malpractice suit brought against a Michigan doctor.[13] Loriann was fourteen and fat. Her mother took her to Dr. Yanga for a medical examination because she was complaining of dizzy spells, fainting, and missed menstrual periods.[14] She saw the doctor six times over four months. Despite the fact that Loriann and her mother both told the doctor that she did not have an irregular menstrual cycle, the physician said that her skipped periods were the result of her weight. He said her other symptoms were related to low blood pressure and did not recommend a pregnancy test. The result of his missed diagnosis was that Loriann was too late to seek an abortion and instead dropped out of high school, foregoing her plans to become a registered nurse, so she could take care of her son.[15]

It is probable that stereotypes about fat children and adults, especially those involving sexuality and food, affect the diagnoses they receive. Loriann's doctor missed the potential of her pregnancy. Concerned that clinicians were missing common bulimia diagnoses in heavier patients, *Journal Watch: Women's Health* published a segment reminding its readers, "Are we missing bulimia in some women?"[16]

The *Internal Medicine World Report* urges healthcare providers to "eliminate complacency" about fat.[17] This call to action is highly offensive given the constant attention focused on "fat" in the doctor's office. Fat people frequently must hound their doctors to focus on the problem they have come to treat. Often, discussions of weight eclipse all other problems, no matter how critical. "Fat must provide phenomenal health protection. I am immune to falls that twist ankles and sprain backs. I can't get migraines and asthma like thin people get. The only problem they ever diagnose me with is a weight problem. If my ankle hurts, if my head hurts, if my period stops, it is always only because I am fat," explains an anonymous health-study participant sarcastically.

The attitude that all health problems fat people have can be traced to their weight translates directly into two treatment regimens for the identical condition—one for fat patients and one for thin. *Dr. Alexander Grant's Health Gazette* discusses treatment for osteoarthritis (OA) of the hip and knee.[18] For fat patients, they say the condition results from obesity. The recommendation for fat patients, thus, is weight loss. If the patient is thin, then the condition is the result of poor posture and poor muscle tone. The prescription for thin people with this condition is exercise to strengthen the related muscles that support the joints. It is completely unreasonable and unscientific to assume that fat people will not suffer from diseases caused the same way as their counterparts. If a condition occurs in a certain percentage of thin people, then it probably also occurs at least that many times in the fat population. Fat only becomes a potential explanation for the condition in those extra cases. For example, assume OA strikes 10 percent of thin people due to their lack of muscle strength. Assume OA strikes 15 percent of fat people. It is reasonable to assume that 10 percent of the fat people will have the condition due to muscle weakness, not weight, and their regimen should reflect that. Otherwise, fat people, who probably will not be able to lose weight, will be denied equal relief. In practice, even moderately fat people are often refused relief as they are frequently denied the hip and knee replacement surgery that can cure severe cases of this condition.

Even when the regimen is the same, the treatment fat people receive can be very different. Betty Rose Dudley, writing in *Fat!So?*, tells her story. When she went to the doctor for a cough, the physician brought up weight loss, which she declined to engage in. When Betty returned for the doctor to interpret her chest X-rays, the doctor presented her with weight-loss program pamphlets and tried to pressure her into joining. Betty again declined, explaining why. When she managed to remind the doctor she was there for the X-ray results, she was told she could have cancer. When Betty went back to find out the results of further testing, the doctor again arrived with even more weight-loss pamphlets. Betty had to refocus the physician, who was angry and disgusted about her lack of interest in dieting, so she could finally find out that she did not have lung cancer.[19] It is unlikely that Betty's physician would have treated cancer concerns in a thin patient in such an offhand manner.

In her dissertation, Jaclyn Packer, Ph.D., lists several examples of missed diagnoses due to fat prejudice. When patients complained of fatigue, pain, and headaches, they were told the symptoms were the result of their weight. In fact, these people had serious medical problems like mononucleosis, fibroid tumors, and eye problems.[20] Because of the bias, their conditions went untreated. If the patients had not been fat, the correct diagnosis might have been made and the problems would have been less severe because of earlier medical intervention. Lack of early intervention is a common problem for fat patients. For example, despite the fact that regular pelvic screenings are of particular importance to fat women due to their higher risk for cervical cancer, a 1993 survey of over 1,300 physicians found that 17 percent were reluctant to perform a pelvic exam on very fat women while none were reluctant to perform the same exam on very thin women.[21] In 1995 researchers found that some physicians listed "obese" as the reason they did not follow standard pap-smear-test procedures on some women.[22] This reluctance can easily translate into delays that are critical.

In a therapy group led by the associate dean of the Indiana School of Nursing, a woman stated,

> Being fat is going to kill me, not because of the strain on my heart but because of the strain on my soul. I am going to have some warning signs and avoid seeking health care until it is too late, because I am sick and tired of the canned speeches from doctors and nurses blaming my weight for everything.[23]

Disrespectful and different healthcare treatment, the result of unchecked bias, creates a legacy of frustration and despair that completely alienates fat people from the medical care system. Packer's work emphasizes the problems of delay and avoidance inspired by the treatment fat people receive in the medical setting. *Every* participant in her survey had avoided a needed medical visit, particularly in relation to gynecological care.[24] Avoiding medical visits make sense because of the rampant fat hostility in the medical profession. A small 1998 study of female nurses' attitudes toward fat patients revealed startling observations about the treatment of fat people by physicians. Verbal humiliation of fat female patients occurred. Nurses noted differences in the way the doctors treated the fat patients and half reported that female patients were more likely to be told to lose weight before having a surgery performed, or refused surgery.[25]

Quality of medical treatment is not affected only on an individual level. The institution of medicine, the industry itself, is infused with fat discrimination. Subtleties like the impact of physician reluctance to treat fat people, the results of alienation, the lack of preventative care, reduced quality of medical care, and less accurate diagnoses are virtually ignored in large studies, even though they might explain why fat people are at higher risk for certain conditions.

While weight is the subject of much attention in the doctor's office, when it comes to research, fat people are often excluded. Rather than studying ways to maximize the health of fat people, researchers only focus on fat people when the goal of the study is the eradication of fat.

Launched in 1993, the National Institutes of Health funded the largest clinical study ever undertaken in the United States. The $625-million-dollar study addressed heart disease, cancer, and osteoporosis in women, following tens of thousands of women for fourteen years. Despite the fact that fat women are told they are at increased risk for heart disease and cancer, they will not benefit from this research. Fat women were excluded from participating in this study. (Furthermore, fat women are at decreased risk for osteoporosis, so the exclusion of fat women from the trial may disadvantage thin women.) A health investigator for the WHI clinical trial, commenting on the ban of fat women, said, "It's my belief that they should be dieting. They need to be dieting, not be in a study where weight loss is not the goal."[26] Ironically, this study is touted as "dramatic action" to address the research gaps that have resulted in the exclusion of women from medical research studies.[27]

The exclusion of fat people from research studies may be preferable to the treatment they receive from the researchers. At Columbia University's

Obesity Research Center, fat people were recruited for an investigation into stomach size and stretchability of the stomach after weight loss. Researchers measured the stomach size of participants before and after putting them on diets. This was accomplished by threading balloons into the stomachs of the fat subjects through their mouths and throats. With the balloon in place, the researchers slowly filled them with water two-fifths of a cup at a time. On a scale of one to ten, the subjects would then rate the sensations of nausea, bloating, and fullness. When the subject registered a "10" of discomfort, the researchers stopped the procedure. The participants were also subjected to another test where a machine measured the pressure on the stomach, rather than relying on their feelings of discomfort.[28]

In a study that exploited the wallets, not the stomachs of fat people, researchers at Rockefeller University recruited eighteen fat and twenty-three thin people.[29] The rigorous study required the subjects to live at the clinic. The first four to six weeks were spent on a liquid-only diet where weight was maintained. Next, they gained 10 percent of their body weight by consuming 5,000 to 6,000 extra calories per day. This was followed by another four to six weeks of liquid diet to maintain weight. Metabolism was measured and the subjects were given diets of only 800 calories per day until they got down to 10 percent below their starting weight. They then spent another four to six weeks maintaining this lower rate. The study was grueling. A study doctor reported that the fat subjects had a harder time than the thin subjects gaining the extra weight and were more uncomfortable with it. When the project was over, the scientific community gained some insight into metabolism. The thin participants gained financially, receiving $40 per day for doing the study. The fat people, however, were not similarly rewarded. Rather than paying the fat subjects for their time, their reimbursement was a promise by the researchers that they could stay on at the clinic with a special diet until they were not fat anymore. Some of them stayed a year. Most of them could not get closer than 20 to 30 percent above average. Not even one of the subjects could maintain the weight loss.

Reinforcement of fatphobia in the medical profession can also be seen in *Clinical Ethics*, a controlling text for ethical decisions in clinical medicine. Under the heading "Failure to Comply with Medical Regimen" the authors discuss the case of Mrs. COPE (Chronic, Outpatient, Palliative,

Efficacious).[30] She suffers from diabetes and has gained sixty pounds, does not take her insulin sufficiently regularly, and has an alcohol problem. They comment on the great frustration for physicians in such cases saying, "Such patients place great strain on the doctor-patient relationship."[31] They determine that if the physician judges that the noncompliance arises from voluntary persistence in health risks and the physician's reasonable efforts in rational persuasion fail, the physician may ethically withdraw from the case.[32] It soon becomes clear in their ethics case study that the major frustration is over the weight issue.

In the next example, entitled "The Problem Patient," they modify Mrs. COPE's situation by having the physician admit her to an inpatient fasting regimen. They then discuss the doctor's role should the patient be found "cheating" on her diet. They hold therapeutic goals may be abandoned since they were "unachievable because of the patient's failure to participate."[33] Remember, she is seeing the physician for treatment of her diabetes. Had she refused to enroll in the starvation-diet program, she would have been "voluntarily persisting in health risks," thus triggering the physician's ability (ethically) to refuse to care for her. Having entered the program and failed, she has been "noncompliant" and thus has triggered the physician's ability to refuse to continue caring for her. Either way, the condition she is seeking treatment for, though arguably related to her weight, has been eclipsed and she has been refused medical care because of her weight.

While the authors mention an ethical obligation for the doctor to first try to persuade her to change her behavior, they do not require any investigation about what went wrong with the treatment program. There is no ethical compulsion to explore any of the other possibilities—the acceptable assumption is that the failure is the fault of the patient, not the treatment regimen. Similarly, there is no ethical requirement to first ascertain success rates for the program before prescribing it.

Further proof of the fatphobia imbedded in the ethical guidelines can be observed in the language used to describe Mrs. COPE. The words chosen are in direct contrast to the language used in a different scenario where the successful weight-loss patient is referred to as "actively involved" and "scrupulous about her eating habits . . . maintain[ing] an ideal body weight."[34]

The treatment of fat people by the medical establishment both institutionally and individually shows great prejudice. The medical ethics text *Clinical Ethics* cautions members of the medical profession that they may be harboring hidden biases regarding disability, disdain for certain kinds of persons or lifestyles, racial prejudice, and repugnance for the aged and retarded. The book commands, "Be aware of the subtle value aspects of objective medical judgments."[35] Not only should the profession heed those words, the authors, too, should incorporate that advice into their own fat-phobic examples of ethical dilemmas.

If the medical profession cannot provide the needed safeguards to correct and address errors and imbalance in the field, then the industry should expect to stand trial for the harm done by its bias. Physicians should be forced to compare risks to benefits whenever they make recommendations for fat people. Given the utter failure of diets, the dangers of weight-loss treatments, and the fact that fat may not be unhealthy, the goal of the health-care industry should be to maximize the health of fat people no matter what their weight. Doctors who casually prescribe diets should be prepared to defend those recommendations in court just the way doctors and drug makers have been forced to defend themselves against various diet-drug-related lawsuits because they cause real harm both to the body and the spirit.

Because bias has existed in the medical field for so long, it is not enough for doctors to monitor their own behavior. They must take affirmative steps to protect the health of fat people. They must insist that equipment like MRI machines and operating instruments are made big enough to accommodate fat patients. And they should take the advice of the *New England Journal of Medicine*: "Doctors should do their part to help end discrimination against overweight people in schools and workplaces. . . . Doctors can help the public regain a sense of proportion."[36]

NOTES

1. Betty Rose Dudley, "Fat Kills," in the 1996 Crossing Press Women Writers Engagement Book, and in Marilyn Wann, *Fat!So?* (Berkeley: Ten Speed Press, 1998), 42.

2. Terry Poulton, *No Fat Chicks: How Big Business Profits by Making Women Hate Their Bodies—And How to Fight Back* (N.J.: Birch Lane Press, 1997), 105–106.

3. Albert J. Stunkard, "Talking With Patients," *Obesity: Theory and Therapy* (New York: Raven Press, 1993), 355.

4. Gladys Agell and Esther Rothblum, "Effects of Clients' Obesity and Gender on the Therapy Judgments of Psychologists," *Professional Psychology Research and Practice* 22, no. 3 (1991): 223, referring to Breytspraak et al., "Sensitizing Medical Students to Impression Formation Processes in the Patient Interview," *Journal of Medical Education* 52 (1977): 24–54.

5. Ibid.

6. Laura Young and Brian Powell, "The Effects of Obesity on the Clinical Judgments of Mental Health Professionals," *Journal of Health and Social Behavior* 26 (September 1985): 233.

7. Ibid., 239.

8. "Choosing the Right Dietitian," *Tufts University Health and Nutrition Newsletter* (June 1997): 3.

9. Shelley Bovey, *The Forbidden Body: Why Being Fat Is Not a Sin* (London: Pandora, 1994). See pages 47–51 for information about a survey similar to Packer's conducted by Bovey. Bovey's survey of 200 people confirms Packer's findings.

10. Jaclyn Packer, "Barriers to Health Care Utilization: The Effect of the Medical Stigma of 'Obesity' on Women" (Summary of Ph.D. diss., City University of New York, 1990), 1–2, 4–5.

11. Poulton, *No Fat Chicks*, 107.

12. Bovey, *The Forbidden Body*, 45.

13. *Clapham* v. *Yanga, M.D.* 102 MICH.APP. 47, 300 N.W. 2d 727 (Court of Appeals of Michigan, 1980).

14. *Clapham* at 50–51, 729.

15. The jury found the defendant liable for damages due to his malpractice. Money was awarded to Loriann for personal damages and for the expense of raising a child. *Clapham* at 50, 729.

16. "Are We Missing Bulimia in Some Women?" *Journal Watch: Women's Health* 1, no. 1 (April 1996): 4.

17. "Obesity Upgraded to 'Major' Risk Factor for Heart Disease," *Internal Medicine World Report* 13, no. 9 (June 1998): 20.

18. "Osteoarthritis (OA) of Hip and Knee," *Dr. Alexander's Health Gazette* 19, no. 1 (January 1996): 2.

19. Dudley, "Fat Kills," 42–43.

20. Jaclyn Packer, "Stigma: Barrier to Quality Health Care," *NAAFA Newsletter* 25, no. 5 (1995): 8.

21. C. H. Adams et al., "The Relationship of Obesity to the Frequency of Pelvic Examinations: Do Physician and Patient Attitudes Make a Difference?" *Women & Health* 20, no. 2 (1993): 45–57.

22. R. M. Lubitz et al., "Is Obesity a Barrier to Physician Screening for Cervical Cancer?" *American Journal of Medicine* 98 (1995): 491–96.

23. Bovey, *The Forbidden Body*, 49.

24. Packer, "Barriers to Health Care Utilization," 6.

25. J. Wright, "Female Nurse's Perceptions of Acceptable Female Body Size: An Exploratory Study," *Journal of Clinical Nursing* 7, no. 4 (1998): 307–15.

26. "WHI Excludes Fat Women," *NAAFA Newsletter* 25, no. 5 (1995): 10.

27. Susan Finn, "Women's Health: Anatomy of an Issue," *Topics of Clinical Nutrition* 11, no. 1 (1995): 2.

28. "Weight-Loss News That's Easy to Stomach," *Tufts University Diet and Nutrition Letter* 14, no. 2 (1996): 1.

29. Gina Kolata, "Metabolism Found to Adjust for a Body's Natural Weight," *New York Times*, 9 March 1995, A1. The study demonstrated that the body's metabolism speeds up or slows down to maintain the natural weight, making continued weight loss and maintenance very difficult.

30. Albert Jonsen, Mark Siegler, and Willaim Winslade, *Clinical Ethics*, 2d ed. (New York: Macmillan, 1986), 39, 86–87.

31. Ibid., 87.

32. Ibid., 88.

33. Ibid., 88–89.

34. Ibid., 39.

35. Ibid., 13.

36. Jerome Kassirer and Marcia Angell, "Losing Weight—An Ill-Fated New Year's Resolution," *NEJM* 338 (January 1998): 53.

CHAPTER 15

THROW AWAY THE KEY

Involuntary Adult Commitment

REMINISCENT OF THE STARVATION ENDURED by political prisoners and concentration camp victims, fat adults with developmental disabilities have been locked in institutions by American courts to force them to lose weight. These people were committed because they were fat. They remained committed because they might get fat again.

Many residential diet programs severely restrict caloric intake, sometimes to 600 calories per day—one-half of the calories considered to be starvation according to the World Health Organization and also less than the 900 calories the Nazis determined were needed to maintain life at Treblinka.[1] While a mentally challenged person may not understand the subtleties of the world or even his own situation, he knows hunger.

In 1982 Michael Pope was "temporarily" committed for institutional supervision to Western State Center at Canonsburg.[2] Pope was removed from the home setting where he had been living because his weight could not be "controlled" there.[3] He was placed instead in an institution until the Allegheny County Mental Health/Mental Retardation program was "able to develop" an alternate living situation where his weight would be controlled.[4] There was no deadline or time frame imposed by the court. Until the Supreme Court's ruling on 22 June 1999, there was no reason to believe that Michael Pope would ever be allowed to leave the institution.

The judge's order was based largely on his finding that Michael Pope's weight was (1) not controllable in the home situation, (2) stemmed from his mental retardation, and (3) constituted an "unquestioned health danger which could be fatal."[5] The determination that Pope's size was a result of his mental abilities is particularly troubling. There was no reason to believe that Pope's size was connected to his mental disability, aside from the commonly held stereotype that both fat people and mentally disabled people are stupid. This finding was legally necessary, however, if Pope was to be committed. Section 406 of the Mental Health and Mental Retardation Act of 1966 allows for the commitment of a mentally disabled person when the person needs care or treatment "by reason of such mental disability."[6] The court may legally exercise authority over Pope in this matter only if the care he needs is required because of his retardation.[7] If Michael Pope is fat not because of his retardation, but for any other reason (like cultural, environmental, or genetic factors), then he is illegally imprisoned.

Millions of Americans who are of average or higher intelligence cannot alter their weight despite vigorous effort. There is no reason to believe that mentally retarded individuals will be any more adept at controlling their weight.

The judge based his decision largely on the health danger posed by Pope's weight. This points to an important consequence of the existing fallacies and misconceptions the public and the medical community hold about the health of fat people.

If Pope's weight is not, in fact, such an unparalleled risk to his health that it could be fatal, or if it is not his weight that puts him at risk but his level of fitness, then Pope is being held against his will, contrary to his best interest and without sufficient cause.

Similarly, Susan McPherson was confined by state actions, remaining committed to a facility that both the state and the medical establishment agree is unnecessary.[8]

Suffering from Prader-Willi syndrome, McPherson allegedly has an "uncontrollable appetite," which can lead to extreme weight gain. She "spent most of her life at foster-home placements" and was removed from that environment by the court to receive treatment for her illness.[9]

Was her illness treated? Her weight was clearly altered. McPherson was committed to the treatment center in October of 1988. By August of

1990, she was ready to be released, having lost over 200 pounds. Neither her syndrome nor her ability to control it changed over the course of the two years. Even so, the courts recognized this as "successful treatment."[10]

Those involved in Susan's case agreed that she was ready to be released. Nevertheless, they would not release her to a regular foster or group home. Instead, the court recommended that she only be placed in a facility made to "deal" with Prader-Willi syndrome. In other words, her facility must be prepared to prevent her from gaining weight. The only group home that could do this was a small facility already at capacity with twelve individuals. Though Susan was on the waiting list, the next opening was not likely to occur until the death of one of the occupants. In the meantime, although Susan requested that she be returned to her regular environment, an environment she grew up in and was comfortable with, the court reissued the commitment petition and forced McPherson to remain in the Cambridge treatment center until the Oakwood facility becomes available.

In Michael Pope's case, the county had no facility to release him to, and possibly never would. Susan remained a prisoner because the only available facility deemed acceptable by the judge was full. In both cases, adult individuals were being held against their will by the state. It didn't matter if they were perfectly healthy. It didn't matter if they were hungry. The state was simply afraid they would get fat.

As of June 1999, people like Susan and Michael may have some recourse. The United States Supreme Court confronted the question of whether the Americans with Disabilities Act, by way of its prohibition against discrimination, requires people with mental disabilities to be housed in community settings rather than institutions. Justice Ginsberg responds, "The answer, we hold, is a qualified yes."[11] Considerations include: whether treatment professionals have determined that community placement is appropriate, the person is not opposed to transfer to the less restrictive environment, it is reasonable for the state to make such a placement in light of realities of available resources and the needs of others with mental disabilities. "Unjustified isolation," writes the Court, "is properly regarded as discrimination based on disability."[12] Continuing, the Court quotes a brief prepared by the American Psychiatric Association explaining that when people, because of their mental disabilities, must "relinquish participation in community life they could enjoy given reasonable accommodations" while their counterparts without mental disabilities can receive medical treatment "without similar sacrifice," this constitutes "dissimilar treatment."[13]

The Court did not require states to offer transfer to all appropriate mentally disabled individuals, but it did mention examples of when a state would *not* have to offer immediate transfer. For example, it could be satisfactory for the state to demonstrate an effective plan for moving people to less restrictive environments, and waiting lists that moved at reasonable rates. It is likely under this decision that Pennsylvania could not keep Michael in an unnecessarily restrictive environment indefinitely and that Minnesota cannot wait for people to die to create movement on the waiting list. Finally, people like Michael and Susan may be literally set free from the fear of fat.

NOTES

1. Nazi calorie maintenance requirement from Marilyn Wann, *Fat!So? Because You Don't Have to Apologize for Your Size* (Berkeley, Calif.: Ten Speed Press, 1998), p. 51.

2. *Pope v. Western Center, Department of Public Welfare, Commonwealth of Pennsylvania*, 69 PA.CMWLTH 572, 452 A.2d 581 (1982).

3. Pope at 581.

4. Pope at 581.

5. Pope at 582.

6. "Mental Health and Retardation Act of 1966," Section 406, P.L. 96, Special Sess. No. 3, Oct. 20, 1966, 50 P>S> 54406.

7. This interpretation is chosen by the court. Appellants argued for a narrower interpretation of the statute, stating that, "A mentally disabled person in need of assistance by reason of such mental disability authorizes commitment only when the disabled person's mental disability itself requires treatment." *Pope* at 582.

8. *Susan McPherson v. Court of Appeals of Minnesota* 476 N.W.2d 520 (Court of Appeals of Minnesota, 1991).

9. McPherson at 521.

10. McPherson at 521.

11. *Olmstead v. L.C.* (98-536) (138 F.3d 893 affirmed in part, vacated in part, and remanded). Quote at line 4.

12. *Olmstead v. L.C.*, sec. III.

13. *Olmstead v. L.C.*, sec. A.

CHAPTER 16

THE FAT LADY'S SCREAMING, NOT SINGING

Continuing the Fight Against Fat Discrimination

How could I live with myself and not fight? No one has the right to go inside you and steal your self-worth. This happens to a lot of people because the prejudice is so acceptable. People go home and feel like losers, like it's their fault. I felt I could not let them get away with making people feel this way.

—Toni Cassista[1]

"ALL I WANTED WAS TO be afforded the same opportunity as everyone else," explains Toni Cassista after being rejected for a position under the assumption her weight would prohibit her from doing the work. She filed an employment discrimination complaint against the Santa Cruz food store and refused a $1,500 offer that prohibited her from speaking about her experience of discrimination. Before her case went to court, ordinary citizens of Santa Cruz, California, took additional measures to prevent acts of discrimination in the future. Spearheaded by the thin Dawn Atkins who had witnessed her mother's weight battle firsthand, a coalition including Toni and several other core members was formed.[2] The goal was to create a city-level general civil rights ordinance that would prevent discrimination on the basis of weight, sexual orientation, physical characteristics, and race, among other things. In building the coalition, members went to

233

every group individually and explained how the ordinance would help them. Pressure was exerted on the coalition, with lawmakers promising to pass the sexual orientation part if they would drop the rest. Dawn stood up and said, "Height and weight discrimination won't be used against me, but I won't take my rights by causing other people to lose theirs." The coalition remained together and the ordinance passed. Since then Dawn has met people who chose to relocate to Santa Cruz because of the protection the ordinance offers.

Courts often have the ability to end unnecessary discrimination against fat people, but lack the vision. Laws specifically prohibiting discrimination on the basis of weight help by making it clear that courts are required to protect the civil liberties of fat people regardless of the judges' personal prejudices. There are a handful of such laws. Like the Santa Cruz ordinance, the state of Michigan prohibits weight discrimination in the Elliot-Larsen Civil Rights Act. Michigan's act applies to the entire state. It's purpose is "to define civil rights; to prohibit discriminatory practices, policies, and customs in the exercise of those rights based upon religion, race, color, national origin, age, sex, height, *weight*, familial status, or marital status" (emphasis added). Washington, D.C., takes a more liberal approach, prohibiting discrimination against an individual on the basis of "race, color, religion, national origin, sex, age, marital status, *personal appearance*, sexual orientation, family responsibilities, physical handicap, matriculation, or political affiliation" (emphasis added).

Just as bias against fat people takes many forms, so, too, can resistance. A college professor recalls her reaction to episodes of discrimination at a local fitness center. After paying her membership, she was told she would not be allowed to use some of the equipment because of her weight. Then, on multiple occasions in the pool, she was harassed by some young men about her weight. Each time she complained immediately. Once the men were ousted from the pool, but the other time the staff would not act. She wrote to the management, insisting she not pay full price for decreased services. Though only a college student at the time, and despite her family's opinion that she "couldn't fight it," she filed in small claims court. For her $10 filing fee she successfully pressured the club into refunding her money. (They probably spent more than the membership price for their own attorney's time.) While a definite victory, the club's behavior had lasting effects. Though she liked to work out and had the potential to be a good athlete, she resisted joining a gym after the incident. "Why would I want to pay money for people to be mean to me? I can get that for free on the street."[3]

With only one month left to go in her family nurse practitioner degree, Leah Strock already has plans to establish a fat-friendly health center in New York. She knows the need. At nineteen, in the gynecologist's office, her feet in stirrups, her doctor said, "You know what your problem is? You're too damn fat!"[4] She kicked him and told the nurse practitioner what he said.

Two careers later, as a registered nurse and six-year veteran of the AIDS field, she expected to be treated with respect as a patient. When she had an injury that required surgery and was lectured about being fat while the surgeon blamed her injury on her weight, Leah again fought back. She sent a letter to the surgeon, the vice president of the hospital, the insurance company, and her doctor. She witnessed her sister's reaction when her sister's new doctor told her that she had to lose weight—she never went back. Leah approached the doctor, who worked at her hospital, and told him to change his approach. When he resisted, she asked how successful he was with that approach. He responded, "Not very." To reduce the alienation he was creating Leah promptly suggested, if he felt he really needed to mention weight, to simply and neutrally ask his patient, "Is there anything I can do to help you lose weight?"

She is currently conducting a study on the experiences of fat women and gynecology. Discussing the documented reluctance of doctors to examine fat women, she explains, "Some may be afraid they won't make a good diagnosis. Beyond that it is prejudice. Just prejudice." Her dreams are big, but she is adamant, "Fat people need preventative health care. They get less than thin people. They need to be able to go for health care in a safe environment."

Also motivated to protect the health and safety of fat people, Elizabeth Fisher became politicized about seatbelt safety for fat passengers. She was affected by the story of newlywed Mara Nesbitt-Aldrich who was propelled into the windshield as she left for her honeymoon. Mara's seatbelt was too small. Like many supersize people, she had no choice but to travel unbelted.

Elizabeth's research into the federal seatbelt size requirements found manufacturers only need to fit up to the 95th percentile of the American male population, which translates to a six-foot-tall, 215-pound body. A seatbelt extender is a simple device which lengthens the seatbelt. Like the seatbelt extenders used on airlines (the items flight attendants hold up before takeoff to demonstrate how the buckle works), it is a piece of seatbelt material with a buckle on one end and a tongue on the other. The buckle matches the installed belt so the device can be attached and give extra length to the seatbelt. This inexpensive gadget allows larger passengers to travel using a seatbelt.

Pointing out that seatbelt regulations leave out 15 million Americans, she argues, "Currently, forty-nine states have laws requiring seatbelt use by 100 percent of front-seat occupants. Federal regulations cover only 95 percent. Do you fall into this 5 percent category? I do."[5] While many car companies do provide these adapters for a modest fee, Honda has refused her repeated requests and demands to make them available for Honda owners and passengers. (See Appendix A: Resources and Activism for more information on how to get involved.)

In response to a fitness center billboard which pictured a space alien and read, "When they come they'll eat the fat ones first," author and activist Marilyn Wann organized a small demonstration. Protesters showed up in alien costumes with signs that read "Eat Me!" and "This Gym Alien-ates Fat People" and did aerobics on the sidewalk.

As a result of the good-natured protest, the San Francisco Human Rights Commission (SFHRC) became educated about the lack of legal protection for fat people. Shortly thereafter activists, attorneys, and politicians joined forces to secure legal protection for fat people in San Francisco. At a hearing before the Human Rights Commission, fat and thin people testified about weight-based discrimination. People described not being hired for jobs, mistreatment by doctors, a death due to lack of medical equipment designed to accommodate large people, being refused apartment rentals, and being unable to fit in courtroom and classroom chairs. They described the social climate of hostility, discussing in particular a local radio advertisement for weight-loss surgery that acknowledged and exploited bias against fat people. Voice-overs acted out scenes of employment and housing discrimination, followed by a pitch that said the company could not change the world, but it could help the patient lose weight through surgical alteration of healthy digestive organs. Perhaps convinced that a medical solution was inappropriate for a social wrong, the SFHRC voted unanimously to prohibit discrimination on the basis of height or weight—the first step to altering the San Francisco law. Commission Chair Henry Low responded, "This is a problem that needs much more attention." Vice-chair Chada Saliba-Malouf endorsed the legal changes enthusiastically, "This ordinance is long overdue in the city of San Francisco."

All of these activists share a common strategy—education. Educating people about fat discrimination is the most important step toward dismantling the prejudice. Education helps fat people repair damage to their self-esteem which in turn prepares them to deal with the very real challenges they face everyday. It helps overcome the stereotypes that prohibit seeing fat people as people. It makes clear the similarities between fat prejudice and other biases like sexism, racism, and ableism. Education entails talking to people about their experiences and challenging biased behavior when it occurs. Toni Cassista explains, "You don't have to be an activist or in a movement. You can just do small, positive things." It can be as complicated as passing a law in your city or as simple as saying "You look good!" instead of "You look like you've lost weight."

As people move to eradicate differential treatment on the basis of weight, legislatures and courts must do their part as well. Verbal, emotional, and physical abuse should be taken seriously whether it happens to children or adults. It must not be tolerated in school, at home, in places of public accommodation, or at work. It is appropriate to compare abuse on the basis of weight to other similar hate crimes, and it is important to recognize that rampant abuse creates a hostile environment for fat people.

The medical profession is riddled with conflicts of interest in the field of weight regulation. This must be understood when relying on the opinions of doctors and other medical workers in court cases involving fat people. The medical establishment has to improve its internal policing and the courts should take a much more active role in requiring this. Judges and government agencies must aggressively hold doctors, researchers, clinics, and centers responsible for fraud when they make promises on which they cannot deliver. Those who damage physical or mental health by making weight-loss recommendations based on prejudice rather than science should be held accountable in the courts and in their profession.

No court should support the denial of rights based on weight without a bona fide reason. This includes the right to work, to be on a jury, to be safe from involuntary commitment, and all the other rights that thin people enjoy.

Children are particularly vulnerable before courts. The substantial power courts hold over their lives should be used to secure equal educational opportunities rather than to force weight loss. Weight should not affect custody decisions except where the child is at risk of abuse due to weight.

Prejudice on the basis of weight is a civil rights issue. It is imperative for every group and every person who supports civil rights to treat it as such. It is time to recognize that progressive politics necessarily involve opposition to weight-based discrimination. We must work toward a kinder, more inclusive culture so that the harassment and resulting isolation that took the life of Christina Corrigan does not take any more lives.

NOTES

1. Toni Cassista, telephone interview, 29 April 1999, Santa Cruz, California.

2. Dawn Atkins, telephone interview, 21 February 1999, El Cerrito, California.

3. Private interview, Leah Strock, New York, New York, October 1999.

4. Elizabeth Fisher, "Honda Says 'No' to Seat Belt Extenders," speech given at the National Association to Advance Fat Acceptance's Everybody Goodbody Festival, 29 July 1999, Boston, Massachusetts.

5. Name withheld to protect privacy, telephone interview, 29 April 1999, San Francisco, California.

RESOURCES AND ACTIVISM

Get Informed, Get Involved, Get Started!

National Association to Advance Fat Acceptance (NAAFA)
NAAFA, P.O. Box 188620, Sacramento, CA 95818.
(800) 442-1214. www.NAAFA.com

NAAFA is a fabulous, thirty-year-old human-rights organization working to end size discrimination and to empower fat people. NAAFA's membership consists of people all sizes of large as well as average-size people. The organization's activities include public education, support, and activism. There is a bimonthly newsletter, a pen-pal program, special interest groups, many other exciting activities all over the country, and shopping! (NAAFA sells cards, political buttons, hospital gowns in sizes 3x and 10x, and fat acceptance books and magazines. Give them a call for details.) There are fifty chapters of NAAFA and each year the organization holds its annual conference in a major city.

Council on Size & Weight Discrimination (CSWD)
P.O. Box 305, Mt. Marion, NY 12456. info@cswd.org,
www.cswd.org

Founded in 1990, the council works behind the scenes as an advocate for large people focusing on health care, children, media, and access issues like physical barriers. They also provide information and referrals.

Weight-Related Legal Issues
Sondra Solovay, 2625 Alcatraz Avenue,
PMB261, Berkeley, CA 94705.
solo@sirius.com

For nondiscrimination trainings, workshops, and education on fat bias and the law, or for help with a weight-related legal problem, contact Sondra Solovay.

Fat Speakers Bureau (FSB)
c/o Fat!So? P.O. Box 423464, San Francisco, CA 94142.
(800) OH FATSO

In an effort to curb fat bias the FSB provides speakers to educate students of all ages. Contact the FSB for information on getting a speaker to talk to your class or group, or to become a speaker yourself!

International Size Acceptance Association (ISAA)
http://www.size-acceptance.org/

ISAA's mission is to promote size acceptance and fight size discrimination throughout the world by means of advocacy and visible, lawful actions.

Seatbelt Safety
http://members.aol.com/nobelts4us

Learn more about Elizabeth Fisher's important campaign!

Amplestuff, P.O. Box 116, Bearsville, NY 12409
fax: (914) 679-1206. www.amplestuff.com. amplestuff@aol.com

Amplestuff is a mail-order company that supplies extra-large items (except clothes) like airline seatbelt extenders, hospital gowns, clothes hangers, books including hard-to-find titles, videos, blood pressure cuffs, and much more.

MINI-LIBRARY

Here are just a few of the many publications available. Educate yourself about the issues!

Shelley Bovey, *The Forbidden Body: Why Being Fat Is Not a Sin* (Great Britain: HarperCollinsManufacturing, 1994).

Laura Brown and Esther Rothblum, *Overcoming Fear of Fat* (New York: Harrington Park Press, 1989).

Charlotte Cooper, *Fat and Proud: The Politics of Size* (London: The Woman's Press, 1998).

Laura Fraser, *Losing It: False Hope and Fat Profits in the Diet Industry* (New York: Plume, 1998).

Glenn Gaesser, *Big Fat Lies: The Truth About Your Health and Weight* (New York: Fawcett Columbine, 1996).

Terry Nicholetti Garrison with David Levitsky, *Fed Up! A Woman's Guide to Freedom from the Diet/Weight Prison* (New York: Carroll & Graf, 1993).

Terry Poulton, *No Fat Chicks: How Big Business Profits by Making Women Hate Their Bodies—And How to Fight Back* (N.J.: Birch Lane Press, 1997).

Hillel Schwartz, *Never Satisfied: A Cultural History of Dieting, Fantasies, and Fat* (New York: Doubleday, 1986).

Judy Sullivan, *Sizewise: A Catalog of More Than 1,000 Resources for Living with Confidence and Comfort at Any Size* (New York: Avon Books, 1997).

Marilynn Wann, *Fat!So? Because You Don't Have to Apologize for Your Size* (Berkeley, Calif.: Ten Speed Press, 1998).

BBW Magazine: Real Women, Real Beauty
11492 Sunrise Gold Circle #D, Rancho Cordova, CA 95742
www.BBWMagazine.com

Belle Magazine: For the plus-sized African American woman
475 Park Avenue South, New York, NY 10016. (212) 689-2830

Radiance: The Magazine for Large Women
P.O. Box 30246, Oakland, CA 94604.
(510) 482-0680. www.radiancemagazine.com

THE LAW

V ERY FEW PLACES SPECIFICALLY PROHIBIT weight-based discrimination. This section provides excerpts from relevant laws. Encourage your state or city to pass similar measures just like the creators of these ordinances did! For up-to-date, complete information, visit a law library or look online. The complete text of the ADA and Michigan's Elliot-Larson Act are easily available on the Web.

SANTA CRUZ, CALIFORNIA

Adopted in 1992, Chapter 9.83 of the Santa Cruz Municipal Code prohibits discrimination on the basis of age, race, color, creed, religion, national origin, ancestry, disability, marital status, sex, gender, sexual orientation, height, weight, or physical characteristics in the areas of employment, housing, real-estate transaction, business establishments, public accommodations, educational institutions, and city services, facilities and transactions.

Santa Cruz City Attorney John G. Barisone:
"The City has incurred no expenses which might be attributable to the fact that the ordinance prohibits discrimination on the basis of height

or weight. . . . The ordinance has been generally well received by the City's residents, landlords, and businesses and the only activity which it has generated since its adoption has been an occasional phone call from an individual or entity inquiring into one's rights under the ordinance or what one must do to ensure that he or she is in compliance with the ordinance's mandates. To my knowledge, there have been no private enforcement actions taken pursuant to the ordinance and the City has not been required to take any formal enforcement actions as a result of ordinance violations."[1]

Santa Cruz Body Image Task Force founder Dawn Atkins:
Multiple people contacted me and told me they relocated to Santa Cruz because of the protection against weight-based discrimination.

WASHINGTON, D.C.

District of Columbia Code, Chapter 25 (Human Rights) provides:
"It is the intent of the Council of the District of Columbia, in enacting this chapter, to secure an end in the District of Columbia to discrimination for any reason other than that of individual merit, including, but not limited to, discrimination by reason of race, color, religion, national origin, sex, age, marital status, personal appearance, sexual orientation, family responsibilities, matriculation, political affiliation, disability, source of income, and place of residence or business." (1-2501. Intent of Council)
"Personal Appearance" means "The outward appearance of any person, irrespective of sex, with regard to bodily condition or characteristics, manner or style of dress, and the manner or style of personal grooming, including, but not limited to, hair style and beards. It shall not relate, however, to the requirement of cleanliness, uniforms, or prescribed standards, when uniformly applied to a class of employees for a reasonable business purpose, or when such bodily conditions or characteristics, or style or manner of less [*sic*] or personal grooming presents a danger to the health, welfare, or safety of any individual." (599. Definitions)

MICHIGAN

Michigan's Elliot-Larson Civil Rights Act prohibits discrimination on the basis of race, color, religion, national origin, age, sex, height, weight, familial status, or marital status. It allows exemptions in cases of bona fide occupational qualification.

Ombudsman Art Stine, Michigan Department of Civil Rights: "Our tradition here in Michigan is that civil rights are vital for all groups of people, that we want to include everyone in the system. These things matter here, perhaps more than they do in other places. . . . In Michigan, we don't track the costs of complying with any civil rights law because, frankly, we don't want to give any credence to the notion that expense might ever be a reason not to include all types of people as participants in our society. With race cases, for example, we don't want people to think that cost might be a reason not to comply with the law that prohibits racial discrimination. Michigan added height and weight to the Civil Rights Act in 1975, and its passage was very easy. Given that certain height and weight characteristics tend to be linked to certain ethnic groups or to women, state legislators decided it was all the more appropriate to include body size as part of a comprehensive antidiscrimination policy. There wasn't even much debate about it. Since then, I'd estimate that eight or ten weight-related cases have come before our commission for a decision. Overall, employers haven't had to do radical accommodations in the workplace and people simply haven't had a big problem with it."[2]

RESOLUTION ON BODY-SIZE DISCRIMINATION SAN FRANCISCO, CALIFORNIA

Whereas, the Human Rights Commission held a public hearing on June 10, 1999 to hear testimony regarding discrimination based on body size; and

Whereas, people experience discrimination based on their body size in employment, resulting in failure to be hired, unfair terminations, denial of promotions, and on-the-job harassment; and

Whereas, people experience discrimination based on their body size in housing and real estate transaction, resulting in denial of rental opportunities by landlords, harassment by landlords and co-tenants, and disadvantages in home-buying and business opportunities; and

Whereas, people experience discrimination based on body size in public accommodations, resulting in denial of services by public and nonprofit agencies, being ignored by commercial retailers, verbal harassment by employees of public and private organizations and businesses, and denial of reasonable accommodation for various body sizes; and

Whereas, discrimination based on body size is a serious social problem in San Francisco and elsewhere, resulting in verbal and physical violence, lack of self-esteem, eating disorders, psychological problems, depression, poor health care, and suicide; and

Whereas, discrimination based on body size robs San Francisco of the talents and skills of many people who otherwise would participate more fully in improving the lives of all San Franciscans; and

Whereas, the Human Rights Commission works to eliminate unfair discrimination against all people;

Therefore, Be It Resolved, that the San Francisco Human Rights Commission encourages the Board of Supervisors and the Mayor to enact legislation adding "body size" or a comparable phrase to San Francisco's anti-discrimination ordinances; and

Therefore, Be It Further Resolved, that the San Francisco Human Rights Commission encourages all City contractors, and all businesses and agencies in San Francisco, to eliminate body size discrimination from their programs and policies.

NOTES

1. Correspondence to Sondra Solovay from Santa Cruz City Attorney John Barisone, 18 May 1999.

2. Interview with Art Stine, Michigan Department of Civil Rights, by Marilyn Wann, March 1999.

EXCERPTS FROM THE AMERICANS WITH DISABILITIES ACT

* * *

An Act: To establish a clear and comprehensive prohibition of discrimination on the basis of disability.

* * *

SECTION 1. SHORT TITLE; TABLE OF CONTENTS. 42 USC 12101 NOTE.

(a) Short Title. This Act may be cited as the Americans with Disabilities Act of 1990.

* * *

SEC. 2. FINDINGS AND PURPOSES.
42USC 12101.

(a) Findings. The Congress finds that

(1) some 43,000,000 Americans have one or more physical or mental disabilities, and this number is increasing as the population as a whole is growing older;

(2) historically, society has tended to isolate and segregate individuals with disabilities, and, despite some improvements, such forms of discrimination against individuals with disabilities continue to be a serious and pervasive social problem;

(3) discrimination against individuals with disabilities persists in such critical areas as employment, housing, public accommodations, education, transportation, communication, recreation, institutionalization, health services, voting, and access to public services;

(4) unlike individuals who have experienced discrimination on the basis of race, color, sex, national origin, religion, or age, individuals who have experienced discrimination on the basis of disability have often had no legal recourse to redress such discrimination;

(5) individuals with disabilities continually encounter various forms of discrimination, including outright intentional exclusion, the discriminatory effects of architectural, transportation, and communication barriers, overprotective rules and policies, failure to make modifications to existing facilities and practices, exclusionary qualification standards and criteria, segregation, and relegation to lesser services, programs, activities, benefits, jobs, or other opportunities;

(6) census data, national polls, and other studies have documented that people with disabilities, as a group, occupy an inferior status in our society, and are severely disadvantaged socially, vocationally, economically, and educationally;

(7) individuals with disabilities are a discrete and insular minority who have been faced with restrictions and limitations, subjected to a history of purposeful unequal treatment, and relegated to a position of political powerlessness in our society, based on characteristics that are beyond the con-

trol of such individuals and resulting from stereotypic assumptions not truly indicative of the individual ability of such individuals to participate in, and contribute to, society;

(8) the Nation's proper goals regarding individuals with disabilities are to assure equality of opportunity, full participation, independent living, and economic self-sufficiency for such individuals; and

(9) the continuing existence of unfair and unnecessary discrimination and prejudice denies people with disabilities the opportunity to compete on an equal basis and to pursue those opportunities for which our free society is justifiably famous, and costs the United States billions of dollars in unnecessary expenses resulting from dependency and nonproductivity.

(b) Purpose. It is the purpose of this Act

(1) to provide a clear and comprehensive national mandate for the elimination of discrimination against individuals with disabilities;

(2) to provide clear, strong, consistent, enforceable standards addressing discrimination against individuals with disabilities;

(3) to ensure that the Federal Government plays a central role in enforcing the standards established in this Act on behalf of individuals with disabilities; and

(4) to invoke the sweep of congressional authority, including the power to enforce the Fourteenth Amendment and to regulate commerce, in order to address the major areas of discrimination faced day-to-day by people with disabilities.

· · ·

SEC. 3. DEFINITIONS. 42 USC 12102

· · ·

(2) Disability. The term disability means, with respect to an individual

(A) a physical or mental impairment that substantially limits one or more of the major life activities of such individual;

(B) a record of such an impairment; or

(C) being regarded as having such an impairment.

. . .

TITLE I EMPLOYMENT

. . .

(8) Qualified individual with a disability. The term qualified individual with a disability means an individual with a disability who, with or without reasonable accommodation, can perform the essential functions of the employment position that such individual holds or desires. For the purposes of this title, consideration shall be given to the employer's judgment as to what functions of a job are essential, and if an employer has prepared a written description before advertising or interviewing applicants for the job, this description shall be considered evidence of the essential functions of the job.

. . .

SEC. 102. DISCRIMINATION. 42 USC 12112.

(a) General Rule. No covered entity shall discriminate against a qualified individual with a disability because of the disability of such individual in regard to job application procedures, the hiring, advancement, or discharge of employees, employee compensation, job training, and other terms, conditions, and privileges of employment.

. . .

SEC. 103. DEFENSES. 42 USC 12113.

(a) In General. It may be a defense to a charge of discrimination under this Act that an alleged application of qualification standards, tests, or selection criteria that screen out or tend to screen out or otherwise deny a job or benefit to an individual with a disability has been shown to be job-related and consistent with business necessity, and such performance cannot be accomplished by reasonable accommodation, as required under this title.

. . .

SEC. 201. DEFINITION. 42 USC 12115.

As used in this title:

(1) Public entity. The term public entity means
  (A) any State or local government;
  (B) any department, agency, special purpose district, or other instrumentality of a State or States or local government; and
  (C) the National Railroad Passenger Corporation, and any commuter authority (as defined in section 103(8) of the Rail Passenger Service Act).

(2) Qualified individual with a disability. The term qualified individual with a disability means an individual with a disability who, with or without reasonable modifications to rules, policies, or practices, the removal of architectural, communication, or transportation barriers, or the provision of auxiliary aids and services, meets the essential eligibility requirements for the receipt of services or the participation in programs or activities provided by a public entity.

SEC. 202. DISCRIMINATION. 42 USC 12132.

Subject to the provisions of this title, no qualified individual with a disability shall, by reason of such disability, be excluded from participation in or be denied the benefits of the services, programs, or activities of a public entity, or be subjected to discrimination by any such entity.

. . .

TITLE III PUBLIC ACCOMMODATIONS AND SERVICES OPERATED BY PRIVATE ENTITIES

. . .

(7) Public accommodation. The following private entities are considered public accommodations for purposes of this title, if the operations of such entities affect commerce

   (A) an inn, hotel, motel, or other place of lodging, except for an establishment located within a building that contains not more than five rooms for rent or hire and that is actually occupied by the proprietor of such establishment as the residence of such proprietor;

   (B) a restaurant, bar, or other establishment serving food or drink;

   (C) a motion picture house, theater, concert hall, stadium, or other place of exhibition or entertainment;

   (D) an auditorium, convention center, lecture hall, or other place of public gathering;

   (E) a bakery, grocery store, clothing store, hardware store, shopping center, or other sales or rental establishment;

   (F) a laundromat, dry-cleaner, bank, barber shop, beauty shop, travel service, shoe repair service, funeral parlor, gas station, office of an accountant or lawyer, pharmacy, insurance office, professional office of a healthcare provider, hospital, or other service establishment;

(G) a terminal, depot, or other station used for specified public transportation;

(H) a museum, library, gallery, or other place of public display or collection;

(I) a park, zoo, amusement park, or other place of recreation;

(J) a nursery, elementary, secondary, undergraduate, or post-graduate private school, or other place of education;

(K) a daycare center, senior citizen center, homeless shelter, food bank, adoption agency, or other social service center establishment; and

(L) a gymnasium, health spa, bowling alley, golf course, or other place of exercise or recreation.

(8) Rail and railroad.

. . .

SEC. 302. PROHIBITION OF DISCRIMINATION BY PUBLIC ACCOMMODATIONS. 42 USC 12182.

(a) General Rule. No individual shall be discriminated against on the basis of disability in the full and equal enjoyment of the goods, services, facilities, privileges, advantages, or accommodations of any place of public accommodation by any person who owns, leases (or leases to), or operates a place of public accommodation.

. . .

TITLE V MISCELLANEOUS PROVISIONS SEC. 501. CONSTRUCTION. 42 USC 12201.

. . .

(c) Insurance. Titles I through IV of this Act shall not be construed to prohibit or restrict

(1) an insurer, hospital or medical service company, health maintenance organization, or any agent, or entity that administers benefit plans, or similar organizations from underwriting risks, classifying risks, or administering such risks that are based on or not inconsistent with State law.

. . .

SEC. 503. PROHIBITION AGAINST RETALIATION AND COERCION. 42 USC 12203.

(a) Retaliation. No person shall discriminate against any individual because such individual has opposed any act or practice made unlawful by this Act or because such individual made a charge, testified, assisted, or participated in any manner in an investigation, proceeding, or hearing under this Act.

(b) Interference, Coercion, or Intimidation. It shall be unlawful to coerce, intimidate, threaten, or interfere with any individual in the exercise or enjoyment of, or on account of his or her having exercised or enjoyed, or on account of his or her having aided or encouraged any other individual in the exercise or enjoyment of, any right granted or protected by this Act.

. . .

SEC. 510. ILLEGAL USE OF DRUGS. 42 USC 12210.

(a) In General. For purposes of this Act, the term individual with a disability does not include an individual who is currently engaging in the illegal use of drugs, when the covered entity acts on the basis of such use.

. . .

SEC. 511. DEFINITIONS. 42 USC 12211.

(a) Homosexuality and Bisexuality. For purposes of the definition of disability in section 3(2), homosexuality and bisexuality are not impairments and as such are not disabilities under this Act.

(b) Certain Conditions. Under this Act, the term disability shall not include

> (1) transvestitism, transsexualism, pedophilia, exhibitionism, voyeurism, gender identity disorders not resulting from physical impairments, or other sexual behavior disorders;
>
> (2) compulsive gambling, kleptomania, or pyromania; or
>
> (3) psychoactive substance-use disorders resulting from current illegal use of drugs.

INDEX